FORGING AHEAD

Austerity to Prosperity in the Black Country, 1945-1968

Simon Briercliffe

Published by West Midlands History Limited
Minerva Mill Innovation Centre, Alcester, Warwickshire, UK.

ISBN: 978-1-905036-84-4

Cover image: From "The World of GKN" – Guest, Keen & Nettlefolds, Ltd., 1964
Courtesy GKN

Caric Press Limited, Merthyr Tydfil, Wales.

Table of Contents

Black
Country
Birmingham
London
N
STAFFORDSHIRE
WEST MIDLANDS
Wolverhampton
Walsall
West
Bromwich
SHROPSHIRE
Dudley
Birmingham
Stourbridge
WORCESTERSHIRE
0
20km
1:400,000
Contains OS data
© Crown copyright and database rights 2017
WARWICKSHIRE

Introduction

VE Day at the Revo Sports Ground, Tipton, 1945.
In the front at right of centre of the picture are Brenda Sheldon and her cousin Vera Pecklow from Tividale wearing the same outfit.

Despite a dire forecast and a drizzly start, Tuesday 8 May 1945 turned into a fine, sunny day in the Black Country. A good day, in fact, for people to pour onto the region's streets for Victory in Europe Day. The long war was all but over, and the Black Country celebrated with street parties, decorations, fireworks, dances and thanksgiving services. Wreaths were laid, effigies of Hitler were burnt, bells were rung, and pictures of King George VI, Winston Churchill and even Joseph Stalin were proudly displayed. People all over the Black Country – and the world – celebrated peace in Europe, and looked forward to the new world to follow.[1]

This book explores the Black Country's journey from that jubilant outbreak of peace, through unprecedented austerity, to an economic boom and a period of affluence in which Britain "had never had it so good". The Black Country is a useful lens through which to view British society in this period. Its historical industrial strength and adaptability kept it going throughout the rigours and shortages of the 1940s, and it contributed significantly to the exports required to keep Britain afloat in the 1950s. It witnessed the re-writing of the social contract between the state and its citizens and helped to drive the economic boom as austerity gave way to prosperity by the 1960s – and it experienced first-hand the fractures in society that arrived alongside this. Yet it was also unique as a region, filled with distinctive localities, industries and landscapes which set it apart from other industrial regions in Britain.

Today, after decades of industrial decline in Britain and particularly in the Black Country, it is common for political and popular rhetoric to look backwards: to the troubled 1970s, to the hungry 1930s, to the age of 'blitz spirit', or to the post-war moment this book describes. The two decades or so following the Second World War are claimed by all sides: as a golden age of social democracy and the welfare state, but also as an unsurpassed show of economic strength built on Britain's industrial and imperial capitalism. As with all historical claims, there is truth and fiction in each interpretation. In 1945, many looked back too, to the 'hungry thirties' of strikes, hunger marches and mass unemployment. The words "Never again" were on everyone's lips, not just referring to the war but to the social conditions that preceded it. 1945 was therefore a time not just to look back, but to look forward to better things.[2]

The Black Country

Telling the history of the Black Country reveals much about the country that emerged from the shadow of war. Despite the national and communal experiences of war, Britain was still a nation where local attachments ran deep, and the Black Country was a perfect example. Prior to the Industrial Revolution, it had been a sparsely populated region, with scattered hamlets across poor agricultural land, and farmers gathering outcropping coal to supplement meagre incomes. The advent of industrial capitalism and steam power in the eighteenth and nineteenth centuries attracted men, women and children to the Black Country for work from across the rural Midlands, Britain, Ireland and Europe. Villages swelled to large towns, but they retained a distinctiveness and local pride that made any collective term one of convenience only. Nevertheless, by the early nineteenth century a distinct mining and manufacturing district, comprising south Staffordshire and north Worcestershire, had begun to be familiar. The epithet 'Black Country' first appeared in print in the 1840s and was soon adopted as a useful shorthand for the area, describing as it did the rich mineral resources below, and the smoke-polluted skies above. It was what lay underneath the ground that turned a sparsely-populated agricultural region into an economic and industrial powerhouse: coal, iron, clay,

Courtesy of Black Country Living Museum

Cobb's Engine House, Windmill End, 1969.

limestone – everything to feed the tens of thousands of foundries, forges and factories close by, which in turn fuelled the Industrial Revolution and imperial expansion of the nation. The Black Country poured forth coal from its thirty-foot seam, iron from its multitude of blast furnaces, and smoke from its forest of chimneys. It manufactured everything from nails and saucepans to the iron girders and plate glass of the Great Exhibition's Crystal Palace.[3]

To begin with, 'Black Country' was a descriptive – and sometimes pejorative – term, evoking the black clouds of pollution above and the mineral riches below. Although the debate about where the Black Country starts and stops is as old as the region itself, it typically referred to an area of less than 100 square miles, encompassing the thick coal seams of the South Staffordshire coalfield and the extensive manufacturing area that – depending on who you asked – stretched in a ring from Wolverhampton to Stourbridge, to Halesowen, Smethwick, West Bromwich and Walsall. Its atmosphere inspired horror amongst many visitors. Charles Dickens described the Black Country's "melancholy air" and its "moral blackness"; Queen Victoria commented that "it is like another world… one of the most dreadful parts of the country one can imagine"; in 1934, the writer JB Priestley still called it "a picture of grimy desolation".[4] Others, more sympathetic to its economy and people, were more circumspect. The American Elihu Burritt praised its industry:

> *The Black Country, black by day and red by night, cannot be matched, for vast and varied production, by any other space of equal radius on the surface of the globe… Never a gold-field on the face of the earth, of ten miles radius, produced such vast values as these subterranean acres have done.*[5]

The Black Country was never a homogenous district. Different towns specialised in different metal trades – chainmaking in Cradley Heath, for example, nuts and bolts in Darlaston – or related trades – saddlery in Walsall, firebricks in Brierley Hill. There were some large businesses, but more common were the 'little masters' operating workshop-sized firms with a small workforce.

After a productive peak in the mid-nineteenth century, the Black Country's traditional heavy industries, and the towns where they were based, faced decline. Industry rallied though: new collieries and new engineering firms began to thrive in other places, and the towns where this new industry was based, like Wolverhampton, grew rapidly. The global depression of the interwar years hit the Black Country hard, if not as hard as some regions, with unemployment reaching over a third of the working population in some parts. Before the Second World War around one tenth of Britain's population worked in metal industries; in much of the Black Country, it was nearly half. This covered a multitude of different industries, however, and it was this diversity and adaptability that enabled the region to survive the rigours of the interwar years. In the 1930s, most Black Country boroughs were decreasing in population, as people moved instead to towns on the fringe. Heavy industrial towns like Tipton and Bilston "ceased to attract outsiders", but Wolverhampton, for instance, developed a young and growing population, so that the experience of this difficult time was not evenly spread.[6]

The Second World War was a catalyst for dramatic change in many ways, but in others this process continued. Towns grew in size and became connected by new residential and industrial estates, and the influence of larger towns increased. There had long been middle-class suburbs on the periphery of the region, in Stourbridge, Aldridge, Warley and elsewhere, and these became increasingly desirable for people from more industrial areas, stretching the older boundaries of the Black Country. With rising post-war wages,

Courtesy of Black Country Living Museum

Open-cast mining behind houses on Garden Walk, Lower Gornal.

people also moved to the Black Country's greener fringes, to overspill areas in Wombourne, Codsall, or the "bungaloid country" of Romsley. In the scythe-making Worcestershire village of Belbroughton, the rural accent was notably mixed with Black Country dialect.[7]

At the same time, mining was in rapid decline – 1968 marked the closure of the last colliery in the Black Country – and the old idea of a Black Country bounded by a coalfield began to seem irrelevant. These borders were certainly still up for debate in the 1960s, and amidst fierce local pride, being part of a broader Black Country was not necessarily seen as a positive thing. Solicitors for Brierley Hill – arguing against amalgamation with Dudley County Borough during one of the many boundary commissions of the 1950s and 1960s – suggested that "the main line of the Black Country was from Birmingham through West Bromwich, Wednesbury and Bilston to Wolverhampton, with a narrow spur running off from Oldbury to Stourbridge". The view identified by the historian Edward Chitham, namely that the Black Country started "at the next village or town to the one you live in" was still much in evidence. The borders of the Black Country were never a fixed entity, but reflect a historical process of expansion, mobility, industrial change and pride in community (and perhaps antagonism towards neighbours) that followed its people as they moved around and out of the region. This pride in distinctiveness was really what defined the Black Country as it boomed: pride in local towns and trades, and a developing pride in the region as a whole.[8]

By telling this post-war story, this book makes the case that, at least until the end of the 1960s, the Black Country was a distinct region within the British industrial, social and cultural economy. Today's Black Country is not just a product of the Industrial Revolution of the eighteenth and nineteenth centuries; it remained dynamic, adaptable and distinctive long after this, and continued to help shape Britain and its relationship with the world long after the narrowboat and steam engine ceased to dominate the industrial world. This focus also provides a way to understand Britain and its place in the world too. The changing political, economic and social tides can all be best understood at local level; likewise, ripples from local events spread to affect the whole country.

Looking at a single generation also helps make sense of the changing face of Britain in the twentieth century. Many of those at work in the Black Country in the 1940s and 1950s were born when Queen Victoria was on the throne. They had known much more economic hardship than affluence, with strikes and large-scale unemployment punctuating their working lives. The gradual introduction of social welfare programmes had made a little difference, and a strong local associational culture was evidence of workers' agency, but social class was still a reality: the interests of industrialists still dominated the

Peter Donnelly

Steelworkers at Round Oak, Brierley Hill, 1961.

lives and livelihoods of their workers. The Second World War precipitated major changes, especially when the people of Britain voted for a programme of comparatively radical change in the form of Clement Attlee's Labour government. It heralded a period of social democratic consensus amongst the world's major economies that lasted, more or less, until 1979, when classical liberal capitalism reasserted itself. For those living in that historical moment, when industry was booming, wages were high and social welfare was at its peak, it must have been a stark contrast to look back at the uncertainties of the pre-war Black Country from the vantage point of their new-found stability.[9]

By studying the Black Country not just on its own terms but as part of the West Midlands, Britain, or a global economy, it is clear that these few square miles of semi-derelict, sooty, industrial land were more than "grimy desolation" and "moral blackness", but were a site where major discourses of technology, progress and society overlapped. It was not insular or inward-looking but porous – people moved in and out from all over the world, and through adaptation and innovation, protest and resistance, they created the Black Country that moved into the 1970s and beyond. And most importantly to those from the Black Country, it was not simply an industrial suburb of Birmingham – it was a distinctive and important place.

Outline

Forging Ahead surveys the challenges and complexities of the Black Country between 1945 – when the outbreak of peace and a landslide Labour victory offered to usher in a new world – and 1968 – when the last colliery in the Black Country finally closed, a symbolic end to one traditional Black Country lifestyle. It also surveys the uniquely Black Country solutions and approaches to life which characterised the transition from austerity to prosperity. Its focus is on the Black Country as an industrial, working-class region. This is not to diminish the importance of its middle classes, but the central story both in the Black Country and across Britain in this period was the rise of the working class as a political, economic and cultural force, and *Forging Ahead* reflects that shift.

Chapter 1 outlines the national and international context in which the Black Country found itself, describing how the enforced austerity of the 1940s gave way to the unprecedented prosperity of the 1950s and 1960s: in particular, it was the working class which benefited from higher wages and bargaining power in the light of a widespread labour shortage.

The remaining chapters are thematic, covering work, landscape, home and society. Chapters 2 to 4 are about industry and work, in the broadest sense. Chapter 2 outlines the vast range of manufacturing in the Black Country, and Chapter 3 the way

Courtesy Black Country Living Museum

Advertisement from *The Ironmonger* magazine, October 1945, demonstrating the durability of Kenrick hollowware .

in which this work was done and the people who made these goods. From raw steel to precision instruments, and from apprenticeship to retirement, Black Country firms had to re-imagine how business was conducted, taking in the demands of a new economy and an empowered workforce. Chapter 4 looks at the chronic labour shortage which defined both the improved conditions for workers, but also the demographic shifts that came as a result. This region had always been, and remained, substantially working class, but as industry began to cry out for labour this working class grew and diversified to embrace people of widely differing backgrounds. In particular, this chapter outlines the growth of European and Commonwealth immigration into the Black Country, including the challenges that these new communities faced on the way. It would not be an exaggeration to suggest that British society in the era of Commonwealth immigration harboured a widespread prejudice towards outsiders, particularly those whose skin was not white, and the Black Country was no exception. Yet this prejudice was not universal, and racism was then, as now, a learned, rather than innate, behaviour. Chapter 4 therefore includes plenty of examples of racism, but they are discussed within local, political and cultural contexts to highlight how such prejudices are created, sustained, or exploited. The stories of those who moved to the Black Country are threaded too throughout the rest of *Forging Ahead.*

Chapter 5 looks at the effects of industry on the unique, sometimes bizarre, landscape of the Black Country in the post-war period. Pitted with mineshafts, marl holes and decaying canals, the Black Country presented a distinct challenge to the planners who sought to reconstruct Britain after the Second World War. Roads and housing estates grew up, railway lines and canals were shut down, but the apparently inevitable march of progress did not meet with unanimous approval.

Chapter 6 takes in one of those battlegrounds – the crippling shortage of housing: here as elsewhere the way that good housing was defined, and who could live there, proved a source of longstanding debate. Chapter 7 moves inside the home itself, which typified the tension between modernity and tradition that characterised this era. Chapters 8 and 9 look at the differing experiences of life within the Black Country. The world experienced from Wolverhampton looked markedly different from the world as seen from Coseley, even though there were only a few miles between them. Chapter 8 shows where and how people shopped and spent their leisure time, and Chapter 9 analyses the relationship between citizen and state in everyday life – a subject that stirred emotions and "local patriotisms" perhaps more than any other topic of conversation in this era, and is key to understanding the growth of a wider pride in the Black Country. Chapter 10 concludes by looking back on the period in the wake of the economic crises and de-industrialisation of the 1970s and 1980s. The book also includes appendices which attempt to map the complexities of the Black Country's industry, politics and society. These include a summary of acronyms and a glossary; a gazetteer of key firms in the region – certainly not exhaustive, but sufficient to give an idea of the range of manufacturing in the Black Country; and an outline of the changing make-up of the Black Country's local government.

This thematic approach seeks to survey each debate that characterised the era. The town planners, for instance, who sought to make the Black Country liveable and modern, were challenged at each step by traditionalists who romanticised older ways of life and railed against the "fetish or orgy of modernising".[10] The council modernisers who proposed mergers and amalgamations between local authorities likewise faced stiff opposition from locals who feared "the dismemberment and death" of local identity and pride. In a less palatable conflict, Chapter 3 looks at how local politicians and the press created and exploited ill-feeling towards immigrants for political gain, and how they too were challenged.[11]

This research has been conducted as part of Black Country Living Museum's (BCLM) 'Forging Ahead' development, a project to take the story of the Black Country that BCLM tells into the period 1945-1968. The Black Country has always been an under-researched region, so this book draws together existing scholarship on this time and place combined with archival and oral primary sources. In an age of planning and reliance upon experts, reports produced by national and local authorities are crucial for statistical detail and for a 'top-down' view of society – but that same viewpoint is also their limitation. Reports by the West Midlands Group for Postwar Reconstruction, Sir Patrick Abercrombie, Staffordshire and Worcestershire County Councils, and so on, are valuable sources for one side of the debate between planners and traditionalists that characterised the era. Likewise, surveys conducted by social scientists such as Doris Rich (on how residents of Coseley spent their leisure time) and Tom Brennan (on the full spectrum of life in Wolverhampton) are full of rich detail, but are influenced by their authors' aims and perspectives as white, middle-class academics studying largely working-class localities. Even those writing on some of the most controversial events of the period, and in the most sympathetic way, came from this world. Paul Foot's campaigning journalism on the racism promoted by Enoch Powell and the Smethwick Conservatives in the 1960s is some of the most useful writing on the period, and his books remain the most important reports of this difficult time. Foot was a committed socialist, but was also the privately and Oxford-educated son of a colonial governor.

It can be difficult to get to the unmediated experiences of the Black Country's diverse working class in this period through such sources. Used with due respect to editorial stance, local newspapers go some way towards this, as do more unusual literary sources like John Petty's unique *Five Fags A Day*, depicting his idiosyncratic life as a scrap picker in Walsall. But this research also draws heavily on a number of oral histories recorded for the BCLM. This project has collected memories relating to specific buildings in the Black Country, using these small places as lenses through which to view the bigger picture. By comparing and contrasting these personal stories with the more official versions in archival sources, it is hoped that *Forging Ahead* gives a representative and accurate picture of the Black Country in this time.

If primary sources provide a range of perspectives, so too do historians. The Black Country lacks a definitive, modern academic history. Many of the attempts have resulted in highly personal, even idiosyncratic accounts. Phil Drabble's *Black Country* is a case in point: published in 1952, Drabble draws a romantic picture of the Black Country as a way of life, fast disappearing under the hand of planners, for whom he had nothing but contempt. Drabble represents an individualism common in Black Country writers, and he held himself representative of a fiercely independent, distinctive Black Country culture. Others who have attempted a Black Country history, such as J Wilson-Jones (1950), Edward Chitham (1972) and Harold Parsons (1986) were not quite so forthright, and produced excellently-researched, very readable histories, but all are characterised by a highly personal idea of the 'real' Black Country.[12]

Post-war Britain has attracted a wide range of historians, who typically identify an era of either radical change or of surprising continuity. Political and economic historians have debated the idea of a post-war consensus pioneered by Paul Addison, who suggested that the Second World War prompted a global social-democratic moment lasting until the late 1970s, characterised by a cross-party acceptance of economic and social policies, a mixed economy, and strong welfare states. Key works by Peter Hennessy and Kenneth O Morgan generally supported this view of the period, although more recently this has been challenged by historians such as Harriet Jones, Noel Whiteside, and James Vernon, who have highlighted the continuing power of conservative ideas, and the making and re-making of industrial capitalism in this new era. Social and cultural historians have had similar debates, with Arthur Marwick's left-wing account of dramatic social change questioned by more recent historians such as Dominic Sandbrook, who argues that much less shifted in society than was presumed. *Forging Ahead* argues that change and continuity were not antithetical but simultaneous. Amidst two centuries of transformation in the physical, social and cultural landscapes of the Black Country, 1945-1968 signalled some of the most dramatic; yet as Rosalind Watkiss Singleton has argued for the region, "old habits" persisted. How the Black Country experienced this combination of change and continuity is the theme of this book.[13]

From Austerity to Prosperity in the Black Country

On 2 March 1968, the last underground coal from the Black Country was brought up from Baggeridge Colliery. It was a quiet end to centuries of the industry that made the Black Country black in the first place and it came at a national tipping point. In 1968, the British Empire with its captive market was giving way to globalisation and

Keith Hodgkins/ Black Country Living Museum

Railway sidings at Baggeridge Colliery standing silent on 18 March 1968.

industrial strategy. Britain's once-mighty manufacturing sector was in decline: from a peak in 1952 when Britain had produced a quarter of the world's manufactured goods, it came to be challenged by competition from the USA, West Germany, Japan and elsewhere. In 1968 too, Britain's social fractures were being revealed – and widened – by the likes of Enoch Powell. It was in this latter part of the 1960s, and the turbulent 1970s, when the fragility of Britain's economic structures became apparent, and the Black Country – for the first time since before the war – really stumbled.

But in the decades before the closure of Baggeridge the picture for Britain and the Black Country was very different. Despite the near bankruptcy of the country and its subsequent austerity, despite social tensions, despite an increasingly tenuous place in global politics, Britain had come out of the Second World War with an industrial sector in full flow. *Forging Ahead* offers two main arguments about the Black Country and post-war Britain. Firstly, place mattered more than ever, typified by the continuing distinctiveness of localities within the region. Secondly, change and continuity could, and did, coexist. The historian Peter Hennessy describes the period after the Second World War as "the twenty golden years": this book aims to explore the complexities of that statement.[14]

Chapter 1

A "great recasting of values"

Britain and the Black Country, 1945-1968

South Staffordshire Water Archives

The bombed Gas Department showroom in West Bromwich High Street, November 1940. The grand interwar building was only partially destroyed – the second floor was removed, the frontage taken back and rebuilt, and the showroom reopened within weeks.

The historic expertise and industrial capacity of the Black Country meant that when the Second World War broke out, its furnaces and forges were turned to support the war effort. In West Bromwich, Archibald Kenrick & Sons switched from cast-iron saucepans to hand grenades, mortars and torpedo cones. Grazebrook's of Netherton moved from pig iron production to 12,000lb 'Blockbuster' bombs. Stewart's & Lloyd's Coombeswood site contributed to Operation Pluto, the 'Pipe-Lines Under The Ocean' that provided fuel to D-Day troops in Normandy. Metallisation Ltd. of Dudley developed metal-coating technology for the uranium isotopes used in the atomic bomb. The Black Country suffered bombing, but nothing like the devastation of near-neighbours Birmingham and Coventry. Towns across the region were hit in the winter of 1940-41, but the bombers were mainly targeting large production sites. The sprawling nature of the region, compared to more densely-packed cities elsewhere in the Midlands, meant that casualties – with a few tragic exceptions – were much lower than in other parts of the country. More demoralising locally were the endless shortages of food and fuel.[15]

Post-war Britain: a "Great Recasting of Values"?

On 5 July 1945, less than two months after VE Day, British voters ousted the Conservative Prime Minister Winston Churchill and returned the country's first majority Labour government under Clement Attlee. Labour in 1945 were, in Tony Benn's famous phrase, less a socialist party than "a party with socialists in it"; nevertheless, their proposals were far more radical than anything the Conservative or Liberal governments of pre-war Britain had attempted. Nearly three quarters of the country considered themselves working class, and they were now in the ascendancy; many held the Conservatives responsible for problems at home and abroad before the war and trusted Labour to turn things around. The new government set about enacting many of the proposals outlined in the Liberal economist William Beveridge's 1942 report on the welfare state, and nationalising many of Britain's industries. The words of Ernest Bevin, Labour's wartime Minister of Labour, must have been music to the ears of the workers of the Black Country: "…there will have to be a great recasting of values. The conception that those who produce or manipulate are inferior and must accept a lower status than the speculator must go."[16]

R Brookes/Black Country Living Museum

Icebreaker *Empress* at work during the severe winter of 1947.

The 1945 election landslide was repeated across the board in the Black Country, unusually for a region which had never voted en masse in this way. Some MPs were returned with huge majorities: John Dugdale in West Bromwich, Stanley Evans in Wednesbury and Arthur Moyle in Stourbridge won by almost 16,000 votes, and Will Nally in Bilston by almost 17,000. Elsewhere, the Black Country was represented by Jennie Lee, Arthur Henderson, John Baird, Billy Hughes, William Wells, George Wigg, and Alfred Dobbs for Smethwick, soon replaced by Patrick Gordon Walker after Dobbs' untimely death. All were Labour.[17]

Austerity under Labour: 1945-1951

As the new government set about fulfilling its manifesto pledges, the country continued to suffer shortages, economic and foreign affairs crises, and ever more stringent rationing. The weather hardly helped: a sodden summer in 1946 necessitated bread rationing for the first time, and the severity of the following winter left Black Country families picking over the spoil heaps of old coal mines for 'nutty slack' to burn. Global aftershocks from the war caused anxieties too. Britain was reliant on $2.7bn of 'Marshall Aid' from the USA – $1bn more than Germany received – and even then had to negotiate a further $5bn loan from the USA and Canada to fund reconstruction, which was only finally repaid in 2006. Money was scarce both in the Exchequer and in the home, but central to the government's platform – an area in which the Black Country was essential – was stimulating manufacturing to expand exports.[18]

Labour's economics combined the progressive aims of full employment and high government spending (as advocated by the Liberal economists Beveridge and John Maynard Keynes) with the more socialist principles of the redistribution of Britain's wealth through high levels of personal taxation (including a marginal top rate of over 90 per cent) and nationalisation of the means of production.[19] Their first big scheme came to fruition on 'Vesting Day,' 1 January 1947. This involved the establishment of the National Coal Board (NCB) after the nationalisation of the coal-mining industry, a totemic achievement for the new socialist government. Although Black Country mining was in decline, productivity – as well as workplace safety – soared. Around a fifth of Britain's industry was also nationalised. By 1951 gas, electricity, rail, waterways, communications, and large parts of the iron and steel and road transport industries had been nationalised as part of a comprehensive industrial policy.[20]

Alongside nationalisation there was an ambitious round of social reform. Perhaps the most lasting contribution of the Attlee administration was the welfare state, particularly the new National Health Service (NHS). Labour set about eradicating what Beveridge labelled the five "giant evils": squalor, ignorance, want, idleness, and disease. Health Minister Aneurin Bevan extended the existing system of national insurance to provide a "cradle to grave" scheme of free, comprehensive medical care to all, regardless of status or income. He also promoted an extensive programme of high-quality council house provision to meet the drastic shortage of decent homes. It could not come soon enough for many: in 1946, around 45,000 people across Britain moved into abandoned military camps such as the Burton Road camp in Dudley, which had been occupied in the war by American GIs. Bevan dreamed of introducing "in our modern villages and towns what was always the lovely feature of English and Welsh villages, where the doctor, the grocer, the butcher and the farm labourer all lived in the same street… the living tapestry of a mixed community".[21] But with a shortage of materials and labour, and a new peak in birth rate (the 'baby boom'), even the million temporary and permanent homes built under his auspices were not able to meet the demand.

Courtesy of Black Country Living Museum

King Street in Darlaston seen from the Bull Stake.

The US loan was one more symbol of Britain's changing role in the world. In 1947, following increased pressure and protests from the subcontinent, Attlee announced the independence of the jewel in Britain's imperial crown, India; and shortly after, plans were set in motion for the creation of a state in British-occupied Palestine, for the Jews who had suffered under Nazi persecution in Europe. Protests and calls for independence across the Empire were increasingly common, and Britain struggled to maintain its place at the top table of international politics once the post-war Soviet Union and the USA came to dominate. Britain's imperial history also affected its domestic policies: in 1948, an Act was passed formally permitting colonial and Commonwealth residents to work in Britain as a way of relieving the labour shortage, a small measure in that year but one that would have a major impact on Britain's changing understanding of itself in years to come.

In 1950, despite an increase in their share of the vote, Labour were returned to power with their huge majority slashed to just five. Little changed in the Black Country, with one exception: the new seat of Wolverhampton South-West elected a young Conservative MP, Enoch Powell. The Liberal Party – once dominant across the Midlands – was almost wiped out. In 1951, however, Attlee's government came to an end. Despite another record share of the popular vote for Labour, and the huge success of that year's Festival of Britain, the Conservatives gained a parliamentary majority and Britain's wartime champion, Winston Churchill, returned to Downing Street.

Britain and the World: the Conservative Years, 1951-1964

If 1940s Britain could be cold, drab and monotonous, the next decade saw the return of a little colour to everyday life. The country was far from inward-looking. Its Empire was still an essential and growing part of the country's trading plans, and stretched from Canada to Malaysia, Jamaica to Kenya. Huge, multi-faceted firms like Rubery Owen and John Thompson made the most of imperial (and later Commonwealth) ties, establishing factories in South Africa, India, Canada and Australia, and welcoming workers from those countries and many more back to their main sites in the Black Country. Among visitors were five Tanganyikan chiefs: their nation became independent from Britain in 1961, but seven years earlier they visited factories and orphanages in Dudley, as well as Dudley Zoo and the Molineux, to see Wolves beat Sunderland. One of them, Chief Amri Dodo of Gorowa, recorded the "unusually friendly" welcome from the Mayor, including a gala dinner at the town's Civic Restaurant. The object of their visit to Britain seems to have been to impress upon these future colonial leaders the importance of 'European' values,

Courtesy of Black Country Living Museum

Coronation celebrations at the White Lion, off King Street, Darlaston in 1953.

WEDNESBURY JOINT CHRISTIAN COUNCIL

A PUBLIC MEETING

in the

TOWN HALL, WEDNESBURY

will be held on

THURSDAY, OCTOBER 10TH, 1946

Subject : "IS CIVILISATION DOOMED?" "The Challenge of the Atomic Age"

Speakers : Dr. H. G. WOOD, D.D.
Prof. P. B. MOON, M.A., Ph.D., Member of the Association for Atomic Research
R. R. STOKES, Esq., M.P.

The Chair will be taken at 8 p.m. by His Worship the Mayor (Councillor Wadsworth)

ADMISSION FREE

Collection to defray expenses. Please bring this ticket with you.

C. H. Bowcott & Sons, Printers, Wednesbury & Darlaston.

Courtesy of Black Country Living Museum

Notice of a public meeting at Wednesbury Town Hall on the subject "Is civilisation doomed? The challenge of the atomic age". October 1946.

and this seemed to have been successful: Dodo came away believing his fellow Africans to be "behind" the Europeans, and with a need to "forge ahead" to emulate "those who have been long civilised."[22]

With the benefit of hindsight, Indian independence appears as the beginning of the end of the British Empire. With the election of Winston Churchill, however – staunch imperialist, scourge of the trade unions, and Britain's war-winning hero – further decolonisation seemed unlikely. Britain's first wholly Conservative government since 1929 arrived with a slim majority, but ushered in thirteen years of Tory rule – and a new monarch, Queen Elizabeth II, whose coronation in 1953 was undoubtedly the first mass-televised event in Britain. Churchill was strongly in favour of Empire, as was Sir Anthony Eden, who succeeded him in 1955. On a wave of affluence and industrial success, Eden promptly won that year's general election. The Empire was increasingly found at home too: successive governments called on workers from across the globe, many of whom saw Britain as not just the metropole of Empire, but the 'Mother Country.' Commonwealth residents from India, Pakistan and the Caribbean could be found working in the Black Country, alongside colleagues from Ireland, Africa, Poland and other parts of Eastern Europe.

It was not until the humiliating withdrawal from the Suez Canal zone in Egypt in 1956 that many finally realised that Britain was no longer the world power it had been. Independence movements across the Empire became increasingly forceful, and Britain's response more desperate: during the Mau Mau uprising, for instance, British soldiers tortured and detained tens of thousands of Kenyans. Power was shifting away from the European colonial powers to the new superpowers, the hyper-capitalist USA and the Communist USSR, and all foreign policy – be it war in Korea in the early 1950s, local appeals to support Hungarian refugees in 1956, or domestic debates over the nuclear deterrent in the 1960s – became caught up in the new, potentially cataclysmic global reality: the 'Cold War'. Eden was forced to resign after Suez. Despite this humiliation, his replacement Harold Macmillan increased the Tory majority to over 100 in 1959.[23]

Churchill had swiftly reversed the nationalisation of the iron and steel industry, but otherwise a social-democratic consensus had been built, providing a foundation for unprecedented economic growth. Despite their different traditions, there was much similarity between the fiscal policies of the outgoing Labour Chancellor of the Exchequer, Hugh Gaitskell (who succeeded Attlee as Labour leader in 1955) and his Conservative successor RA 'Rab' Butler. Under this new stability, the traumas of 1930s economic instability and the disruption of war in the 1940s began to give way to a newly affluent society, leading Macmillan to tell the British people in 1957 that "most of our people have never had it so good".[24] If this was true in the broadest terms, it also masked widespread inequalities. As later chapters will show, women, immigrants and others who fell outside an increasingly restrictive nuclear family norm did not share this prosperity evenly.

The national economy was not always as buoyant as Macmillan's words suggest, but on the whole exports, consumption and wages grew. The period experienced rapid changes in consumption and culture, Change was everywhere, from increasing car ownership to the birth of rock 'n' roll, from high-rise flats to ring roads, from nuclear power to nuclear bombs. By the end of the decade, a pragmatic Macmillan was ready to recognise the "growth of national consciousness" in Britain's African, South-East Asian, and Caribbean colonies in his famous "Wind of Change" speech in Cape Town, which symbolised the rapid dismantling of the British Empire. In 1961, Britain also began negotiations with the new European Economic Community (EEC), though membership was initially vetoed by the French President Charles de Gaulle, who believed Britain had a "deep-seated hostility" towards Europe. As the historian Eric Hobsbawm commented, the 1950s were a pivotal moment: "Suez and the coming of rock 'n' roll divide twentieth-century British history."[25]

"White Heat": Labour Returns, 1964-1970

The 1960s represented the beginnings of the long decline of Britain as a world power. Macmillan resigned in 1963 – ostensibly due to ill health, but with spy scandals raging around him, economic difficulties, and declining support in government. His successor Alec Douglas-Home, an aristocrat mocked by the opposition as an "elegant anachronism", lasted just a year. In the Black Country though, wages continued to grow; industrial improvements meant that output rose too, and there appeared little sign of decline. Disillusionment with the Tories finally bore fruit when Harold Wilson, adopted from the left of the Labour Party when their previous leader Hugh Gaitskell

Courtesy of Black Country Living Museum

Crowds awaiting election results outside Wednesbury Town Hall, Holyhead Road, in the 1950s. The couple facing each other are the Fletchers, parents of Dr John Fletcher, one of the founders of the Black Country Society.

died in 1963, led his party back to power in the 1964 general election. A key plank of Wilson's platform was his insistence that Britain was going to be "forged in the white heat" of a scientific and technological revolution. It represented the trajectory of the Black Country: traditional labour-intensive industries such as chainmaking or saddlery were in decline, to be replaced by mechanisation and automation in engineering.

Labour's return coincided with an era in which British popular culture stormed the world. The cultural history of the 'Swinging Sixties' is one of working-class heroes from The Beatles to Michael Caine, of sexual and social liberation, and of Britain's growing place in the artistic and creative worlds. Locally, the "Swinging Sixties" took somewhat longer to arrive in Dudley or Bilston than in Carnaby Street, although Black Country bands formed in this era went on to global success by the end of the decade.[26] Nationally though, an outpouring of creativity in music, literature, fashion and film was matched by a growing liberalism towards sex and contraception, racial discrimination and gender roles.[27]

The Black Country: the "Hub of a Universe"

The Black Country was, above everything else, an industrial region. Its expertise, infrastructure and skilled workforce placed it at the forefront of British industry. In the words of the West Midland Group on Post-War Reconstruction and Planning in

Courtesy of Black Country Living Museum

A completed lighthouse at the huge Chance Bros. glassworks in Smethwick.

1948, the Black Country was "a national asset of high value". For historian David Kynaston, it was the "hub… not only of a nation, but of a universe".[28] From the post-war Black Country emerged coal and cookers, saucepans and scales, firebricks and phosphorus, washing machines and windows, cookers and keys, sausages and springs, boilers and bicycles. Wages and working conditions improved like never before during this time of economic consensus. The days of exploitative middlemen and widespread poverty appeared gone in the Black Country, replaced by workplace welfare and working-class affluence. The following chapters explore the world of industry and work in the Black Country, by analysing what it produced and who produced it. Just as new materials and new processes changed the face of industry, so too did the prospect of labour being in a commanding position. This was to have significant ramifications for the everyday experience of work, but also for who was called upon to do that work.

Chapter 2

A "national asset"

Industry in the Black Country

Courtesy of Rachel E Waterhouse/Black Country Living Museum

Heavy machine shop at Tangyes, Smethwick, in 1957.

The roots of Black Country society in the mid-twentieth century were solidly industrial. 300 years of heavy industry had been built upon massive natural reserves of coal, iron, lime and clay. However, economic depression in the late nineteenth century, and the dwindling local availability of raw materials, brought about the decline of many of the region's traditional heavy industries in the early twentieth century and the expansion of the economies in other parts of the country: South Wales, the North-East, Central Scotland. But the Black Country reinvented itself. It diversified into light and medium-scale engineering, and businesses were – comparatively – prosperous during the turbulent inter-war years. They remained so after the Second World War. This chapter demonstrates that compared to the monolithic industries of some other industrial regions – textiles in Manchester or Yorkshire, coalmining or shipbuilding elsewhere – the Black Country's strength lay in its diversity. It made things that people wanted, from bricks to car parts to washing machines, and it therefore contributed tremendously to Britain's post-war recovery and prosperity. The region also experienced the tide of amalgamations and acquisitions that characterised the era too: the day of the backyard chainshop or small family business was passing; the mechanised foundry and integrated supply chain were on the rise. Yet the distinctive local and regional industrial diversity that had always set it apart was still in evidence.

The demands of war provided a boost for much of British industry, particularly in metalworking regions like the Black Country. Many local jobs were reserved occupations, alongside the famous 'Bevin Boys' in the region's collieries, and other firms manufactured bombs, munitions, and tank and aircraft components. When VE Day came, new use had to be found for this productive capacity. Britain was staring into an economic abyss at the end of the war as the US Lend-Lease agreement ended, and there was a massive balance of payments shortfall, coupled with huge debts as a result of borrowing to finance the war effort. As a result, the new Labour government asked manufacturers to devote all their resources to increasing exports. By the 1950s, Britain had increased its share of world trade to 25 per cent and rising. The Cradley Heath hollowware manufacturer Ernest Stevens informed its domestic customers that "owing to export efforts, 'Judge' Ware is not as plentiful as we all would like, but home production is progressing and your supplies will tend to improve".[29]

So Black Country firms became increasingly integrated within a global market: Guy Motors sent buses to South Africa, Pakistan and the Netherlands; Henry Hope Ltd. exported windows to 37 countries; the Mount Works in Cradley Heath made specialist saddlery staples demanded by Fiji; and Fred Done, trapmaker at Sidebotham's in Wednesfield,[30] claimed to have caught "more lions than any man alive" – including in the service of the Ethiopian Emperor, Haile Selassie. "If a man sets traps for rats in a West African warehouse," it was suggested, or "for coypus on a South American ranch, for lions in the East African bush or tigers in the Indian jungle, it is very likely that the trap comes from Wednesfield." The Britain of the 1950s was responsible for a quarter of the world's trade in manufactured goods, was the biggest producer of coal and steel in Europe, and built more than half of the world's exported cars. The West Midlands, with Black Country production at its centre, was at the heart of the manufacturing economy, making up around 40 per cent of British exports by value.[31]

Courtesy of Black Country Living Museum

Jim Parkes (left) and colleagues at Baggeridge Colliery in the 1950s. Jim, from Mushroom Green, Dudley Wood, began at the colliery in 1932 and worked there for thirty years.

Extractive Industry

By the end of the Second World War, mining in the Black Country was in its final days. Coal was still responsible for more than 90 per cent of the nation's heat and energy, but it was an industry in trouble, and mining it in the Black Country had become uneconomical. It was one of the first industries to be nationalised by Labour, in 1947, but the new NCB inherited an industry crippled by under-investment and poor labour relations. The NCB, based locally at the Earl of Dudley's former home of Himley Hall, poured money into the Black Country's remaining collieries. Mechanical cutters and conveyors were installed and for the first time, the Black Country saw the high, conical spoil banks so familiar in other parts of the country. Some smaller pits continued too. Beech Tree Colliery in Cradley provided work for 118 men and 27 pit ponies in 1957, producing 80,000 tons per year of the best coal in its 60-year history. It was so productive that Polish, Latvian and Czech workers had to be drafted in, but its demise was brought about by a classic Black Country problem: flooding. A sudden seepage of water forced its closure in 1958, with an estimated half a million tons of coal left underground. Within ten years, all of the Black Country's nationalised collieries were closed, having proved unviable compared to the vast, modern pits in South Wales, Nottinghamshire and Yorkshire. At 5:30am on 2 March 1968, the winding gear at Baggeridge Colliery, in Himley, cranked into action for the last time, raising a cage of miners up 800 feet – the last shift to mine coal underground in the Black Country.[32]

A number of small pits owed their continued existence to the presence of fireclay around the coal seams, and these were licensed by the NCB rather than nationalised. Brickmaking was still a major concern in the Black Country and was now "the only major industry still rooted to its raw material".[33] Alongside the production of huge quantities of ordinary bricks across the region, the south-west of the Black Country, in and around Amblecote, Brierley Hill, Pensnett and Gornal, produced large quantities of high-quality fireclay used for firebricks, retorts and refractories (bespoke firebricks used for lining furnaces and kilns). The quality of this clay had been a draw for industry for hundreds of years. When made into bricks, its ability to withstand extreme temperatures made it ideal for building kilns and furnaces.

Dreadnought Tile Works

Barrow girls at Hinton, Perry & Davenhill, Pensnett, in 1961, makers of Ketley Bricks and Dreadnought Tiles. The Dreadnought Tile Works is still going strong in 2020, 215 years after it was founded.

Of the 25 firebrick manufacturers in the Black Country, 23 were in the south-west: Amblecote, Brierley Hill, and the surrounding villages. The biggest was Gibbons Brothers of Dibdale, Lower Gornal, whose specialism was gas retorts used in the production and distribution of the coal gas that powered streetlights and cookers across the world. Their 21 kilns, branch line and locomotives, colliery and engineering division meant that they could manufacture an entire gasworks on site and transport it across the country. This specialisation was typical: it was estimated that only around a tenth of production in this part of the Black Country was for ordinary, production-line firebricks. EJ & J Pearson of the Delph, Brierley Hill, for example, was able to produce a firebrick for the local glass industry measuring an enormous 6ft by 2ft by 18 inches, taking two months to fire in the kiln. This firm and its distant relation Harris & Pearson, on Brettell Lane, were just two of many smaller, family-run firms in the area and like many British businesses were subject to a succession of mergers as the decades passed. Despite their tremendous success in this period, this kind of specialisation proved dangerous. When Britain made the switch from coal gas to natural gas in the late 1960s, for example, much of Gibbons' work was rendered redundant. Most Black Country brickworks had closed by the 1980s – the only twenty-first-century survivor is Hinton, Perry & Davenhill of Pensnett, producers of the famous Ketley bricks and Dreadnought tiles.[34]

Heavy Metal

Wherever coal was found, so too was the iron and steel industry. Although the Black Country's own ironstone deposits were depleted, the expertise of local iron and steelworkers ensured that by 1952, although none of Britain's largest steelworks were in the West Midlands, a fifth of the nation's early-stage metalworkers were. Attlee's Labour government attempted a partial nationalisation of the highly complex iron and steel industry in February 1951, forming the Iron and Steel Corporation (ISC) to acquire the share capital, not the works, of 80 key iron and steel companies. After the Conservative victory that year, however, this policy was swiftly reversed, and most were sold back into private ownership.[35]

Round Oak Steelworks, for instance – founded by the Earl of Dudley in the 1870s – was bought by the Tube Investments (TI) group, based in Oldbury. This large concern had arms all around the country but added Round Oak as its key early-stage producer, dealing with a huge amount of scrap metal – in abundance in the Black Country – and producing cold-formed bars and sections in its new 50-ton arc furnaces. Similarly, the massive Spring Vale Steelworks in Bilston was re-purchased by

Peter Donnelly

Round Oak Steelworks and the Dudley Canal, 1962.

its previous owners, Stewart's & Lloyd's. They poured investment in, most famously in the form of a huge new blast furnace called 'Elisabeth' (after the owner's daughter, not the new monarch) in 1954, capable of producing 275,000 tonnes of steel per year. Bilston, though small in comparison to giant steelworks like Port Talbot or Corby, served the specialist demand for hot-rolled sections within Britain's steel industry. The other major steel producer was Wednesbury's Patent Shaft & Axletree Co., which was re-purchased by the related shipbuilding firms Cammell-Laird and Metro-Cammell and continued to produce plate steel and railway rolling stock.[36]

All of these firms were highly successful into the 1960s, increasing the region's output by half a million ingot tons between 1957 and 1967, and taking market share from the North-East and elsewhere. Their success encouraged Harold Wilson's Labour government to enact a much more comprehensive nationalisation in 1967, and Round Oak, Patent Shaft and Bilston Steelworks all became part of the new British Steel Corporation.[37]

Manufacturing

The uses of iron and steel fall into two broad categories: casting – pouring molten metal into moulds – and forging – working the metal by rolling or striking. Rolling mills were found at steelworks and other sites across the region, and enabled metal to be formed into anything a customer might require. The commonest products were steel sections, or pre-rolled lengths of steel suitable for a variety of uses. Constructional engineers like Coseley Buildings or Rubery Owen turned these into huge structures, from everyday factory buildings to entire London Underground stations. Other manufacturers turned this heavy metal into an overwhelming range of products. When the Institute of Mechanical Engineers visited the Accles and Pollock tube works in Oldbury in 1950, for instance, they found 4,500 employees making everything from huge aircraft undercarriages to scientific tubes, including the world's smallest tube, at one quarter the diameter of a human hair. Accles & Pollock proudly boasted that when an American firm sent their engineers what was claimed to be the smallest tube in the world, they returned it with one of their own inside, a friendly rivalry that continued for nearly 40 years. New products for the post-war boom in leisure included javelins, archery equipment, golf clubs and billiards cues; at the same time, they were leaping into the future, creating cans for nuclear fuel elements.[38]

Black Country goods were sold locally and globally. Walter Somers' Haywood Forge, in Halesowen, was well known for some of the largest forgings in the region. The Queen and Prince Philip visited the Forge on their tour of the Black Country in 1957 and were shown the 3,600-ton press known as the 'Somers 'Ommer.' There were also locally-made Wellman and Gibbons charging cars, 'Glyso' corebinders and Fordath sand-mixers on site. At the same time, many Black Country products travelled the world. Tangye Brothers made vast numbers of diesel engines, pumps and hydraulic equipment in Smethwick, but were always concerned with their export market. The firm had expected to sell across India and the Middle East after the war, but India's independence in 1947 (with its attendant tariff controls) and the Suez crisis in 1956 changed this dramatically. Tangye's diverse portfolio helped it weather the storm, however: they sold engines to Spain for irrigating vineyards, hydraulics to Calder Hall (now Sellafield), hydraulic jacks to Canada, and industrial heaters to South Africa and Australia, "where problems of factory heating would not at first sight appear to be a major worry". The Commonwealth clearly remained their major marketplace, although "the problems and potentialities of the European Common Market offer a new challenge to those equipped and ready to meet it".[39]

Other firms prepared to greet the atomic age. The Wolverhampton firm John Thompson took its first step into this new industry in 1955 with a contract for the Dounreay nuclear power station in the north of Scotland, followed by Berkeley in Gloucestershire in 1959. They went on to contribute to nuclear power stations at Bradwell, Dungeness, Hinkley Point, Hunterston and Latina, Italy. The Cold War dominated global politics by the 1950s, and military and aeronautical contracts were won across the Black Country. William Mills of Wednesbury and Herman Smith of Netherton both produced castings for guided missiles such as Bristol-Ferranti's 'Bloodhound' system, and Wolverhampton's Boulton-Paul produced specialist parts for the most famous planes of the 1960s, including the Harrier jump jet and Concorde.

Nevertheless, East-West relations were not always so hostile. John Thompson was one of several firms that sought out trade with Communist countries. Representatives were joined at the 1962 Leipzig Trade Fair (which West Germany boycotted) by Wednesbury's MP John Stonehouse, and held long discussions with the German Democratic Republic and USSR; other Black Country firms such as GWB Furnaces in Dudley did work for Soviet installations too.[40]

The distinctive human and physical geography of the Black Country has long led to local specialisations and distinct urban identities: Stourbridge glass, Cradley Heath chains, Willenhall locks. This remained true in the post-war period,

Courtesy of Black Country Living Museum

Stainless steel vessel for Britain's full-scale fast breeder reactor, departing John Thompson's works in Ettingshall for Dounreay nuclear power station.

although mergers and acquisitions spread some industries around the Black Country a little more evenly. The area around Oldbury, for instance, was home to a plethora of small and large tool manufacturers. William Hunt & Sons' (WHS) huge Brades Works made every kind of tool, and its success led to mergers first with the Stourbridge firm Nash Tyzack, then the Sheffield-based Spear & Jackson, who themselves merged with Eva Brothers, a tool-making group including the well-known firms Edward Elwell (Wednesbury) and Chillington (Wolverhampton). Hunt's acronym prompted the nickname 'Work Hard or Starve' given by bricklayers dependent on their tools, but another speciality was the 4-inch pointing trowel – it became famous as the industry standard trowel for archaeological excavations. It came recommended by Stonehenge's archaeologist Richard JC Atkinson and remained the most-used archaeological trowel for the rest of the century.[41]

Chainmaking was also concentrated in the hilly southern Black Country, particularly in Cradley Heath. Both the handmade chain factories and the exploitative employment practices that had characterised this industry were dying out. By 1953, machine-made chains comprised half of the output of Griffin-Woodhouse, Cradley Heath, and the puddled iron which was hammered into hand-made chain was increasingly hard to come by. By the end of the 1960s, the last wrought-iron chain firm in Worcestershire closed down: "The lines of hearths in the chainshop now stand cold and the 90ft bed for testing chain is unused."[42]

One firm that rode the wave of mergers and acquisitions was the famous Noah Hingley & Sons of Netherton. Founded in 1820, Hingley's was most famous for its work on the *Titanic*'s anchor in 1911, but by the early 1950s it was at the head of one of the biggest industrial groups in the region, and still making chains, anchors and steel. At the group's headquarters in Netherton, puddled wrought iron was still made, chains were still hand-made and tested, and the steam hammer plant still made forgings up to 6 tons; but modern drop hammers, heat-treatment plants, machine shops, a research laboratory, and a well-appointed athletics ground joined them. Hingley's had a swathe of subsidiaries, including famous names like Wright's Forge (Tipton), John Bagnall (West Bromwich), and John Bradley (Stourbridge) and in 1961 made its largest acquisition yet, taking over M & W Grazebrook of Peartree Lane, Netherton. Just five years later, however, with some branches beginning to struggle, the group was finally taken over itself by Wednesbury's FH Lloyd.[43]

Springs provided historical continuity in West Bromwich. The Salter brothers had produced weighing equipment in the town since 1770, and there were still over 30 spring manufacturers based there in the 1960s. The growth of the British car industry was a particular catalyst, but West Bromwich made springs for everything from heavy railway rolling stock, to theatre seats and precise electronic measuring equipment. Salter's remained the biggest, literally: its factory was the highest building in town, and its 2,000 workers produced weighing scales as well as springs. Salter's main competitor was another Black Country firm: Avery, based in Smethwick.[44]

Courtesy of Black Country Living Museum

Harper's of Willenhall had moved from the town's traditional lock industry into iron castings for the motor industry. Traditional hand casting continued as an essential part of the work.

Willenhall still made more than 90 per cent of the world's locks: no fewer than 18 million per year. The American firm Yale had bought out the biggest Willenhall lock manufacturer, H & T Vaughan, and it joined Josiah Parkes & Sons and Chubb as the biggest lock firms in the Black Country. They relied on locally produced iron and steel, and keys from another specialist town, Wednesfield. There, a key could be cut to fit any lock: experts like Tom Mason could make them for anything from ancient gates to the Marquis of Bath's Russian chest and Lord Derby's kennels.[45]

Other traditionally local industries suffered during this period, sometimes due to changing legislation. Wednesfield's longstanding trap industry went into steep decline immediately after myxomatosis was introduced to control the rabbit population. Other traditional industries grew. The small town of Darlaston had some of the best-paid workers in the country working in engineering firms, many of which specialised in the high-quality fastenings which were essential to the Black Country's other manufacturing industries. Locally-owned Darlaston firms including the Steel Nut & Joseph Hampton Co. and Charles Richards competed with industrial giants like Rubery Owen's Nuts & Bolts (Darlaston) Ltd., and GKN's Nuts & Bolts Division.

GKN has its roots outside the Black Country, at the vast eighteenth-century iron works at Dowlais, South Wales, and the screw factory of Nettlefold & Son in Birmingham (later Nettlefold & Chamberlain, where the future mayor of Birmingham Joseph Chamberlain made his career). But the major innovator in the firm was Arthur Keen – founder of Patent Nut & Bolt of Heath Street, Smethwick. He was an ambitious businessman, acquiring Dowlais in 1900 and Nettlefold & Chamberlain in 1902 to form one of the biggest companies in the country. Guest, Keen & Nettlefold (GKN) took over coal mines and steelworks, and absorbed other nut, bolt and screw producers like FW Cotterill, Enoch Wilks, Tolley Sons & Bostock, Staffordshire Bolt & Nut Co. and Jabez Yardley – all in Darlaston.

The firm underwent substantial modernisation and further expansion after the war. This was very necessary. Its headquarters at Heath Street, Smethwick, was home to some seriously outdated practices: when a new accountant arrived in 1946, he found a budget line for "steak for dogs" – they had only just stopped delivering screws by dog cart. But two decades later they were proudly proclaiming their vast range of modern manufactures: steel and iron works at Baldwin's, Swindon, near Himley; rolled and bright steel at Smethwick; forgings and castings at Garrington's in Darlaston and Bromsgrove; motor and aviation components at BRD in Aldridge, C & B Smith in Wolverhampton, and Joseph Sankey's in Bilston; reinforced concrete at Twisteel, Smethwick; metal plating at Ionic, also in Smethwick; Nettlefold's screws in Smethwick; and of course nuts and bolts in Darlaston. By the 1960s GKN was one of the region's largest employers.[46]

Courtesy of Black Country Living Museum

Nettlefolds screws being packed for shipping across the world at GKN's Heath Street Works, Smethwick.

Geographical specialisation extended beyond metal too. Hundreds continued to be employed in Walsall's leatherworks and Stourbridge's glassworks, although the largest single glassmaking firm was Chance Brothers in Spon Lane, Smethwick. Chance already had a fearsome reputation, having made the glass for the Crystal Palace, Houses of Parliament and the White House, and specialist equipment and structures from microscopes to lighthouses. The firm also produced cathode ray tubes, car windscreens, precision glass tubing, 90 per cent of Hollywood's camera lenses, domestic glassware, and even re-glazed Westminster Clock Tower, home to Big Ben, to correct damage sustained during the war.[47]

Oldbury was famous for its chemical industries, such as Albright & Wilson and Imperial Chemical Industries (ICI), located next to each other between Park Lane and the Titford Canal, and British Industrial Plastics (BIP), makers of polymers of all kinds, from industrial resins to Melmex melamine. Walsall also developed a thriving electrical engineering industry, the biggest firm being Crabtree, opposite the Arboretum. Crabtree employed around 1,800 people in 1946 and – apart from being one of the country's largest consumers of porcelain – manufactured everything on site, from chemicals to castings. Producing for the domestic market, it benefited from the boom in housebuilding, from prefabs to new towns.[48]

Courtesy of Black Country Living Museum

An advertisement for the chair and couch range produced by Tipton's Vono. Established in 1896 by Ernest Vaughan (Vono stood for "Vaughan Only, No Others"), by this time the famous firm was part of the Duport industrial group.

Everything for the Modern Home

Domestic affluence overtook austerity in the mid-1950s. Compared to other manufacturing areas, the Black Country had a diversity of manufacturing and engineering expertise, meaning that it was already producing household items in greater quantities than many other manufacturing regions. So, almost uniquely, it was possible to source almost everything for the modern home from the local area. A front door could be adorned by a Kenrick knocker and a Kirkpatrick letterbox, with a Vulcan front gate. Decorating inside and out was possible with Mander's paint made in Heath Town – after all, it was good enough for the Queen and the Prime Minister. Best & Lloyd balustrades and Smith & Davis 'Clipper' carpet holders provided furnishings for stairs, whilst a bedroom might include a Tipton-made Vono bedstead, and the bathroom a Bilston Foundries bath and Thomas Dudley toilet. The front room could house a grand Wordsley or James Smellie coal fireplace, or a humbler Triplex or Chatwin grate, tended by a Bilston Knight companion set with a shovel, poker and hearth brush; unless a household had a modern 'Gasmiser' fire, produced by Cannon in Coseley. In the evening, once the rayon curtains, made at Courtauld's, Wolverhampton were drawn, the family could gather around an Ever Ready radio, a new television containing a cathode ray tube made by Chance or listen to a record on a Dansette with a BSR turntable changer.

British Sound Reproducers (BSR) was founded by Dr Daniel McLean McDonald in a small building on Perry Park Road, Rowley Regis, in 1932. By the end of the war they were manufacturing high-quality sound reproducing equipment including tannoys, intercoms and laboratory testing equipment. In 1952, McDonald offered his turntable autochanger to Morris Margolin, who had until then been producing large radiograms, but with this cheap, reliable component they were suddenly in a position to revolutionise home entertainment. Margolin trademarked the name 'Dansette' in 1952 and immediately began to sell out of their new turntable.

This transformed BSR. From one small factory at Old Hill they expanded to employ 2,600 staff by 1961, including a large proportion of women. Margolin's (and McDonald's) timing was excellent. The introduction of the 7" single in 1949, the first Top 12 chart in 1952, and the birth of rock 'n' roll in the mid-1950s all combined to make the affordable, easy-to-use Dansette a household staple for families and teenagers all over the country. In the Black Country, BSR also produced their own record player, the Monarch, and expanded to a huge new factory at Wollaston Mills in 1959, on the site of Isaac Nash & Son's edge-tools works. At its height in the 1970s, BSR produced 250,000 units per week, and held no less than 87 per cent of the world market for turntable changers.[49]

The newly middle-class – or aspirational working-class – housewife was also expected to be the perfect hostess. Her Daintymaid kitchen, made by Grovewood Products at Dudley Port, could be installed with a gas or an electric cooker, from Coseley's Cannon or Tipton's Revo. Kitchen ingredients could be weighed on Avery or Salter's scales and a Kenrick mincer would be used to prepare dinner. There was a bewildering choice of pots and pans: pressure cookers from Presto (Wolverhampton) and steam cookers from MCL & Repetition (Oldbury) competed with traditional metal hollowware, in which the Black Country had the biggest names in the business – Kenrick, Izons and the competing 'Judge' and 'Jury' brands of the Stevens brothers. Meals might be served on Taylor Law's "Matched Colourware… the perfect help for hostess and housewife all the year round". Taylor Law, better known as Tala, operated a large factory in Stourbridge, and epitomised the domestic expectations of the post-war housewife: the "lasting gifts for the bride" section of their catalogue featured icing syringes, hand whisks, and bread bins.[50]

Even Black Country food and drink was served. One of the largest meat producers in the country was Marsh & Baxter, whose huge meat-processing factory dominated the skyline in Brierley Hill and slaughtered 2,000 pigs a day. Soft drinks were made by T Mason & Sons, whose slogan was 'Fizziness is our Bizziness' – while beer was available from one of the biggest manufacturing sectors in the whole area, brewing. Smethwick's Mitchell's & Butler's, and Wolverhampton & Dudley Breweries dominated the industry across the Midlands. When all was done, the Servis washing machine, built by Wilkins & Mitchell of Darlaston, took much of the strain out of the previously back-breaking wash day. Rubery Owen produced the Rowen dishwasher, plumbed in with Evered tubing, and one of their subsidiaries made the Easiclene gas refrigerator.

The Black Country never managed to gain a reputation for complete prefabricated houses, although some firms did make an attempt. A joint venture between Gyproc, West Bromwich's Brockhouse and Bilston's Sankey's produced a handful of 'Keyhouse Unibuilt' houses made of cold-rolled steel sections produced on site. A few were built in Canley, near Coventry, in 1943, and another pair in Edinburgh. Despite an initial flurry of enthusiasm, they were superseded by other firms' hot-rolled production methods, and the experiment went no further.[51] A similar fate seemed to have occurred to Rubery Owen's prototype houses: two of these were built in the new Bentley estate, built for workers at Owen's huge Darlaston works, but no more.[52]

The Motor Industry

The motor industry, however, overshadowed everything else. Before the Second World War, cars were a luxury item, primarily for the well-to-do and middle classes. Wolverhampton, in particular, had a brief spell as a major motor manufacturing centre in the early twentieth century, although it collapsed as quickly as it had risen. It was a major gamble, then, for the new Labour government to pin its hopes on the motor trade as a lynchpin for the export drive, but Sir Stafford Cripps, Labour's President of the Board of Trade, was bullish. He was proved right. Domestic car production rocketed from a few thousand per year before the war to half a million by 1950 – reflecting a similar growth in domestic car ownership – and this was by no means the peak: production grew year on year into the 1970s, topping over two million vehicles per year. The West Midlands was the centre of this industry. Rover was based in Solihull, Austin's huge Longbridge works were in Birmingham, and Rootes, Jaguar, Daimler, Standard-Triumph and Alvis had their headquarters in Coventry. These firms formed the backbone of the British motor industry alongside Ford in Dagenham, Morris in Oxford, and Vauxhall in Luton. These massive assembly lines were not replicated in the Black Country, however, which specialised in components. Some older Black Country makers remained, but this was not where the mass-produced "cheap, tough, good-looking car of decent size" that Cripps desired was built.[53]

Courtesy of Black Country Living Museum

A prototype prefabricated house constructed by Rubery Owen in Darlaston. Only two of these steel-framed homes were built, as part of the new Bentley estate north of Darlaston.

Courtesy of GKN/ Black Country Living Museum

GKN boasted that although they did not make complete cars themselves, they made virtually everything that went in them.

The most famous car manufacturer in the Black Country was Sunbeam. Established in Wolverhampton in 1905, the struggling firm was acquired by Rootes in 1936 which moved much of its manufacture to Coventry. The Sunbeam Trolleybus Company, however, stayed in Wolverhampton. It was acquired by Brockhouse in 1944 then by Guy Motors in 1948, creating probably the largest trolleybus manufacturer in the world. Guy's 14-acre factory in Fallings Park employed 1,500 people building the famous Arab buses as well as lorries and trolleybuses. London Transport, and local operators in Wolverhampton, Walsall, Birmingham, including Midland Red, were all Guy customers and their Sunbeam-branded trolleybuses were used from Pontypridd to Pretoria, and Rotherham to Rangoon. Although Guy's products performed well into the 1960s, poor financial decisions led to a takeover by Jaguar in 1961. By the time the latter was subsumed into British Leyland in 1968, the Guy badge was on borrowed time, and the last vehicle branded as a Guy rolled off the line in 1972.[54]

Jensen sports cars, built in West Bromwich, were for a wealthier clientele: in 1953, a new Jensen 541 at £2,346 cost more than the average house.[55] Several other manufacturers made less successful attempts in this sector: Walsall's Swallow Doretti and Wolverhampton's Turner A30 never caught on. Wolverhampton's Kieft also tried, though they had more luck with racing cars, such as that driven by Don Parker to two Formula 3 championships in the early 1950s. Even more successful in that field were British Racing Motors (BRM), a small, unsuccessful, team when they were taken over by one of their trustees – Alfred Owen of the massive Rubery Owen organisation, based in Darlaston. With Owen's might behind it, BRM went on to win 17 *grands prix* between 1959 and 1972, with Graham Hill, Juan Fangio, Jackie Stewart, who won his first ever Grand Prix in a BRM, and Stirling Moss. The high point came in 1962, when Hill won the Drivers' Championship and BRM the Constructors' Championship.[56]

It was in parts for other car makers, however, that the Black Country excelled. The motor industry's requirements for small, mass-produced castings ensured that by the mid-1950s, half of the country's component manufacture employment was in the West Midlands. This prompted investment in mechanisation too, so that foundries which had operated in a traditional way since the Victorian era finally began to embrace modern processes including plastics, production lines and pressure die-casting.[57]

This modern supply chain became central to how the motor industry operated. Few manufacturers fabricated every part of a car themselves – it made better economic sense to source the best and cheapest components from wherever they could be supplied. The region's proximity to the major assembly lines meant that a rapid turnaround was possible. The *Foundry Trade Journal* reported on the Birmid Industries works in 1960:

> *Frequently castings arrive at a point of despatch at a temperature so high as to render handling decidedly uncomfortable. Indeed, the wooden bases of lorries and pallets have, on occasion, been fired... Even when they arrived at the vehicle assemblers, many of Birmid's castings were said to still be warm.*[58]

The Austin-Healey 100 demonstrated this supply chain to its fullest extent. This sports car was introduced in 1952 and final assembly was completed at Austin's Longbridge plant. But before it got there, it started as a chassis built at John Thompson's Motor Pressings site in Wolverhampton. From there, it was shipped to Jensen's factory in West Bromwich – they built on the primed body panels which had been supplied by Dowty Boulton Paul of Wolverhampton, installed wiring and some of the trim, then shipped it off to Longbridge where it gained an engine from Coventry and transmission from elsewhere in Birmingham.[59]

The Observer described the supply chain of over 100 firms to Jaguar's Coventry factory in 1961 as "perched on the shoulder of a whole pyramid of suppliers… [including] hordes of tiny firms in the jewellery district of Birmingham and 'the Black Country'". Production was at full capacity and order times were short, and the newspaper was worried about the fragility of this so-called "vertical disintegration". A series of strikes in the early 1960s proved them right. Among others, 800 foundry workers at Midland Motor Cylinder in Smethwick, and 500 at G Clancey in Halesowen struck in September 1961: as a result, thousands of assembly line workers at Cowley, Longbridge, Solihull and Coventry had to be sent home. When 550 press shop workers at Sankey's went on an unofficial strike in 1962, production of the Mini at Longbridge ground to a halt.[60]

As businesses attempted to create an internal supply chain to counteract this fragility, mergers and acquisitions became commonplace. GKN, the Triplex Group and Birmid Industries of Smethwick – from whose foundries came transmission casings for the Austin Princess, auxiliary castings for the Mini, suspension arms for the Ford Zephyr, cylinder blocks for Rolls-Royces and Jaguars, engines for the Commer TS3, even zinc alloys for Dinky toys – were examples. Similarly, Beans Industries of Hurst Lane, Tipton, was snapped up by Standard-Triumph in 1956: its fully-mechanised, 300,000 square foot foundry could produce 500 tons of iron castings per week, from large engine blocks for heavy commercial vehicles, to precise brake drums, flywheels and cylinders.[61] Standard-Triumph was itself acquired by Leyland Motors in 1960, and merged with British Motor Holdings in 1968 to form British Leyland, the largest business in the British motor industry (see Appendix 2).

The industrial history of the post-war Black Country was one of prosperity and growth, but also the decline of traditional small industry in favour of bigger corporations and more advanced technology. The skill and expertise which the region had developed over two centuries of industrialisation stood it in good stead for this change, and it served the worker as well as the master. Sweated trades and disregard for employee well-being were becoming things of the past, and the exploited woman chainmaker and puddler risking life and limb were no longer the characteristic working people of the Black Country. Instead, the production engineer, the Punjabi foundryman, the skilled steelworker were the workers who powered the booming Black Country in the 'golden years' after the war. This chapter has showcased many of the Black Country's most recognisable names and shows how the geographical distinctions and skills that had long characterised the region persisted. The region's place in a global supply chain was assured in this period, and despite occasional strikes, there seemed no reason for this growth and prosperity to end.

Rubery Owen and the Mini

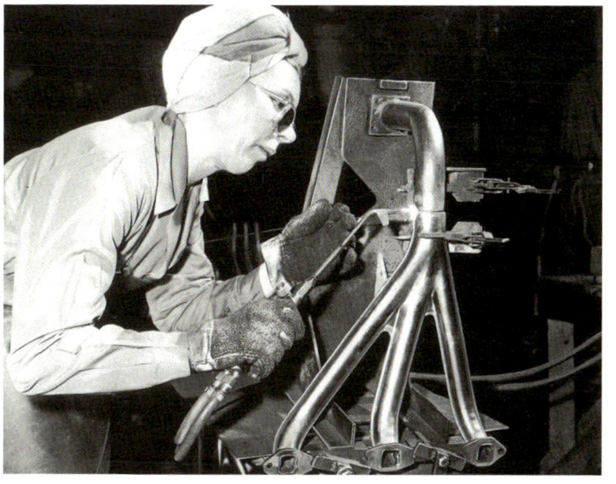

At work on the exhaust manifold for the Mini Cooper S, at Rubery Owen's Darlaston works in 1965.

Courtesy David Owen/Black Country Living Museum

Perhaps the biggest component manufacturer of them all was the Rubery Owen organisation. The firm had become experts in production engineering for the motor industry, and by the post-war boom were building chassis, axles, wheel arches, brakes, wheels, ploughs, and even complete racing cars. The Darlaston factory was so large that when director Alfred Owen welcomed the Duke and Duchess of Gloucester to the works, he greeted them in Willenhall and, halfway through, donned his ceremonial chains as Chairman of Darlaston Urban District Council, as they entered another district. By the end of the 1940s, the firm was still growing: in 1950 its 100,000th Ferguson plough rolled off the line, just four years after production started. The works made aircraft sections and vehicle parts: double-decker Midland Red chassis, Austin axle casings, MG fuel tanks, and millions of 'RO-style' wheels for Jensen, Rover and the Ford Cortina Mk II. The comings and goings were so substantial that three locomotives and 150 rail wagons operated from the firm's sidings, and over 200 road vehicles were pioneers in the logistics field.[62]

Like many firms, Rubery Owen's fortunes were tied to the British motor industry. While this would eventually prove fateful, the mid-1950s saw Rubery Owen's place in history confirmed. The political crisis in Suez, in 1956, had led to petrol rationing and a slump in car sales. The resultant boom in sales of more fuel-efficient German 'bubble cars' prompted the British Motor Corporation (BMC) to design a new, smaller and more efficient car. The result was alternatively known as the Morris Mini-Minor or the Austin 7 – but quickly became just the Mini. Alec Issigonis' iconic 1959 design featured an innovative transverse, front-wheel drive engine, but to build that an entire new subframe was required. This was designed and built at Darlaston by Rubery Owen, and just six years later, the millionth Mini came off the production lines at BMC's Longbridge plant.[63]

Chapter 3

"Jobs for all"

Working life in the Black Country

Courtesy of Black Country Living Museum

Fred Done (left) and Teddy Tonks, trapmakers at Sidebotham's in Wednesfield, holding examples of the company's famous lion traps.

Many workers in these prosperous post-war years defined their living standards in contrast to the insecurities and powerlessness of the turbulent 1930s, when unemployment was rife and hunger marches and protests were a feature of everyday life. One character in Colin MacInnes' period-defining 1959 novel *Absolute Beginners* summed it up: the 1930s were "poverty, unemployment, fascism and disaster and, worst of all, no chance, no opportunity, no sunlight at the end of the corridor". Labour's 1945 manifesto, *Let Us Face The Future*, featured many bold promises, but most important was "jobs for all": a reaction to previous mass unemployment, and a crucial part of financing the new welfare state. These promises were evidently popular, and Labour were elected in a landslide in July 1945. Despite the difficulties of post-war austerity and a shortage of materials and money, a decade later full employment had been all but achieved. By that time a Conservative government was in power, but the political and economic tone had been set by Attlee's government of 1945-1951, and power lay as much with the worker as with the employer – trade unions sat at the heart of the government, particularly under Labour, and workers had more say in the running of the country than ever before.[65]

Full Employment

Labour's first solution to finding "jobs for all" was a major programme of industrial reform. Central to this was public ownership of fuel and power, inland transport, and iron and steel, all of which had a major impact in the Black Country. After bringing the war in Asia to a close, Clement Attee's new government set about the nationalisation schemes on which they had swept to power. The NCB took over coal mining on 'Vesting Day', 1947: gas and electric, iron and steel, telecommunications, road haulage, rail, waterways and even Thomas Cook & Son's famous travel agency followed.[66] Such changes brought new efficiency and public benefit, and made a difference to the lives and prospects of many employees: for Ernie Timmins, for example, who started work at West Bromwich Corporation's Albion Gasworks in 1936, nationalisation opened up a career in the gas industry that could never have been possible had the West Bromwich Municipal Gas Department remained in local hands. For him, trade unions and the Labour party were a part of everyday life: he was a member of the National Association of Local Government Officers (NALGO) and Clem Attlee, he recalls, was his "blue-eyed boy". [67]

Trade unions were at the heart of local and national life. Nationally, union membership had leapt from 6.3m in 1939 to nearly 9.4m in 1949, and unions were represented on 60 government committees. They were generally seen as patriotic, benevolent and respectable, on their way to becoming a "great and permanent estate of the realm".[68] Even under the Conservative government of the 1950s, unions continued to grow. Trade unions were never monolithic in the Black Country – fewer than half the manufacturing workforce were unionised in the 1950s – but they remained a ubiquitous feature of everyday life: Wolverhampton, Bilston & District Trades Union Congress, for example, had committees not just for employment but for Sports & Social, Schools, Youth and Women, and fought for medical as well as wage improvements.[69]

By May 1950, fewer than 10,000 people were registered unemployed in the entire West Midlands – just 0.5 per cent of the population. Tipton's Employment Committee believed there was just one person "wholly unemployed" in the entire town. The number stayed this low until the 1970s: consistently below one per cent and consistently lower than the national average. Skilled workmen were in short supply, and it was well-known that a workman could leave a job in the morning and find a new one that afternoon. Censuses revealed the level of skilled labour employment: in West Bromwich, for instance, nearly two-thirds of the workforce were in skilled industrial jobs. By the mid-1950s, Wolverhampton alone had 1,200 vacancies. Throughout the 1950s and 1960s unemployment stayed low, rarely breaching two per cent even in years of recession in the steel industry. As the economy boomed, the working population of the Black Country became, in general, the beneficiary of a newly affluent Britain. Full employment was achieved, which enabled trade unions to fight successfully for improved conditions: education and skill levels increased, wages rose, health and housing improved, but there was still a shortage of workers.[70]

Working Life

Full employment did not solve all of society's problems. But now, employers had to compete for a limited workforce, so exploitation and low pay became an untenable way to run a business. Perks that had formerly only been associated with 'progressive' companies – high-quality apprenticeships, social provision, pension plans – became the norm.

Although school was compulsory until age fifteen, the route into work was decided at the age of eleven. The 11-plus test decided whether students would go on to grammar schools, where most would then go on to white collar or managerial roles; technical schools, where students

Courtesy of Black Country Living Museum

John Munslow, apprentice coremaker at Sandwell Castings, West Bromwich, 1955.

were equipped for skilled engineering jobs; or secondary moderns, which – with many exceptions – fitted students for less skilled jobs, or at least a longer training route.[71] Despite the many jobs available, however, the best way to get a good job was still to know someone who could provide an employment opportunity. Innumerable Black Country teenagers began their working lives where their father had got them a job. That was the case for one of the Black Country's best-loved entertainers, Dolly Allen, who spent 40 years making nuts and bolts for Hackett Brothers of Halesowen, just like her father, her uncle, her husband and later her son.[72] But it was also well-known that the best way to get a job at Gibbons' – the large refractory and firebrick firm in Gornal – was to join the choir at St Mark's, Pensnett. Eric Gibbons and works manager Albert Morris sang there, and the foundry manager Richard Morris was choirmaster and organist.[73]

One of the best ways to secure a well-paid career in industry was an apprenticeship, although they were not without their own challenges. Foremost was pay: although £2 or £3 was a lot to a 15-year-old starter, almost all apprentices expected to hand over most of their pay packet to their mothers. Netherton-born Pete Cox, for instance, remembers his excitement on receiving his first salary from J Barnsley & Son of £3.7s.6d in 1960 – but his shock at only getting to keep 7s.6d of it after his mother had taken the household share.[74] School-leavers were thus often pushed by their families towards a readily-available low-skilled job – well-paid, but with limited prospects, which entrenched a class divide between skilled and unskilled work.[75]

Apprenticeships were also often secured through family connections, which many firms cultivated. Chance Bros. employed a Personnel Manager who kept in touch with apprentices' parents, and at Birmid Industries, families were invited to an annual sports and presentation day.[76] In 1962 Bilston Steelworks had 200 apprentices, and almost a quarter were the sons of current employees.[77] Smaller employers' apprenticeships were usually less grand, however: Michael Plant, from Blackheath, had an apprenticeship with a small electrical contractor which helped his training, but the wages were so low he had to take on a second job as a projectionist's mate at the King's Cinema in Blackheath.[78]

Apprenticeships were usually five years plus a short probation. George Mills signed with John Thompson on his sixteenth birthday (his uncle was a foreman at Beacon Windows, a Thompson subsidiary) and was paid £2.18s.6d for a 44-hour week. By his graduation, after rotating through several different divisions, he was earning £6.2s.2d and went on to become a training officer.[79] This involved not only work but day release, night school, homework, sometimes even PE lessons – FH Lloyd's engineering apprentices had to endure a 7:30am run before their lectures.[80] An apprentice expected to work hard – as one firm put it, "working for Chance certainly means *working* for Chance" – but with dinner dances, camping and coach trips they came with social, as well as employment, opportunities.[81] This system was a major investment for a firm, potentially costing thousands of pounds, but apprenticeships ensured a continuity of service, expertise and loyalty to the firm. The symbiotic relationship between families, localities and employers knit Black Country towns and firms together as industrial communities.

Tangyes Apprenticeships

Tangyes apprenticeships were reckoned some of the best, and there were usually around 88 apprentices to be found at the Cornwall Works, Smethwick. New recruits (mostly local, although a link was retained with West Hill School in St Austell, Cornwall, harking back to the Tangye family's roots) were given special brown boiler suits and shown the sign: "Tangye apprentices are wanted all over the world." This was true – graduating apprentices went on to important jobs at ICI, GKN and many other firms across the globe. Apprentices rotated through the firm's many departments. This meant they worked at everything: running errands, hand-filing castings, performance-testing pumps, fitting 12-foot flywheels onto 12" shafts, and designing new parts in the drawing office. When not at work, the young men had a day and several evenings at the Chance Technical College in Piddock Road, Smethwick, originally founded by the glassmaking family.

Apprentices were key to the company's success not just in business, but in sports: the Tangye Football Club ranked high in the Birmingham Works League, and was narrowly pipped to the Works Cup in 1954. Other activities available for the young men – and apprenticeships were almost exclusively for men – included angling, horticulture, archery, table tennis and cricket. The year culminated in Apprentices Day, when the director Sir Basil Tangye joined the apprentices and their families in Smethwick. The young men showed their parents around the works in the morning, and the afternoon was set aside for sports at the company's ground on the Birmingham Road, and presentation of the Technical Apprentices' Cup, and the Trade & Commercial Apprentices' Cup.[82]

Courtesy of Black Country Living Museum

Apprentices at Tangyes Cornwall Works, Smethwick, in 1956.

The Workplace

Wages rose faster in the Black Country than elsewhere, reflecting its importance within the new manufacturing economy – by 1961, household incomes in the West Midlands were 13 per cent higher than the national average. A car assembly worker could earn up to £30 per week, a typical foundry job – during the better spells – around £20.[83] High wages often represented back-breaking work in dangerous conditions, however, with large amounts of overtime required to make up the sums. Brockhouse foundryman Harry Butler recalled that even though there was plenty of work about, "the company wanted every ounce out of you they could get".[84] The clocking-in card and the 'bull' horn still governed many lives and signalled a hard day's work ahead.

Foundry and forge work was famously tough. Clocking on was essential, and if an employee was three minutes late their pay would likely be docked. Vera Weigh of Tipton remembers visiting her father's work as a child to see "black smoke and this red-hot molten metal running down and he'd got leather fitted over his shirt

Gurdev Rai at work in 1961 at Goodyear, Wolverhampton.

Alice Griffiths demonstrating the advances in chainmaking at the Joseph Woodhouse chainworks, Cradley Heath, 1961.

and I thought no wonder he likes a pint". For many, drinking on the job was not only normal, it was essential to restore fluids lost in sweat. Another Tipton resident recalls a colleague who "used to drink a crate of Guinness a day when he was working on the foundries". The first job for the apprentices at Bean's foundry each day was to visit the pub for the first of up to 18 pints of Ansell's Mild. When temperatures in the foundry reached 54°C (130°F), this level of drinking becomes understandable. Although some works still had a 'beer boy' – typically an older worker – soft drinks were becoming more widely preferred. Tom Smith at Griffin-Woodhouse chainworks in Cradley Heath still made pub trips in the 1950s, but the chainmakers preferred cold tea, mineral water or Coca-Cola. Some workplaces even relied on more traditional drinks: at one foundry "they used to have a bucket of water with barley in and blokes used to have to put something [fluids] back. With salt and barley you know."[85]

Women had been an essential part of the industrial war effort in the Black Country, but as the war drew to a close, many were demobilised and expected to return to the home. The government's view was that "the attitude of the housewife to gainful employment outside the home should not be the same as that of the single woman," and "in the next thirty years housewives as mothers have vital work to do in ensuring the adequate continuance of the British Race and of British ideals in the world".[86]

The Black Country has a long history of women's work. Chainmaking, for instance, had historically relied on women working at backyard forges for rates of pay which were a fraction of their male counterparts'. This type of exploitative employment had mostly fallen away, although there was still a large wage disparity, and the number of women engaged in chainmaking was on the decline. Nevertheless in the Black Country, the proportion of women in the workforce was generally higher than elsewhere in the country, although most of these jobs were in workplaces already dominated by women, particularly light industries like saddlery, lockmaking and fasteners. Light assembly work at BSR in Stourbridge and Old Hill, for example, was a major local employer of women in the Black Country.

Although some women could be found in male-dominated workplaces like foundries, a skilled female moulder in this environment could still expect to earn a full third less than a man doing the same work, even earning less than an unskilled male labourer. Women's pay could be as little as half that of a man. One couple in Coseley were interviewed in 1949 by the sociologist Doris Rich: the husband worked full-time as an acetylene burner in Tipton and earned £6.10s; his wife earned £3.13s.8d as a gas cooker assembler at the Cannon foundry. There was a generational divide here too. They lived with the wife's parents: her mother did not work; her father, a handlesmith, refused to give his wages with his wife present, as he did not wish her to know what he earnt. Women often had to take on the 'unofficial' tasks of the business too: Hylda Cliff, the 'Voice of BRD' (Blade Research & Development, a GKN subsidiary) at the company's factory in Aldridge, had to place brewery orders for the staff canteen, pass on personal messages, provide needle and thread and manage "a personal supply of aspirins [which] is regularly called upon by sufferers from a morning-after" – all in addition to her paid role as a telephonist. Parity with men was very distant.[87]

Part of this was society's expectations of a woman's role. Work for women was common before marriage, but many firms enforced unofficial marriage bars, where women left employment as soon as they married. Female apprenticeships were extremely rare, and men were expected to be the main breadwinner. Those who needed extra income could take up 'outwork' like laundry, catalogue clubs, midwifery, or carding pins and needles for firms like Newey Brothers of Tipton. Mrs Sheldon of Tipton, for example, collected hair grips from Newey's factory in a pushchair or pram in the morning, and spent the day placing them on cards for sale. But this sometimes proved embarrassing for husbands, who did not like others to know their wives worked; Mr Sheldon ended up giving his wife an extra 10 shillings housekeeping money to save face. Such factors often combined to draw women out of the workplace and into the home-centred, domestic life of the nuclear family.[88]

Although accurate figures are

Ellen Coleman, otherwise known as 'Nellie the Bricklady', working on 'specials' – bespoke firebricks produced to order by Harris & Pearson, Brierley Hill. Coleman was reputedly the oldest woman brickmaker in the Black Country, still working well into her 80s.

Brickmaking was a huge employer of female labour: women were generally far better at the skilful work than men. Perhaps the most famous brickmaker in Brierley Hill was 'Nellie the Bricklady' of Harris & Pearson. Ellen Coleman was born in Brockmoor in 1886 and began 'setting' – carrying bricks to the kiln on a sackcloth bustle around her waist – as a 'brickyard wench' at Harris & Pearson in 1902. She soon moved onto moulding where she stayed until 1970 making, at her peak, 1,600 bricks a day. Standing only 1.45m (4 feet 9 inches) tall, she worked barefoot in the warm drying room, and stood on a box to reach her bench. She fetched water from the canal to get the clay moist, but also to wash her face – she believed that the clay and canal water kept her skin in remarkably good condition. She wore a white calico top tied at the back of the neck, with a sacking apron and another piece of calico to cover her hair (or a woolly hat in cold weather). Perhaps most importantly, she kept herself hydrated: at 10:30am she would have a bottle of stout; and in the evening, she would have another.[89]

impossible to ascertain when so much employment was still on a casual basis, the employment of workers from outside the UK was not consistent across all workplaces. Some professions employed no 'coloured workers' at all. Even by 1968 there were no Caribbean or South Asian bank clerks in the Black Country, few shop salespeople, no police in the entire West Midlands and not a single person of colour amongst the 1,000 employees at Beatties in Wolverhampton. Instead, immigrant labour was initially concentrated in public transport, nationalised health care, and unskilled industrial labour.[90]

Single employers could often be catalysts for immigration into specific towns. The proportion of Indian workers at Smethwick's Birmid Industries, for instance, rose from one fifth in 1947 to

John Bulmer/Popperfoto/Getty Images

Foundry workers pictured in 1961 as part of the photographer John Bulmer's Black Country exhibition.

nearly half by the end of the 1960s. The cyclical and demand-led nature of the car industry meant that new workers were frequently required, and foremen came to rely on their Indian workers, especially those, including former army servicemen, who could speak English. They were able to send messages to India seeking more workers for the foundries in Smethwick, with the result that large groups of single men moved there for work. When the Indian High Commissioner, Mrs Pandit, visited Birmid, the management told her that they "thought very highly of their Indian and Pakistani workers, and also that the workers were quite satisfied with the conditions in the factory and had no complaints".[91] A similar story could be told of other works: Goodyear, Guy Motors and Qualcast in Wolverhampton, the Conygre and Beans foundries in Tipton, and Rubery Owen in Darlaston all employed immigrant workers in the 1950s. The latter even appointed a 'coloured welfare officer' in 1961 and proudly asserted that it had no employment quotas or colour bar, and its cricket team was predominantly black. This was often attributable to the prompting of the employer: Alfred Owen was a Conservative but distanced himself from the provocative language of politicians like Peter Griffiths and Enoch Powell. At West Bromwich's Kenrick works, immigrant workers made up 40 per cent of the workforce by 1964, although William Kenrick appears to have been a more reluctant employer. That feeling evidently filtered down to the workforce – one team bound and threatened a Caribbean worker at knife point when they deemed her to be working too slowly.[92]

Workplace racism could be expressed in different ways. At the Conygre foundry in Dudley Port, for instance, part of the Birmid group, managers began to refer to their large South Asian workforce by number rather than name, and even operated separate toilets for them. Immigrant workers tended to be at the back of the queue for advancement too: foremen and shop stewards were disproportionately white. Frequently, everyday ignorance and racism affected workplace relationships. One Jamaican-born worker remembers a work colleague showing surprise after he cut himself making bucket handles – "she didn't think that my blood would be red".[93] But in other places, relations between British and immigrant workers were strong, and close friendships established – the Jamaican moulder Roderick Ansine told the *Wolverhampton Chronicle* in 1952 that although he did not enjoy his work; "I like the people. They have been swell to me – fair, you know, which is all we ask."[94]

The New World of Work

In 1950, the Institution of Mechanical Engineers organised a tour of some of the West Midlands' major factories. Sankey's of Bilston, they noted, "realises the necessity for welfare activities and has a first-class social and sports club, excellent canteens and first aid rooms". The firm boasted of its long-serving staff, with 47 employees having completed 50 years' service. Other big firms like GKN and Noah Hingley Hingley were proud of their apprenticeship schemes, sports facilities, superannuation schemes and industrial relations records; Mitchells & Butlers, for instance, offered a staff benevolent fund, two pension schemes, and prided itself that "in fifty years the company has not experienced a strike or lockout".[95]

Such facilities certainly influenced employment decisions: a job where "there was everything there for you" was evidently attractive. Salter's company history sums up the tone of the period, describing those "distant days when so many employers were more concerned with the improving of their own fortunes than with the welfare of their workpeople", before extolling their own commendable record in this area. Firms had to compete for staff on these grounds, and while it would be wrong to suggest that businesses were any less concerned with profits, this was still a whole new world for many workers: a

Courtesy of Black Country Living Museum

Bill Tombs tapping the furnace at Shotton Brothers, Oldbury, 1949.

world where they were invested in and valued, not exploited and expendable.[96]

Work, however, remained hard, hours long and conditions tough. Factories were noisy, filthy, hot and fumy places: many knew the experience of a father dying young from occupational health problems. Accidents were still commonplace with modern health and safety measures a long way off: no gloves, no safety glasses, no hard hats, no steel toe-caps – often just a leather apron and scarred arms. The British Iron & Steel Federation, for instance, advocated for improved foot and shin guards for rolling mill workers in 1959, but accepted that "flannel shirts and moleskin trousers" were still the norm.[97] Bill Tombs was the main furnaceman at Shotton Brothers, Oldbury, having worked his way up over 25 years. In 1949 he was featured in the *Made in Oldbury* exhibition brochure tapping the furnace, but while doing the same job a year later, a colleague's hammerhead dislodged and flew off, hitting Tombs so hard that he died of his injuries.[98]

Many of the larger firms recognised the health problems associated with the workplace and opened clinics or surgeries on site. Tangyes opened a Dispensary in 1865, appointed a Welfare Officer in the 1920s, and offered a full medical service until the birth of the NHS rendered this unnecessary, but others implemented this kind of service for the first time. Garrington's of Darlaston replaced their old washhouse with a new one, their old surgery with a state-of-the-art medical centre, nurse and doctor. Rubery Owen's brand-new clinic was run by the NHS and even offered dentistry and ophthalmology.[99]

Tangyes was a pioneer in nutritional health too, having built a dining room in 1877, but the company was not typical. Only 1,500 firms nationally had a canteen at the outbreak of the Second World War. However, the wartime government ordered all firms with over 250 workers to provide somewhere for the workers to eat and by the end of the war, the number had risen to 20,000. Vono, of Dudley Port, had a canteen but found it little used. The firm that decided that another attempt was in order and employed a Catering Manager to refit their canteen and kitchen in 1950. Under the new regime the canteen took off, and twelve months later it was serving 520 hot dinners a day, with the bulk served in the first ten minutes. Diners could choose from three or four main courses, and six or seven puddings, and if anyone was worried about standards, they were assured that everything was utterly hygienic: "Canteen Assistants are all trained to be proud of their appearance and personal cleanliness — there is a routine inspection of each girl's hair, nails and uniform before she starts her day's work."[100]

Such provisions served several purposes: as well as attracting workers in a competitive labour market, firms saw such provisions as improving productivity and creating a wholesome local community too. Oldbury's Hughes-Johnson provided a good example: having built a canteen and sports ground during the First World War, they were proud that a large proportion of

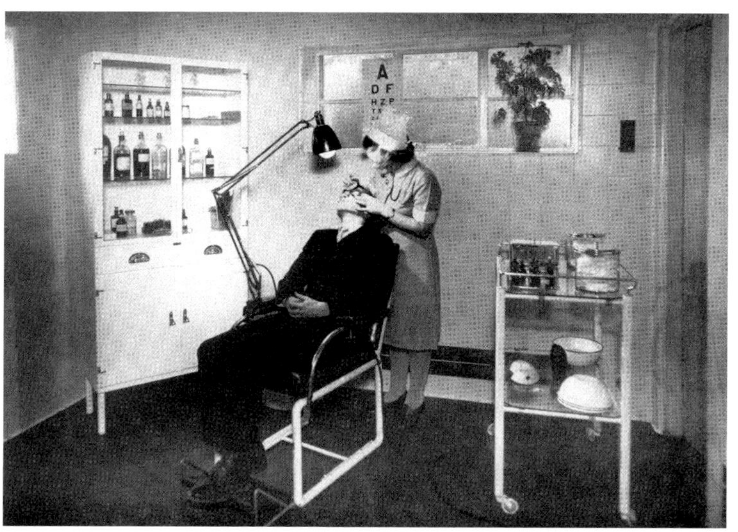

Courtesy of Black Country Living Museum

Ambulance Room at FH Lloyd's steel foundry, Wednesbury.

its workers had "spent a lifetime in the service of the company" and saw those amenities as an important local facility for its staff, most of whom lived close by in Langley Green. Company holidays, sports, clubs and societies became a major part of social life for those who worked there, as well as their families. Most large firms had somewhere for their workers to play at a variety of sports, from snooker to football, and the resulting regional Works Leagues were a major source of entertainment. There was typically a social club or recreation area too. Tube Investments built a ballroom in Oldbury which became home not just to the firm's social events – including productions of *Oklahoma!* and *South Pacific* – but for local schools and community groups too. The company dance could even be the highlight of the year: Crabtree's directors hosted an impressive night at Walsall Town Hall each year, with a band, decoration and buffet, and even chartered buses to get the cheerful revellers home at midnight. Company magazines like Rubery Owen's *Goodwill* also demonstrate the interest such firms took in the social, professional and moral development of their staff – Alfred Owen prefaced most issues with a short Christian message, and built a new place of worship (Emmanuel Church) on the new housing estate the firm sponsored at Bentley.[101]

Many firms even provided for employees into retirement. Tangyes began a 'staff superannuation pension scheme' ("This at once makes employment with the firm more attractive and removes that burden of insecurity in old age which hangs over all non-pensionable posts"), while Mitchells & Butlers had both a non-contributory superannuation fund and a contributory pension. Typically, Rubery Owen went even further. Based on the 'Sons of Rest' movement for retired working men, Alfred Owen opened a Sons of Rest workshop at Darlaston. Here, men of retirement age could carry out light workshop activities at their own pace, earning a small wage to supplement their pension. These new schemes were of particular value to those who had devoted their lives to individual firms: Jack Nicholls, dressing-shop foreman at Archibald Kenrick's, for example, retired at 81 having spent no less than 69 years with the firm.[102]

Being in a position of power was a new experience for many of the Black Country's working class, but it was far from universal. Prospects were affected by social class long before working life began, so that for those who could not access a grammar school or an apprenticeship, this brave new world was less radically different from pre-war life. Many still had to scrape to make ends meet and for

Courtesy of Black Country Living Museum

Annual Pensioners' Dinner for Tipton's Horseley Bridge & Thomas Piggott Ltd., 1955.

some, life could still be extremely tough. While few women chainmakers remained, for instance, many women's lives were still dictated by a limited budget, and they relied on insecure work and community networks to help them through. Immigrants too were pushed into unskilled jobs and endured constant prejudice. The headline figures showing increased prosperity did not reflect every experience.

Nevertheless, for many the world of work was greatly improved from conditions before the war, and the post-war period was when a 'job for life' became closer to the norm. Companies became an integral part of individual and collective identity in the Black Country. Workers were happy to define themselves as Rubery Owen men, or Tangyes men, or Sankey's men, because they felt genuinely valued. The social life that went with working at one of these big employers could be full, and even when the work was hard, it was well recompensed. Firms too came to rely on a supply of labour rooted in local and personal connections. With such mutually beneficial interconnections, this period represents the height of the symbiotic relationship between employer, employee and locality: work, leisure, family and place were inseparable strands of what it meant to be from the Black Country.

Chapter 4

"Loads of work and loads of jobs"

Overcoming the Labour Shortage

Courtesy of Black Country Living Museum

Steelworkers at the Patent Shaft Steelworks, Wednesbury. The photograph was taken by Alan Price in November 1968. With the permission of the management, he visited to take a picture of the steelworks nearly five decades after he had been in a similar photograph himself, as a boy on the same site.

For some industries, however, relying on family and local connections was not enough to meet the demands of the post-war economy. Industry was now globalised. Rubery Owen, for instance, spread across the UK and opened factories across the British Commonwealth, in South Africa, India, Canada and Australia; they also encouraged employees to emigrate and share their expertise in these new markets. FH Lloyd went a step further in 1960, setting up a large steel foundry at the Chittaranjan Locomotive Works in West Bengal, in collaboration with the Indian Railway Board. The process was a significant cultural exchange on both sides: FH Lloyd staff spent time in India, and the Indian foundry superintendent and chief engineer brought their families to Wednesbury for a year.[103] In the Black Country though, the biggest demand was for unskilled labour, and this period witnessed the globalisation of capital being matched by an increasingly global workforce.

This chapter charts the post-war labour shortage, the attempts to solve it, and the new working class that resulted – more diverse but every bit as central to the Black Country's culture and regional uniqueness. The variety of local economies, employers and cultures meant that for both the existing working class, and for those who came to meet this shortage, the experience of life in the post-war Black Country varied. Nevertheless, there were substantial shared experiences too in the demands of work, paying the rent and feeding the family, and the Black Country's unique working-class culture – with all its local and social complexities – persisted and thrived through all the twists, turns and changes of the next decades.

The 1940s: Labour Crisis

The Second World War had an immediate impact on Britain's industry. Suddenly, where earlier unemployment had meant that many people were glad to get any job, labour was at a premium. Many of the Black

Used with the permission of Wolverhampton Archives

In most workplaces, even if a formal marriage bar was not in place, most women left once they were married. Here, June Bowater (second from right) is celebrating with colleagues from GKN-Sankey in Bilston, before leaving to get married.

Country's distinctive industries – coal, brickmaking, anchor-making, foundry work of all descriptions – were 'reserved' because of their great importance to the nation's industrial output, and workers in these industries were not called up into the military. Just as in the First World War, women were called into service in industry; they were joined by small numbers of workers from British India, the Caribbean and elsewhere to keep Britain on a war footing.[104]

After the war, however, many of these new workers left the workplace. The war had, of course, taken its toll on the working men of the region, through casualty or through continued post-war service, and with demand for production soaring Britain found itself with a shortage of labour estimated at about 1.35m in 1945. Demobilised men could pick and choose the better-paid, more skilled jobs, and they were less keen on the lower-paid, unskilled jobs that were so necessary to the running of many workplaces. These were still desperately needed though. The region's foundries and factories cried out for workers, but so often these – rather than the skilled workers in reserved occupations – were the ones who did not return from the war. It was estimated that Britain was still over 1.3 million workers short at the end of 1946, and the situation did not look like improving. In the face of this shortage, the government tried something new: bringing workers in.[105]

The first formal attempt at targeted overseas recruitment was that of Displaced Persons (DPs) from Europe, where the aftermath of the war had brought food shortages, political upheaval and the displacement of people from their homes. There were many DPs in Britain already, as soldiers, refugees and workers: in Wolverhampton alone there were up to 12,000. A large number of refugees from Eastern Europe were resettled in camps around the edge of the Black Country, including Merry Hill in Wolverhampton, Perton, Bobbington Airfield, Coven, Pendeford Hall, and Brinsford Lodge in Featherstone. Polish soldiers had fought alongside the British throughout the war, and although encouraged to return to Poland in 1945, many were fearful of the new Communist government there. In 1947, the Polish Resettlement Act allowed 120,000 former soldiers to settle in Britain. Poles worked at many of the larger factories in the Wolverhampton area: those housed at Brinsford Lodge were bussed to Courtauld's in Wolverhampton, and Sankey's in Bilston, among others. At Stewart's & Lloyd's steelworks, Bilston, the 'Polish Camp' – a hostel overlooking the works sports ground – provided an alternative home for many Polish steelworkers. Workers there included Jozef Chudzik, a decorated veteran of the Free Polish Army and survivor of the Soviet gulags, and Josef Stawinoga, later to become famous for his makeshift camp in the middle of

Wolverhampton's ring road. By 1955 around 2,000 Poles lived in Wolverhampton alone, forming close bonds as a community in exile: Polish clubs, ex-combatants' associations, trade unions and services at SS Peter & Paul led by Father Feliks Kaminski, a concentration camp survivor, helped knit the community together.[106]

Other Eastern Europeans were recruited directly by the government. Around 80,000 people, known as European Voluntary Workers (EVWs), were brought to Britain from Ukraine, Poland and the Baltic states between 1946 and 1949, under schemes codenamed 'Balt Cygnet' and 'Westward Ho'. They too were stationed in camps and bussed to work. For women workers from Lithuania, for example, the main employer was Courtauld's textile factory in Wolverhampton; for the men, the main employers were Goodyear or NCB collieries. A close-knit Lithuanian community developed with an Orthodox Sunday School near the Molineux stadium, the 'Viltis' sports club, and a Lithuanian reading room at Courtauld's. Within the Black Country itself, other groups were recruited to aid the post-war reconstruction of the Midlands. Poles and EVWs lived alongside Jamaican and Irish workers at National Services Hostels Corporation (NSHC) hostels on Tenscore Street, West Bromwich, Willenhall Road, Wolverhampton, and Causeway Green, Oldbury.[107]

Courtesy of AUGB, Wolverhampton Branch

Bishop Ivan Buchko visiting Wolverhampton in 1955. Bishop Buchko was appointed Apostolic Visitator for the Ukrainians in Western Europe by the Ukrainian Greek Catholic Church in 1945.

The Black Country was also home to several Prisoner of War (POW) camps, which remained into the late 1940s. The continued imprisonment of German and Italian POWs was justified on the grounds of labour shortage, and prisoners were employed in all kinds of industry. At the Ravensitch Farm camp on Woods Lane, Amblecote, Italian prisoners walked to EJ & J Pearson's brickworks, and although they wore uniforms denoting their status, often stopped to chat with their neighbours. Members of the Ambrose family – who had emigrated from Italy in the 1890s to live in Kingswinford – recall talking with POWs in Brockmoor; Josephine Ambrose even met her future husband Salvatore Terrana this way. Relations were friendly too at the Bromley Lane camp in Kingswinford. Prisoners there included Herbert Langer, who worked in the Rector of Wordsley's garden. Langer was so taken with the Black Country that he returned and set up a business in Stourbridge, selling army and navy surplus supplies from a store on Enville Street. His advertisements featured an imperial German helmet and the legend 'Achtung!' Many POWs were interned until the late 1940s, and some even longer.[108]

The resulting mix meant that the Black Country of the 1940s was far more diverse than is often assumed. Public transport had one of the most acute labour shortages, and Wolverhampton Corporation Transport's employment roster gives an example of how many people in Europe had been displaced by the war, and how diverse some workplaces had become: in 1949 it employed 70 overseas staff including 12 Bachelors of Science, a Master of Literature from the Sorbonne, a professor from the University of Krakow, a Hungarian wrestling champion, and a number of Jamaican men. But these workers were usually segregated from the rest of the Black Country: most lived apart, in camps or hostels, and even those with high qualifications were restricted in the work they could do. It soon became apparent too that no matter how many European recruits were drafted in, the labour shortage was not close to being filled.[109]

The demand for jobs in Britain also held a strong attraction for Irish workers, who faced a stagnating economy at home. Around half a million Irish people emigrated in the 1950s, sometimes 60,000 a year, boosting the Irish-born population in Britain to 726,000 by 1961, and sending back something like £7 million per year in remittances. The West Midlands, with its booming industries and reconstruction programmes, was a particular draw in this era, something that was exploited by Black Country-based firms like ICI and Midland Red, who opened recruiting centres in Ireland. Factories and building sites were common places of employment. Contractors such as John Laing, Wimpey, McAlpine or the Wolverhampton-based Tarmac all employed scores of Irishmen. Luke Kelly was

Used with the permission of Wolverhampton Archives

Tarmac employees working on the Ettingshall Brook Culvert. Tarmac, a Wolverhampton firm, was a major employer of Irish workers in the construction industry.

one of these itinerant workers: he arrived in Wolverhampton in 1957 where his brother Paddy, already in the town, found him a home and a construction job. Kelly was fired in 1958 for confronting his bosses when he discovered that English workers were being paid more. His experiences fuelled first his Communist politics and later his successful career with Ireland's most famous traditional music group The Dubliners: His repertoire included songs like 'Hot Asphalt' and 'McAlpine's Fusiliers' about the experiences of men just like himself. Irish women made a huge contribution too, notably forming about a tenth of the nursing workforce of the new NHS from its formation in 1948.[110]

Emigrant life could be tough, however. In 1951, Maurice Foley of the Young Christian Workers' Association (and later MP for West Bromwich) drew the attention of the Irish Ambassador to poor housing, health and spiritual conditions amongst the Irish in Birmingham, Coventry and Wolverhampton. Foley's report found its way to Taoiseach Éamon de Valera, who claimed in a speech that Irish workers were being exploited in the Midlands, living in "absolute degradation", and that they should seek work in their home country. His speech aroused great controversy, but backfired: there was precious little work in Ireland, and the occasion drew attention to that as the reason so many were emigrating in the first place. De Valera drew reproach from local newspapers, and correspondence revealed that more than the economy was driving people from Ireland. Margaret Feeney of Smethwick wrote to the *Birmingham Daily Gazette* that "Mr de Valera has made, and is making life impossible for Irish people in Ireland," alluding to his "dictatorial attitude" – a remnant of the bitter political divisions played out in Ireland in the preceding decades.[111]

Irish immigration was thus male and female, skilled and unskilled, and often the subject of prejudice and discrimination. However, the long tradition of Irish workers in Britain meant that despite their numbers, their presence in the Black Country was less remarked upon than the more unusual Eastern European or Commonwealth migrants. Like Eastern European migrants though, they were white and to some degree able to blend in with local communities – a privilege not afforded to those arriving from some parts of the British Commonwealth.

"He (and She) has Travelled Far"

The diversity of the Black Country in the early 1950s was demonstrated in a series of portraits by the journalist Colin Cross, published in the *Express & Star* in 1953. The brief interviews showed the range of work, home and leisure life. Joe Fenech – a 27-year-old Maltese electrician – worked at Goodyear but his chief enjoyment in life was following Wolves all over the country. "I like England best," said Fenech, a sentiment repeated by Dutchman Walter Veenendaal – except for the weather and the beer. Veenendaal worked as a grinder at Fischer Bearings, having been stationed with the Dutch regiments at Wrottesley Park during the war. He had met his German wife at Fischer and settled into a flat on Kingsland Road. Liselotte Coulson had also settled in the Black Country after meeting her partner, but in her case, she had met the Wolverhampton man abroad after having fled Soviet-occupied Poland. Denis Beston represented Wolverhampton's Ukrainians. He worked at Ever Ready and was again struck by the unpredictability of British weather. Unlike the others though, he was not keen to talk about his past: "I want to forget some of the things that have happened to me." Sayyad G Shah, "an Indian who loves Bilston", was in fact from Pakistani Kashmir, and claimed, somewhat optimistically, that the countryside around Wolverhampton was "just like Kashmir". Likewise, regarding the local people, "some of them are nice; some of them I don't like; just like the people of Kashmir". Another Commonwealth citizen with a positive experience of Wolverhampton was H Heman-Mensah, from the Gold Coast, at that point on the verge of dominion status. Heman-Mensah was studying electrical engineering at Wolverhampton Technical College and the Electric Construction Company, and hoped to use his skill in the service of his home country. His vision of the future was a positive one: "you cannot play a piano on the black keys alone," he noted, "nor on the white" – he believed in cooperation between the races in both the Empire and the Metropole.[112]

Jubilee Arts Archive/Sandwell Community History Archives Service

Glassworkers at Chance Brothers, Smethwick, in the 1960s.

Although the arrival of the *Empire Windrush* at Tilbury Docks in 1948 has come to represent the symbolic beginning of Caribbean immigration to Britain, small numbers of Jamaican workers had been living in the Black Country since the war, at hostels such as Causeway Green in Oldbury. The 1948 British Nationality Act was an attempt to meet the ongoing labour shortage by formalising the rights of imperial subjects to settle elsewhere in the Empire. Those from the Caribbean were endorsed as "citizens of the United Kingdom and its Colonies", equal in rights with the English and not immigrants from a foreign nation; while those from newly independent nations like India and Pakistan were "Commonwealth Citizens", Many saw Britain as a land of opportunity, the "mother country"; themselves as "children of the Empire"; and the British as the "most level-headed in the world". Wages and economic prospects were at rock bottom in the Caribbean, and the promise of "loads of work and loads of jobs" in Britain overruled many emigrants' fears. One group arriving in Wolverhampton in 1955 summed up the feelings of so many when they told the *Express & Star* that they arrived with "a mixture of hope and anxiety".[113]

By 1958, around 125,000 people from the Caribbean had arrived in Britain, where industry was still crying out for labour. When Bill Orgill moved from Jamaica in 1960, he arrived in Princes End on a Monday and started at Foster Bros. in Wednesbury on Wednesday. He went on to spend 35 years at Tipton's Bean Foundry. Most were single men, though not all. Winnie Henry emigrated from Jamaica to Dudley in 1957. She shared a bedsit with her brother Clifton in Wellington Road to begin with (later cleared as a slum), before moving to Vicar Street, then Himley Road where her husband joined her in the early 1960s, and finally Douglas Road near Buffery Park. Winston Henry worked at Bean too, making parts for British Leyland vehicles. Winnie's son Lenworth recalled his father's experience of employment in Dudley: "You could quit one job in the morning and be in work by the early afternoon." Lenworth – better known as Lenny – went on to become Dudley's most famous export as a comedian and actor.[114]

People's lives prior to arrival in Britain counted for little once they were here. Even the well-educated usually had to take hard, unskilled, low-paid work. Calvert Hutchinson recalls his first job in the region after moving to Dudley in 1959. Well-qualified but with severely limited prospects in Jamaica, he moved to Britain for "survival" and found a job at Bright Steel, on Castle Hill, on his first day in the town. Wearing only his best suit he was asked to start there and then, and ended up covered, head to toe, in the slurry that was sprayed onto the grinding machinery – a long walk home followed through the first snow he had ever seen, and the suit had to be scrubbed and the day repeated until his first wages arrived, and he could buy some work clothes.[115]

Causeway Green

These early pioneers were not always treated kindly, in person or in the press, and racial stereotypes were common. A disturbance in 1949 at the Causeway Green hostel, off the Birmingham New Road near Oldbury, illustrates this. When Polish residents attacked a Jamaican group, ostensibly for dancing with white women, many officials were in favour of removing the Jamaican men from the hostel completely, as well as blaming the "women of an undesirable class" who had been fraternising with them. The Jamaican men present at the time included the musician Sammy 'Banjo' Walker, who was described as "chocolate-coloured Sam Walker" in the *Daily Mirror*; the jazz musician Andy Hamilton; and Horace Halliburton, who outlined their case: "We are little better than nomads, and consider it very unfair that, though we are British, we are the people to suffer." He described the difficulty in finding work because of his colour, and how heartbroken he was to hear mothers pointing him out on the street, saying: "I'll set the black bogey man on you if you are not well-behaved." Many of his fellow-residents stuck up for the Jamaican group, however, laying the blame elsewhere: Welshman Edward Harvey said: "We think it extremely unfair that the Poles should be allowed to remain at the expense of the Jamaicans." It was a sad reminder to those present that in the eyes of many Britons, skin colour outweighed British citizenship when making moral judgements.[116]

Express & Star/Wolverhampton Archives

Daphne Dundass cleaning cookware at the Midland Metal Spinning works, Tower Street, Wolverhampton.

Often firms were proud of their new employees. Accles & Pollock in Oldbury employed a Trinidadian airman named Prince Albert Jacob, who lodged at Causeway Green. A fine sprinter, he won the 100 yards dash at the 1948 Birchley Sport Day, when employees of Accles & Pollock and related businesses competed against each other – he was described as "Broadwell's Brown Bullet" in the company magazine, after the firm's address.[116] Difficulties came less in finding work than in finding a home. In 1949, Wolverhampton was described as a town where there were "several hundred coloured workers working happily and successfully in factories, and these areas could absorb more… [but] it is almost impossible to find accommodation for them". There was a shortage of homes, but as the paper pointed out, also a reluctance by landlords to let to people of colour. Those who did sometimes exploited their tenants by over-filling old, unsuitable houses and some areas of towns eventually gained reputations as immigrant areas, characterised by overcrowding and poverty. Waterloo Road in Wolverhampton, and in Dudley the crumbling Victorian terraces of Himley Road, Wellington Road and North Street became areas known for their Caribbean population.[118]

Workers from the Indian subcontinent were also drawn to the foundries and factories of the Black Country. Although the economy of India and Pakistan was not in as parlous a state as that of the Caribbean

Express & Star/Wolverhampton Archives

Mohamed Sadiq making chains in 1965.

or Ireland, the longstanding imperial connections between Britain and South Asia, the encouragement of pioneer British Asians, political upheaval following the traumatic Partition of the subcontinent, and the potential for sending remittances home encouraged these Commonwealth citizens to migrate. Their settlement was geographically uneven: it centred on urban areas with large employers seeking unskilled labour – the iron and steel foundries of Smethwick and West Bromwich, and the large factories of Wolverhampton. In Smethwick, the huge Birmid Industries foundry complex had recruited many Indian workers during the war, and the workforce remained around one fifth Indian in 1947. Post-independence South Asia was a turbulent place, and Britain was often seen as an economically more attractive option than staying put.[119]

Despite these growing concentrations, South Asian workers could be found across the Black Country. One 1950 estimate suggested that around half of the region's iron foundries employed some foreign workers, most of whom were Indian men in unskilled positions. As time went on, workers from other parts of India and Pakistan joined them, so that by the 1960s "16 languages and 24 dialects" were spoken at the Birmid and there was a substantial Indian community in the town. Unions were slower to embrace this diversity. Although by the 1960s some were producing recruitment information in Urdu and Punjabi, some major unions were hostile to immigrant labour. In 1967, some 350 Indian workers at Tipton's Conygre foundry struck for four weeks over racially-discriminatory redundancies, supported by students from Birmingham and Aston Universities, and other members of the new Indian Workers' Association (IWA). Yet the Transport & General Workers' Union (TGWU), the Indian strikers' own union, refused to support them, and the white workers' union (the Amalgamated Union of Foundry Workers, AUFW) even instructed their white colleagues to cross the picket line. Conygre's management eventually conceded, marking an important milestone in the self-organisation of the immigrant workforce in the Black Country, but it had been a discomfiting experience for all sides.[120]

The 1950s: Growing Communities

The labour shortage remained severe in the 1950s. Throughout the decade, Ireland and Poland remained the largest sources of immigration into Britain. Communities of Commonwealth immigrants began to settle around large employers like Villiers and Goodyear in Wolverhampton, Bilston steelworks, Vowles in West Bromwich, Shotton Brothers in Oldbury, Lee Howl, Duport and Conygre in Tipton, and others across the region. The new NHS was another major employer. Several Indian doctors in the Black Country already had long-established practices, with many taking prominent roles in the local community: Dorabji Saklatvala and Hiron Roy in West Bromwich, Vitesh Lambah in Bilston, and Dhani Prem in Great Barr and Smethwick, who was also Birmingham's first Asian councillor and an important advocate of the rights and welfare of Indian immigrants in Birmingham and Smethwick. Nurses too were in demand, particularly from the Caribbean and Ireland. By 1960, nearly 40 per cent of new NHS junior doctors were recruited from the Indian subcontinent; in 1963 Enoch Powell, now Minister of Health, sanctioned the recruitment of 18,000 NHS staff from South Asia. Class continued to affect perceptions of 'race', however: researchers found that white residents were more likely to tolerate an Asian neighbour if they were a doctor.[121]

One further group joined the diversifying Black Country in 1956, as global politics again sent out ripples. In October, Soviet tanks rolled into Budapest following an uprising against Communist rule in Hungary. 200,000 Hungarians fled the country and resettled across the world as refugees. In Britain, local branches of the Women's Voluntary Service (WVS) played a significant role in helping the refugees, and the WVS *Bulletin* in 1957 carried a proud report from the Wolverhampton branch:

We were issuing clothing to Hungarian refugees, our last customers being a husband and wife. After they had received their clothing they still lingered, obviously wanting something and saying some unpronounceable word over and over again. We were nonplussed. The husband, a nice cheery man, having gesticulated without success (No, not pants, long or short) suddenly rushed out of the hut, and presently appeared with a doll in his arms, which he carefully laid on the counter. Then, solemnly folding his handkerchief, he proceeded to fit the doll with a neat nappy. "Napkins," we shouted in unison, "Ja napkeen," he answered triumphantly, very pleased with his ingenious solving of the difficulty.[122]

However, Britain's international role shifted in the 1950s, from an imperial to a post-colonial power as former territories of the Empire fought for and gained independence. Attitudes towards immigrants – particularly those of colour – which had been built on Britain's imperial dominance, began to change. In 1948, the British public believed themselves on top of a mighty empire, yet more than half the population could not name one British colony; two-thirds believed that "native peoples in the Colonies have a lower standard of living than ourselves"; and 95 per cent had no "first-hand knowledge of coloured people".[123] Despite the comprehensive defeat of the fascist powers in the war, a minority persisted with far-right politics too – in 1947, a speech by Minister of Health Aneurin Bevan at Dudley Town Hall was interrupted by a heckler imitating a Nazi salute. But Britain's international role was increasingly threatened during the 1950s, and some historians have suggested that this anxiety about 'national decline', which accompanied decolonisation and diplomatic embarrassments like the Suez Crisis in 1956, prompted some to find scapegoats in the small immigrant population.[124] Government was not immune to this: Sir Winston Churchill was wary of what he called "coloured immigration", suggesting shortly before leaving office in 1955 that "Keep England White" would be a good slogan to adopt.[125]

As the 1950s progressed, uncomfortable local evidence began to emerge of official discrimination and everyday prejudice. Willenhall Baths was accused of operating a colour bar at its Saturday night dances in 1952, prompting a letter of protest to the *Express & Star* from representatives of the local Jamaican population:

We were made to understand that because we are Jamaicans or coloured men we are barred. Is this fair to us as British subjects to be treated like this because of another man's action? We are protesting against this discrimination.[126]

Black Country Visual Arts - Apna Heritage Archive, 1960s-1980s
Punjabi Migration: a Photographic Journey

Kuldip Aujla with Perminder Hayre in Cross Street, Wolverhampton *c.*1961.

The men were within their rights as British citizens to attend, but although Willenhall Council strenuously denied putting up a colour bar, they allowed dance organisers to set their own policies with regard to admittance and "several coloured men were refused admission" on the night in question. The *Express & Star*'s reporter believed that "exception was taken to their method of dancing", and "there were indications, too, of a few white people showing some feeling towards them". Threats of violence, real or potential, were to become part of the lives of people of colour in the Black Country.

Elsewhere, when the Jamaican Moody family was offered a council house in Bilston in 1958, some neighbours petitioned the council, stating: "We are all against this move. We don't want coloured people living by us."[127] This was true for those buying their own houses too: Calvert Hutchison faced similar opposition when he tried to buy near his place of work, at Bilston Steelworks. New Black Country residents soon learned which pubs, social clubs, trade unions, workplaces and shops operated colour bars. This was by no means universal, and individuals like Hutchison continued to resist such discrimination; but the 1950s revealed that potential problems lay ahead.[128]

Colour bar: Strike on the West Bromwich Buses

Sometimes trade unions, newspapers, local authorities and the public came together to condemn racism. In 1955, West Bromwich Transport Committee appointed an Indian man, Bhikai Patel, as a bus conductor – a role in which he had worked in his hometown of Bombay (now Mumbai). Public transport was acutely short of workers and employed many immigrant staff, first in behind-the-scenes roles, and later as drivers and conductors. Wolverhampton was already employing 68 people referred to as "coloured", out of a workforce of 900. West Bromwich's Transport Committee praised the good reputation "which had been earned by the coloured workers who have been in town for the last five years. They have never caused any trouble and they have solved a great number of problems for local employers."

However, following a previous (unsuccessful) vote by Birmingham Transport workers to operate an unofficial workplace colour bar, drivers and conductors in West Bromwich voted in favour of strikes against Patel's employment. They vehemently denied they were operating a colour bar, claiming rather that their overtime would be affected, although the strike leaders told their local TGWU secretary that "if one coloured man was allowed to work a flood of them would follow". The TGWU (of which Patel was a member) condemned the strike, which went ahead unofficially on 19 February 1955. 450 workers stayed off work. Further disruption was caused by drivers from neighbouring municipal transport authorities, including Birmingham, Wolverhampton and Walsall, who turned back at the Borough boundary in solidarity.

The strike was condemned from every angle. The decision to strike was taken against the advice of the TGWU, and the chair of West Bromwich Transport Committee, George Jones, expressed his disgust at the actions of both his own and neighbouring borough transport workers. The West Bromwich and Birmingham Trade Councils, Birmingham Transport Committee, local mayors, MPs and councillors from political parties across the spectrum and – most importantly – the West Bromwich public all strongly criticised the actions of the busmen. The bishops of Birmingham and Lichfield wrote:

> *"All men are the children of God no matter what the colour of their skins [and] we must state plainly that efforts to enforce a colour bar are not reconcilable with Christianity… We rely on the kindliness of the British working man to uphold the cause of human freedom and realise that a colour bar is morally indefensible."*

The Transport Committee held firm against the strikers, and public opinion moved ever more strongly to their side. On 26 February the busmen struck again, although seven (out of 115) buses were run mostly by inspectors, indoor staff, and Arthur Horton, the sole driver to vote against the strike action. Several newspapers ran editorials on that Saturday suggesting the strike was also motivated by generous overtime payments which the workers were keen to protect. A strike the next Saturday was called off after a long TGWU meeting, and the busmen agreed to talk with the transport committee. Although they stated that they were willing to work with Mr Patel, at his first shift the driver refused to leave with him on board, again restating the unofficial colour bar. He later apologised and no further strikes were held.

Later that year, bus drivers in Wolverhampton struck for similar reasons: ostensibly citing overtime issues, in fact workers wanted a five per cent quota on 'coloured labour'. The strike gave confidence to far-right organisations like the Birmingham Nationalist Club, which distributed stickers proclaiming "Keep Britain White" and "Coloured Invasion Threatens Britain" at the town's bus garages. Nevertheless, the incident demonstrated that while ignorance and prejudice were present in the Black Country as in the rest of the UK, with the support of politicians, unions and the public, discrimination on the grounds of colour could be met with firm rejection. However, such resistance was not consistent nationally: the Bristol Omnibus Company's infamous colour bar arose in similar circumstances and was only faced down by organised resistance from the black community there in 1963.[129]

The 1960s: Prejudice and Resistance

The 1960s witnessed a change in the tone of debates around immigration. The labour boom of the 1950s was slowing down following intermittent economic worries; continuing decolonisation of the British Empire meant that Britain's global role continued to change; and pressure from the right wing of the Conservative Party to restrict numbers resulted in the first restrictive legislation since the war, the 1962 Commonwealth Immigration Act. This limited immigration from the Commonwealth but not Ireland – an exemption many commentators described as "racially discriminatory". Precise figures for the Black Country are impossible to ascertain, although it was estimated that by 1961, the immigrant population of the built-up West Midlands comprised just over 50,000 born in the present or former

British Empire, and 58,000 from Ireland. Nationally too, there were as many Polish people arriving as there were from the Caribbean. The Commonwealth Immigration Act prompted a spike in applications to come to Britain, and many Commonwealth citizens already here – most of whom were hoping to return to their home countries at the earliest opportunity – decided to settle on a more permanent basis because of the Act. Gradually the idea of 'immigrants' as a problem was applied increasingly to those from the Commonwealth. As many observed at the time, people's origins became blurred: immigrants found that it mattered little in this country whether they were from Jamaica or Barbados, Trinidad or St Kitts, they were all 'West Indians' or 'Jamaicans'; or whichever part of the South Asian subcontinent they were from, they were 'Indians' or even 'Asiatics'; despite considerable cultural and religious differences, to sum this up in the parlance of the day, they were all 'coloured'.[130]

In the Black Country, immigration continued even after the 1962 Act, but unevenly. The personal, social and employment factors attracting immigrants for work were strong in Smethwick, West Bromwich, Wolverhampton and Walsall, but less so in Dudley, Stourbridge, Halesowen or Sedgley. The reaction to immigration varied too. Although parts of the Black Country became notorious during the 1960s, it should be stressed that these occurrences were usually responses to the local political and economic weather, rather than an inevitable response to immigration. Racism was certainly not uncommon, across political or social divides, but it was just one reaction to the broader social changes affecting the Black Country, and politicians and press frequently encouraged or exploited tensions for their own ends.

In 1958, Britain experienced its first mass disturbances focused on the skin colour of those involved in decades: violence towards immigrant communities in Nottingham and Notting Hill became known as 'race riots', appropriating language from the long history of such events in the USA, and were followed by small-scale copycat violence across the country, including in Dudley and Blackheath. The violence was roundly condemned, and the blame laid largely at the feet of the now-notorious Teddy Boys by police and press. Further disturbances in Middlesbrough in 1961 preceded the progress of the Commonwealth Immigration Bill through Parliament, and in July 1962, when it became law, far-right agitators, including Oswald Mosley and the Coventry schoolteacher (and leader of the new National Socialist Movement) Colin Jordan, attempted to whip up racial violence. Both held rallies in Trafalgar Square which were broken up by anti-fascist protestors, though Jordan was still given space on ATV's

Graham Gough/Dudley Archives and Local History Centre

Police employed dogs to quell the violence in North Street, Dudley during the disturbances in 1962.

Midlands News, claiming that "the majority of people in this country are sick and tired of coloured immigration, sick and tired of Jewish control".[131]

This heightened atmosphere broke out into violence in Dudley after allegations began to circulate that a black man had injured a white man in the 'Green Dragon', Dudley, on Saturday 28 July 1962. Fights broke out the following evening when a group described as "rowdies" *The Times* went "on the hunt for coloured persons" but were frustrated by a heightened police presence led by Superintendent Hullah. Monday night brought more fights and a coordinated attack on two Sikh brothers, Jamuil and Bharpur Singh, on Castle Hill. Given the violence of the previous nights, the brothers had taken to carrying knives for their own protection, so that when a large group attacked them with belts, chains and bricks, it was one of the attackers who ended in hospital. Given the intense provocation, the Singhs were cleared of any wrongdoing. The group continued though, smashing windows, throwing bottles, and trying to storm North Street where the police had formed a cordon.

North Street was described by national newspapers as Dudley's "Negro quarter". This was something of an exaggeration: Dudley had just a small immigrant population of around 1,000 (in a town of

65,000), spread between older houses at the foot of Kates Hill, and around Wellington and Himley Roads. North Street street was the centre of attention for the crowd on Tuesday 31 July, probably the worst night of rioting. Twenty-nine people had been in court during the day from arrests over the weekend, and police were stationed around the town to deal with the cheering, jeering crowds waiting outside. Newspaper accounts of that evening differ wildly: estimates range from 100 to over 1,000 people in Market Place when pubs closed at 10:30pm, taunting the 150 police they had surrounded. Crowds marched to North Street with "iron bars, belts, bricks and rubber coshes" and damaged a number of homes. Smaller disturbances followed the next night, but the combination of dogs and arrests appears to have calmed the situation down. Most of those arrested were young men in low-skilled work on their summer break – some of them perhaps the Teddy Boys causing so much alarm nationally – though there were older ringleaders identified too: Derek Anslow, 34 and unemployed, waving his two walking sticks and shouting for others to get the "black'uns"; and 44-year-old William Lawley from the Priory estate who told PC Evans: "I'm going to do them, Taff," before wading in swinging a chain.

The disturbances were widely reported, and many explanations suggested. *The Observer* was mystified, and unable to see past stereotypical explanations of racial violence: "Of the usual things that have caused racial tension in other towns (women, jobs, houses, immigration in dominating numbers) there is no one thing that sticks out here as an obvious provocative factor." Many newspapers discussed the possibility of organised far-right politics at work but concluded that "race relations at Dudley were probably rather better than in many other West Midland areas", a conclusion supported by Dudley MP George Wigg, who claimed it was "nothing but nihilism… I find no evidence of ill-will to the coloured people of this town." The riots stand against the backdrop of national immigration debates as a reflection of prejudice amongst small sections of the Black Country working class, but – as in Nottingham and Notting Hill – they were systematically condemned by press, politicians and commentators. Elsewhere in the Black Country though, local press and politics were colluding to stoke up racial tension.[132]

Smethwick: "The Poisonous Mouthings of the Racialists"

The clearest example of this was in Smethwick. Despite a comparatively large amount of Commonwealth immigration – up to 4,000 out of 70,000, or less than six per cent of the town's population in the early 1960s – Smethwick actually had a declining population and an ageing housing stock, as residents moved away from a town "dingy with factories, smoke, and old housing", to modern estates in other parts of the Black Country or elsewhere. [133] Relations were mostly cordial, although around ten pubs enforced a colour bar, and even shops and churches participated in similar discrimination. Anti-immigrant attitudes could be found amongst all political persuasions – Smethwick Labour Club operated a colour bar, for instance – but from 1960 the local newspaper, the *Smethwick Telephone,* and the local Conservative Party colluded to stigmatise and demonise the town's immigrant population in a particularly extreme way.[134]

The *Telephone*'s editor Katie Billingsley was an outspoken supporter of the local Tories and began publishing letters and opinion pieces making lurid claims about the town's immigrants, suggesting they brought tuberculosis, overcrowded their homes, and disturbed the town. These were not published without opposition, although the printing of ongoing correspondence in the letters pages did little to lower the tension of the debate. One of the key letter-writers, Donald Finney, wrote to the *Telephone* in March 1961 to announce the foundation of a branch of the far-right Birmingham Immigration Control Association (BICA): "Something has got to be done now," he wrote, "to stop this influx of thousands upon thousands of foreigners coming into England."[135]

There were predictably stormy scenes at the first BICA meeting in April when John Jackson – who had consistently written to the *Telephone* to oppose Finney's views – took the platform to cries of "N*****-lover" and "Throw him out". Soon after, the newspaper published an extraordinarily leading editorial:

> *…to those of our readers living in areas in which immigrants have congregated: if you know of a house which is obviously overcrowded and/or insanitary, give us the fullest details and we'll confront an apparently complacent authority with what's going on… The* Telephone *has no colour prejudice. But we recognise that Smethwick does have a colour problem, and that an all-out effort must be made to solve it NOW.* [136]

The appeal was met with correspondence given titles like "Smethwick will soon be like Mecca", "Diseases returning" and "The new 'Black Hole'". Headlines talked of colour bars, rent strikes by white council tenants, and "heathen rites" and "temples for the black people," referring to the recent conversion of a closed church into the first dedicated gurdwara in Europe. Yet though the agitators made the headlines, there was support for the immigrants too, from immigrant community groups like the Pakistan Welfare Association, community

SWNS

Racist graffiti on Victoria Road, Smethwick, in 1962.

organisers like Avtar Singh Jouhl and Jagmohan Joshi, church-led organisations like the Community Club, and letter-writers like GW Baker of Middlemore Avenue, who complained about "the poisonous mouthings of the racialists".[137]

The town's Labour MP, Patrick Gordon Walker, was not tremendously popular in Smethwick; seen as an outsider and a career politician, his majority had decreased in successive elections during the 1950s. In 1960, Peter Griffiths became leader of Smethwick Conservatives. As a headmaster in West Bromwich, he was particularly interested in education and it was this that provided him with his first taste of notoriety. In 1963 he proposed that Indian children in Smethwick be taught separately for part of the day, in English, mathematics and science. The suggestion drew widespread criticism and comparison to school segregation in the American South.[138]

The *Smethwick Telephone* continued to stir up debate, publishing lurid and speculative accounts conflating overcrowding and poverty with prostitution, street crime and disease. The newspaper and Griffiths claimed that people were afraid of immigrants, afraid to go out after dark, afraid of "miscegenation" – that people of different races might cause Smethwick people to lose "our English characteristics, perhaps our very heritage, eventually to become a nation of half-breeds".[139] Griffiths' language was always evasive and suggestive, claiming that his rhetoric just reproduced what 'people' were saying, rather than his own opinions. In 1962, for example, he said "people resent them for what they term 'living on our welfare services'… they regard these large numbers of unskilled immigrants as a threat to their own standards of living".[140] Spoken on the same weekend of the Dudley riots, his words carried an undertone of threat not to the 'people', but to the immigrants themselves. In fact, most people were not nearly so fearful. In one survey, around half accepted that some people were afraid to go out after dark, yet only a tenth were afraid themselves. In the words of Smethwick Young Socialists' Derek Harper: "People have been conditioned by publicity to believe in this fear – in other people. When it comes to themselves, they have to admit they don't feel it." Even Donald Finney's vigilante group failed to find any evidence to support accusations of immigrants accosting white girls.[141]

The bitterness peaked after the Conservatives won the municipal elections in June 1964, and Griffiths was adopted as parliamentary candidate for the 1964 general election. Posters and street graffiti began to appear in the town, including the most infamous: "If you want a n***** for a neighbour, vote Labour." "I would not condemn anyone who said that," said Griffiths; "I would say that is how people see the situation in Smethwick."[142] Griffiths entered the election campaign with stridently racist policies. He claimed to have no colour bar, but a "squalor bar", blaming certain sections of the immigrant community for having "made no attempt to live up to the social and moral standards the people expect", He sought to ban unskilled immigrants, those in poor health and those who did not work. He refused to condemn the pubs and barber shops that refused to serve people of colour, and predicted "an explosion" in the town if Gordon Walker was re-elected. He opposed allowing any immigrants a council house and accused immigrant children of holding the English back. *The Sunday Times* summed up his careful use of language: "Mr Griffiths never *quite* calls spades, spades. But the implication is always very clear."[143]

Griffiths was castigated in the national press by groups such as the Birmingham Co-ordinating Committee Against Racial Discrimination and the IWA, by churches, by local politicians like Dr Prem, and by his political opponents in Smethwick. Even the Conservative Prime Minister, Alec Douglas-Home, was forced to repudiate Griffiths' tactics in a television interview before the election. Griffiths' victory in November 1964 came as a shock. The Smethwick result went strongly against the national swing, which returned Labour to power after thirteen years. The humiliated Patrick Gordon Walker – widely expected to become Foreign Secretary – was forced to stand in Leyton, East London in a by-election the following January, and lost again. Further scandal followed when it was revealed that the Smethwick Labour Club he had booked for his outgoing speech was itself operating a colour bar.

Mirrorpix/Reach Licensing

The American civil rights leader Malcolm X visiting Marshall Street, Smethwick, in February 1965.

The following year, residents of Marshall Street petitioned the council to impose a policy of buying up houses on the street as they became vacant so that they could be let to white tenants only. The Conservative-controlled town council seized on the idea and applied to Housing Minister Richard Crossman for permission to borrow money for the scheme. The policy raised a storm of protest and Crossman, deeply opposed to its principle, rejected it. Among those protesting was Malcolm X, who visited Smethwick in February 1965. The American civil rights leader had been invited by the IWA whilst on a tour of universities, although controversy followed him at every step. The Mayor of Smethwick said that "it makes my blood boil that this man should be allowed into this country", and the chairman of the Standing Conference of West Indian Organisations in Birmingham thought that his compatriots were probably "not the sort of people who would want to follow Malcolm X". X had a different view: "As long as it is the Fascists and Nazis, it seems everything's OK, but when I go to Smethwick there are protests." He had come, he told reporters, "because I am disturbed by reports that coloured people in Smethwick are being treated badly – like Hitler treated the Jews". Malcolm X stopped for a drink at the Ivy Bush, close to Marshall Street, before speaking at the University of Birmingham later that day; nine days later he was shot dead in New York. Griffiths lost his seat in the 1966 general election.[144]

Enoch Powell and Wolverhampton

The Smethwick election heightened the pitch of the immigration debate in Britain. Many – including the new Labour Prime Minister Harold Wilson, who suggested that Griffiths should sit out his time as a "parliamentary leper" – were disgusted at the events and called for fairer treatment for immigrants, resulting in Britain's first anti-discrimination legislation in 1965. Politicians like Griffiths and his friend, Kidderminster MP Gerald Nabarro, maintained strident calls for an "absolute ban" on immigration, and watching in the wings was Enoch Powell, MP for Wolverhampton South-West. Although he later claimed to have been concerned about immigration from the mid-1950s, Powell had avoided Smethwick and as Minister for Health had held pragmatic, uncontroversial views about the need for immigration to meet labour demands: notably, he had overseen NHS recruitment campaigns across the Commonwealth during his tenure. As Wolverhampton resident Surjit Singh Sandhu recalled, Powell was also often happy to support constituents in organising visas – Sandhu moved to the town with Powell's help in 1965. However, following a very unsuccessful campaign to become leader of the Conservative Party in 1965, and a council election scare in which the chairman of BICA's Wolverhampton branch nearly won a council seat in Powell's constituency, he began to heighten his rhetoric.[145]

Results in the 1966 general election appeared to suggest that 'race' as a political issue was on the decline. Across the board in the Black Country, Labour candidates – generally intentionally eschewing talk of immigration – increased their majorities; in Smethwick's case, the actor Andrew Faulds won back the seat for Labour. The exception was Enoch Powell, who increased his share of the vote. But this proved a temporary lull rather than a sea-change in public opinion. In 1967 the political mood shifted again. The catalyst this time was the potential arrival of many East African Asians in the UK – around 100,000 people who had been granted British citizenship when Kenya was made independent in 1963, but were now threatened with expulsion by the Kenyan government. The British government rushed through a new immigration bill, requiring new immigrants to have had a parent or grandparent born or naturalised in the UK. As with the 1961 bill, it prompted another round of racialised, anti-immigrant rhetoric.

In August 1967, Tarsem Singh Sandhu was sent home by Wolverhampton Corporation Transport for wearing a beard and turban to work, in contravention of the Transport Committee's uniform policy. There followed nearly two years of back and forth between Wolverhampton's Sikhs and the town council, played out once again in the letter pages of the local newspaper, the *Express & Star*. The newspaper's editor, Clem Jones – a close friend of Powell's – attempted to ensure that both sides of the debate were represented fairly; nevertheless, this allowed extreme views to resurface in the town. Immigrants again found themselves castigated in print as "parasites", as "a thankless crowd of workshy malingerers", as devaluing property, as blocking hospital beds. The degree to which this affected Powell's thinking, or how Powell affected the debate, is difficult to ascertain; however, the protracted argument certainly added to the feeling that the Black Country was home to a distinct 'race' problem. The Transport Committee eventually backed down after months of pressure from Sikh campaigners.[146]

In February 1968, Enoch Powell spoke at a Conservative party dinner in Walsall. Despite some highly questionable statistics, his arguments for a moratorium on immigration were nonetheless praised in the tabloid press. A few weeks later, and just after the publication of the updated Race Relations Bill, Powell stood up at the Midland Hotel in Birmingham and made his most famous speech, one he thought would "go up 'fizz' like a rocket".[147] The journalist Paul Foot, in his book on Powell, considered that what made this speech unique was how it represented the relationship between Powell – rarely considered a model constituency MP – and the ordinary people of Wolverhampton. Powell employed anonymous anecdotes and stories that he claimed came from his constituents, to argue that – in the words of one anonymous interlocutor – "in this country in 15 or 20 years' time the black man will have the whip hand over the white man". No trace was ever found of Powell's informants, only echoes of rumours that had floated around far-right groups for years.[148]

If tensions had been simmering in the Black Country, they threatened to boil over after the 'Rivers of Blood' speech, nicknamed after Powell's more verifiable quote from Virgil. Powell was swiftly sacked from the Shadow Cabinet by Edward Heath, leader of the Conservative Party, over the speech, and wildcat strikes were reported in his support amongst dockers in London, construction workers at Rugeley, motor workers in Coventry, Smithfield meat market workers, and elsewhere. In the Black Country, small strikes occurred among tanker drivers in West Bromwich, and brewery workers at the Park Brewery, Wolverhampton; workers from Villiers and Victoria Sheet Metal in Wolverhampton, Sankey's in Bilston, and Eaton Yale & Towne in Wednesfield, signed petitions of support; and a procession from Wolverhampton to Dudley displayed banners like "We support Powell and Britain", singing "We have the best MP in the land".[149] These grabbed the headlines, although engineer Mick Powis's experience at Turner Manufacturing was probably more common:

> *It was the main topic of conversation for several days… probably summed up by this quote, 'Enoch Powell is a fine gentleman, who is saying what everybody thinks'… There was talk of a token strike to support Powell… which ended with a unanimous decision not to support it.*[150]

An uglier side of support for Powell showed through though, with multiple violent attacks against Wolverhampton's immigrant population in the following days. Wade and Albert Crooks were hospitalised by a group shouting "Powell! Powell!" in a pub near East Park, Wolverhampton – for many immigrants, it was a time of fear of violence, abuse, even deportation. Powell was not put off. A speech in Eastbourne later in 1968 showed that he had moved from an argument about numbers to one about habits and customs – in warning of "the transformation of whole areas… into alien territory", he clearly had his representation of Wolverhampton in mind.[151]

Powell's speeches were to usher in an era of unprecedented aggression towards African-Caribbean and South Asian communities in Britain, but they also provoked anti-racist activism in opposition. Resistance came in particular from students at Wolverhampton Polytechnic and community groups like the IWA and the West Midlands Caribbean Association. "Let no man deceive himself into thinking that Enoch Powell speaks for Wolverhampton," said Aaron Haynes, secretary of the Wolverhampton Council for Racial Harmony. "It should not be forgotten that there is inter-racial friendship to be found in this town among all sections of population."[152] Black and Asian workers continued to fight for their own rights in the workplace too: the Conygre strike the year before Powell's speech was matched by others at Midland Motor Cylinder and the Newby Foundry in West Bromwich.[153]

"Race relations"

What would come to be known as "race relations" in the Black Country reflected national events and debates. It is no coincidence that the racist violence in Dudley occurred as the first Commonwealth Immigration Act came into force, or that Enoch Powell seized the opportunity to ramp up his rhetoric as the second Immigration Bill was being discussed, in light of a potential influx of British citizens from elsewhere in the Commonwealth. Yet too often the Black Country was also making the news. The national press was eager to latch onto stories like the bus strike in West Bromwich, the Dudley riots, or the racist politicking in Smethwick. These major stories around immigration – and by this most meant Commonwealth, or 'coloured' immigration – were rewarding sources of publicity for newspapers and politicians in the 1960s. Their presentation as somehow representative of commonplace viewpoints enabled others to exploit this feeling, far more so than when press, politicians and civil society decisively identified racism and condemned it. Such coverage played a huge part in the everyday experience of immigrants in the Black Country, creating fear and prompting community organisation as a bulwark against racism. But it should not be seen as accurately representing the ordinary opinions of Black Country people either, the vast majority of whom never signed a petition in support of Powell, or attended a BICA meeting, or supported a pub or club in the operation of a colour bar, or shouted racial slurs at their neighbours.

Although the 1960s had been a traumatic decade, it also saw the birth of resistance to racism, both within immigrant communities who organised themselves, and from other groups. While racism – physical and verbal, subtle and blatant – existed, so too did its opponents in the Black Country. Crucially, when local government, press and other institutions stood up to racism, as in West Bromwich and Dudley, it was pushed back. When politicians equivocated, and newspapers claimed to report both sides of the debate – as in Wolverhampton and Smethwick – racism festered. But in the end, the bus strike collapsed; Peter Griffiths failed to segregate Marshall Street; the Dudley rioters were dispersed or arrested; and Enoch Powell was sacked from the Shadow Cabinet, his career never to recover. And as the Conygre strike showed, immigrant workers were more than capable of standing up for themselves. By the 1960s, workers from all over the world were part of the Black Country working class, not separate from it, and without them, the region could not have been as strong as it was.

Chapter 5

An "unlovely heritage"

The changing Black Country

Bournville Village Trust

The Portway Branch of the Titford Canal, with Birchley Rolling Mills in the foreground and the Rowley Hills to the rear, *c.*1945.

There were few things which tied the diverse Black Country together in these years, but its unique landscape was arguably one. The industrialisation of the Black Country environment had been rapid and unplanned throughout the eighteenth and nineteenth centuries, and its late Victorian decline was similarly haphazard. Exhausted or flooded coal mines were simply abandoned, leaving a honeycomb of underground tunnels and a surface too unstable to build on, while elsewhere water became polluted, empty factories were left to rot and cavernous marl holes turned into death traps. This legacy of industrialisation enchanted some and frustrated others. For all the beauty of land in the midst of reclamation by nature, such dereliction presented a massive hurdle to the planners and reconstruction committees of local authorities who, faced with a substantial housing shortage and an expanding economy, needed somewhere to build. This tension between nostalgia and progress eventually left its own legacy. By the end of the 1960s the Black Country had been transformed, but only partially: Victorian shops abutted modernist precincts; ring roads were constructed over decades; and traffic was increasingly clogging an unreformed road network. The Black Country had been pulled into modernity but, as some argued, risked losing its unique identity.

Courtesy of Black Country Living Museum

Slag heaps at Bloxwich.

"Neither Industrial nor Rural but Derelict"

The Black Country is a geographically varied region, with a unique geology. Divided by a "knobbly backbone" of hills from Sedgley in the north-west to Rowley Regis in the south-east, it has two distinct landscapes. The north and east of the Black Country, a "sober patchwork of duns and browns, and browny-greens and slate blues, and dull reds", is generally flatter and drained by the nascent, meandering River Tame. This was where the coal was most easily accessible to early industrialists, resulting in what the Black Country author Francis Brett Young called a "lunar landscape" emerging around towns like Bilston, Tipton and Wednesbury. The south and west, where ironstone proliferated in addition to coal, drain into the quicker Stour, with steep valleys and high hills that lent themselves to water power – it was no accident that the Black Country's early tool forging industry focused on the upper reaches of the Tame in Oldbury and the Stour valley in Stourbridge. This ridge between the two forms part of the country's major watershed: rain falling on one side of Dudley High Street is said to flow to the North Sea, on the other to the Bristol Channel.[154]

Nevertheless, the whole region industrialised rapidly, and the environment was rarely considered. As mining began to decline in the late nineteenth century, some parts of the Black Country took on an appearance that was shocking to many onlookers. JB Priestley wrote in 1934 that "there are signs of atrocities everywhere; the earth has been left gaping and bleeding".[155] The historian WG Hoskins – no admirer of industrialisation – put it even more succinctly, describing the Black Country as a "landscape of Hell". In other parts of Britain, bombsites from the war provided a playground. In the Black Country, bomb damage had been limited but these industrial ruins provided a ready substitute. In 1945, the writer Walter Allen found booming industry in the towns but increasingly abandoned wasteland between them, with little thought to its future use: "a country neither industrial nor rural but derelict". Stanley Beaver, an industrial geographer who toured the Black Country by bicycle in the 1940s, believed that almost 14 out of the 53 square miles of exposed coalfield could be called derelict, and that "nowhere outside the Black Country is derelict land so concentrated and in quite such intimate relationship to urban development".[156]

This was, for the most part, a legacy of mining. The high, conical spoil banks visible at Sandwell Park or Hamstead collieries were the result of large-scale mechanisation, but they were not characteristic of the mining that made the Black Country's fortune. Instead, older, smaller spoil heaps resulted in swathes of

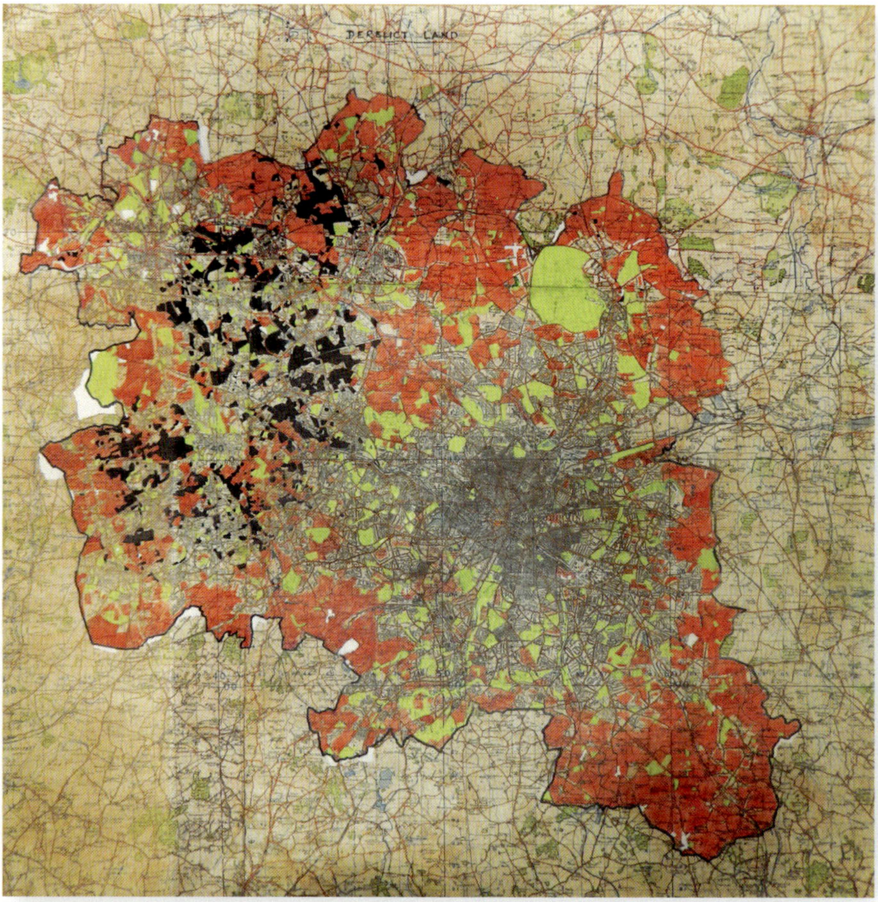

Bournville Village Trust/Cadbury Research Library: Special Collections, University of Birmingham(WMG 2/20)

Plan showing the concentration of derelict land in the West Midlands conurbation in 1948. Undeveloped land is marked in red, open space in green, and derelict land in black.

pitted, uneven ground referred to as "hills and hollows". Leaving ground unstable and awkward, this landscape caused innumerable problems for councils and developers; it had "carved", "mangled", and "tortured" the Black Country landscape, left "disfigured by an endless succession of spoil banks, dumps, abandoned works".[157] Slag heaps produced by the iron-smelting industry, though sometimes removed for road-metal, littered the landscape. "Swags", pools formed by land subsidence, abounded; quarries pockmarked the Rowley hills; huge "marl 'oles" scarred the region wherever clay was dug for brickmaking, the cause of numerous deaths by drowning or injury. Bricks were the last local industry to rely on material extracted from the Black Country, as the arc of massive brickworks running along the clay seam from Bromley Brickworks through Corbyn's Hall, Stourbridge Refractories, Himley Bricks and Oak Farm testified.

Where some saw only dereliction and

decay, others more attuned to the history and culture of the Black Country found this landscape fascinating. The local journalist WE Hall visited Cobb's Engine House at Bumble Hole in 1965, and saw industry giving way to wilderness. The chimney stack towered over a "secret world full of plant and insect mysteries" – despite its engine having been shipped to the Henry Ford Museum in Detroit in 1928. His "fey, lost world, with the willow-herb growing up by narrow, twisting paths" could have described many parts of the region. This wildflower, known as fireweed, was symbolic in the post-war period: its pink flowers, a fiery red in the autumn, thrived in burnt-out places where bombs – or unregulated industry – had struck.[158]

In clay country, Amblecote, there were "buttercup meadows and woods"; in Coseley, industrial decay was balanced by "rich greenery, and ruralness". In the journalist J Wilson Jones' poetic language: "The sound of drop hammers is giving way to the lark's melody. The rattle of the colliery incline is being replaced by the nightjar… even now in the heart of the Black Country, beauty lingers on." Nevertheless, most visitors, officials, perhaps even Black Country folk, would agree with the conclusion that the Black Country was "dominated by the unlovely heritage of industrial revolution", forming "as great a scenic blot on the face of England as it is a monument to industrial productivity".[159]

Peter Donnelly

Anglers on the Stourbridge Canal near George King Harrison's firebrick works, Brierley Hill, 1962.

"Planning is in the Air"

The writer and television presenter Phil Drabble, in particular, exemplified a nostalgic, romantic localism in his 1952 history of the Black Country, and lost no opportunity to bemoan the distant bureaucrats he was sure would destroy it:

> *Unkempt, craggy land it is, full of surprising hillocks and hollows, and the planners would bulldoze it flat so that their sentinels could observe all that went on. But I like these rough, wild places as they are. I want no lidos or mass entertainment demanding no initiative… I hope more land may be thrown open to the public as it is, without vast expense on formal laying-out.*[160]

Drabble was echoing national debates between modernisers like the Conservative housing minister Keith Joseph, and romantics like the architectural critic Ian Nairn or WG Hoskins, who complained about the "black-hatted officers of This and That".[161] Drabble was writing in 1952, in the midst of a wave of post-war reconstruction seen by many as essential. As early as 1943, the councils of Black Country towns were thinking about what should come after the war. Dudley's *Blocksidge's Almanack* noted: "Plans are being prepared for the great reconstruction which we are told is going to bring about a new world… like other towns, Dudley is preparing and she has a vast programme to consider."[162] Wolverhampton's Reconstruction Committee employed the University of Birmingham's Tom Brennan for a full social survey and published sweeping plans produced by the architect Ernest Berry Webber for the redevelopment of its historic, but cluttered, town centre. Both were a sign of the new power and authority vested in both social scientists and local authorities after 1945. Even more influential was the West Midland Group for Post-War Reconstruction and Planning, based at the University of Birmingham and consisting of, amongst others, Stanley Beaver and members of the Cadbury family. They, like others, found the Black Country landscape fascinating:

> *While the observer may understand readily the relationship of a Bath crescent or a Bloomsbury square with the scene of its heigh-day, he is confused and bewildered at the prospect of, say, the Black Country shopping street, the view at one end closed by a murderous hump back canal bridge, the busy shops and banks terminating at the other end with a level crossing and another canal bridge. Flanking these may be a decayed railway station, alongside, a blue brick Gothic church jostles a black bitumastic sheeted factory built on land from which the inhabitants have been driven away because their cottages were slums by modern standards. And yet how pregnant with recent history is every word of this unexaggerated description.*[163]

The West Midland Group proposed plans at local and regional levels and came to sweeping conclusions about the hindrances of the old-fashioned landscape. The demolition of 'slum' property was the first thing on many councils' minds, but infrastructure was not far behind: for Wolverhampton, "construction of the inner-ring road will afford an opportunity for the gradual rebuilding and improvement of some of the older parts of the central business area of town". Zoning was recommended too. Residential areas were to be "self-contained neighbourhood units, freed from intersecting main trunk roads and provided with communal facilities, local shopping and… open spaces". Many towns could have repeated Brennan's description of Wolverhampton in 1948: "Factories are closely packed together, they are often obnoxious or noisy, and many thousands of them were, at some period in the last hundred years or so, converted from dwelling houses to the purposes of manufacture."[164] New industrial zones were mooted too, "to provide not only for an industrial use proportionate to the available labour pool, but also to enable industry to be re-sited and re-developed along modern lines".[165] Most radical were plans for the commercial centre of town, resulting in a new market and shopping centre over the next few decades. Reports like Brennan's and the West Midland Group's landmark *Conurbation* in 1948 accompanied a major overhaul of planning laws, giving local authorities substantial power. Such plans were a radical departure for the Black Country: instead of unchecked expansion by private capital the state, both local and

Courtesy of Black Country Living Museum

Brierley Hill's Chapel Street Estate under construction in 1956, overlooked by the remains of coal and fireclay mining in Amblecote.

national, was to play a much greater part in preparing for the post-war future. As the West Midlands Group put it: "Planning is in the air."[166]

Such radical transformations had wider impacts than just on the built environment. Black Country councils were in constant competition with one another, particularly in the light of ongoing boundary reviews, and town planning was one way of presenting a case for continued local control. The small town of Darlaston, for example, embraced innovative urban planning as a way of fending off the expansion ambitions of the nearby, and much larger, borough of Walsall. In 1944, Darlaston Urban District Council (UDC) approved a scheme by Sir Alfred Owen (of Rubery Owen – one of several socially concerned, or paternalistic, industrialists in the region) to build the "garden city of the Black Country" on the rubbish tip that had been Bentley Common, with thousands of homes surrounding a new church and community amenities. For this, the borough surveyor HN Hughes convened a "council of experts" to work with the surrounding boroughs. A growth in the trust and emphasis placed upon expertise was key to the town planning movement, reflecting a more general move away from private provision towards a more publicly-minded local governance: a comment on the Bentley scheme in the *Walsall Observer* suggested that it would rectify some of the "many mistakes made when men were too exclusively self-centred". In 1962, the town again promoted an ambitious new scheme

Courtesy of Black Country Living Museum

Plans for the "The New Darlaston" published in 1962.

Used with the permission of Wolverhampton Archives

"Gap in the fence", from the Wolverhampton Photographic Society's 1966 exhibition.

to completely reorganise the town centre – it included pedestrianised zones, high-rise social housing, and a new motorway. Darlaston UDC considered this less an experiment than a duty: it felt "a legal obligation to plan; a moral obligation to promote good town development; a redevelopment obligation to replace areas which were substantially worn out; [and] an obligation to hand on to the next generation a town which is flourishing and attractive". Darlaston UDC outlined the town's flaws and proclaimed the remedies, albeit with one eye on fending off the ambitions of nearby, larger local authorities to swallow up the town. As elsewhere though, the town's grand plans were only half-completed and its struggle for independence was unsuccessful – Darlaston was subsumed into Walsall County Borough in 1966. The craze for town planning was not universally successful, and for most of the 1940s, 1950s and 1960s, the Black Country was a transitional environment, the result of an unplanned industrial past faced with the competing realities of modern life.[167]

Canals

Perhaps nothing illustrates the battles between ancient and modern better than the Black Country's famous waterways. From 1769, when the original Birmingham Canal opened from Wednesbury to Birmingham, the Black Country developed one of the largest networks of waterways in the world. Even in 1949, Rev F Brighton

Canal & River Trust Waterways Archive

The Wednesbury Oak Loop of the Birmingham Canal, pictured here in 1958, was formally closed in 1954.

considered Ocker Hill the "Venice of the Midlands".[168] But the advent of efficient rail and road transport heralded the decline of the canals as commercially viable entities. Traffic on the Birmingham Canal Navigations (BCN) fell from 3 million tons in 1930 to 1.2 million in 1947. Half of this was on the main line from Birmingham to Wolverhampton, but the 600,000 tons carried there diminished to just 150,000 by 1964. The limitations of the locks and narrow canals were only too evident and despite nationalisation in 1948, the Black Country's canals were abandoned. Dudley tunnel closed to commercial traffic in 1950, followed by many of the smaller branches: the branch to the Izons foundry in West Bromwich, the Neachells Branch of the Bentley Canal, the Portway and Causeway Green branches. Others followed, often with good reason. The journalist David Smith recalled the fate of the Bentley Canal:

> *When I was born [in 1954], the canal was still in use; it carried coal barges to feed coal-fired furnaces. By the time I was aware of it, however, it had fallen into disuse, but it was still filled with its characteristic bright orange water, said to be the result of a continuous discharge from a local firm, Ductile Steel, and later embellished by the rust of abandoned prams and other detritus.*[169]

Canals were dangerous places and sources of disease, and many residents were relieved when the canal was formally closed and filled in.[170] By the end of the 1950s, only the main waterways of the region remained in infrequent use, a story repeated across the country: from a peak of 4,500 miles of waterway network in Britain, by 1969 there were just 1,400 remaining. In the Black Country, over 100 miles of canal were reduced to around 70. A few carrying firms still plied their trade after nationalisation, mostly bringing coal from the Cannock Chase coalfield to the power stations of the West Midlands. Famous firms like Fellows, Morton & Clayton limped into voluntary administration, although smaller ones like Tipton's Alfred Matty's continued into the 1970s, carrying, dredging, and disposing of waste oil from Round Oak and phosphorus from Albright & Wilson. The job came with its challenges, particularly during winter. Not only did the ice have to be broken up, but pirates roamed the Black Country canals – in 1950 several boats reported thieves dropping onto boats from bridges on lonely stretches of canal, holding up the boatmen and shovelling coal before leaping off at the next bridge. Perhaps only the few remaining boat families really mourned the decline. 70-year-old Tom Shackleton did not look forward to his retirement "on the bank" after a lifetime on the "cut". As he relayed his story to *John Bull*'s Harry Hopkins in 1953, he still thrilled to show the journalist the "snake of glowing steel" that could be seen "leaping" out of the rolling mills at Bayliss, Jones and Bayliss, near Wolverhampton.[171]

That this decline did not prove terminal for the Black Country's canals was attributable to a small number of campaigners dedicated to saving them. In 1944, the writer and campaigner LTC "Tom" Rolt published *Narrow Boat*, an account of a long cruise across the near-abandoned waterways of the Midlands. Although he avoided the Black Country – mostly for its 84 locks and the "dolorous region" of the Wyrley & Essington Canal – his struggles against the wind, rain, and pollution and his encounters with Black Country day boats proved inspirational for leisure boaters. Two years later, he formed the Inland Waterways Association (IWA). By the end of the 1950s, leisure boats were more common than working boats on many parts of the network. The Dudley Canal Preservation Society was formed in 1964, the Birmingham Canal Navigations Society in 1968, and although the transformation of the Black Country's canals from dereliction to public amenity would take many decades to complete, the roots of the change can be found in the 1960s.[172]

The Battle of Stourbridge

Eighteen years after the publication of *Narrow Boat* the movement had gathered enough momentum for 118 boats to arrive on the Town Arm of the Stourbridge Canal for a rally. This was deliberate: the British Transport Commission (BTC) was eager to close the waterway down and was supported by Amblecote UDC which was keen for a canal that "had outlived its usefulness" to be filled. Despite obstruction and legal threats from the BTC, volunteers spent the fortnight before the rally clearing the canal and repairing the flight of 16 locks between Wordsley and Brierley Hill. A dragline was hired to dredge the canal, borrowed from ongoing restoration on the Stratford-upon-Avon Canal. At a cost of £74 to hire, this was the only expense for the restoration of the canal, compared to the £20,000 proposed by the BTC to fill the canal in. The latter's secretary, a Mr Ives, arrived with police and lawyers and ordered the work to cease, threatening that if the dragline's bucket touched the water he would have the workers arrested for trespass. David Hutchings, the rally's chairman, responded by pulling the policeman behind the dragline and ordering the driver to continue dredging. At this, the driver raised his bucket to the highest extent and released it – unfortunately for Ives, who was standing close by and found himself covered in mud and silt from the canal bed. The first boat traversed the length of the Stourbridge Town Arm on 30 July 1962. The "Battle of Stourbridge" made the front page of *The Times* and the rally was a huge success, paving the way for a wave of restorations which followed across the Black Country and Britain.[173]

Canal & River Trust Waterways Archive

Rally on the Stourbridge Canal, August 1962.

Clean Air, Dirty Water

One of the main stumbling-blocks for the more romantically-minded observer was the sheer toxicity of the place. Industrial pollution had long been a major problem for the Black Country, both in the air and in the waters. The region was littered with spoil, from coal waste to marl holes to Oldbury's famous 'Blue Billy', a by-product of sulphuric acid containing cyanide, heaps of which towered behind the town's many chemical works. Both the Tame and the Stour were once major sources of power and water for the Black Country, but by this period, waste from Oldbury chemical works, Tipton brickworks or Lye hollowware works combined to create brightly-coloured but highly polluted waterways. Perhaps neither river was quite as noxious as the infamous Rattlechain Lagoon in Tividale, once the marl hole for Samuel Barnett's brickworks, then a waste dump for Albright & Wilson, but by the 1950s so polluted that even hardened boatmen could be completely overcome by its fumes.[174]

Courtesy o' Black Country Living Museum

Looking towards Albright & Wilson's chemical works, Oldbury, 1959.

In 1860, the Victorian author Walter White described Oldbury as "a place of smother amid smother", full of chimneys "which pour forth their cloudy contributions". By the time the children's author Allan Ahlberg was growing up in Oldbury nearly a century later, the town was still a "hot and sulphurous cup". The pall of smoke that hung over the Black Country is difficult to imagine today, but Ahlberg's description of "a lid upon the town" matches the findings of a study in 1945, that smoke pollution blocked up to half of the sunlight in the region around Birmingham.[175] A Black Country smog could shut down all operations: Stanley Simms, who had recently arrived from Jamaica, remembered the novelty of a man leading buses through West Bromwich town centre: "If I put my hand out in front of me, I couldn't see my own hand."[176] As well as the toxic contents of the smoke, the pollution affected everything from germination of seeds to corrosion of metals, caused rickets and respiratory problems, and even "bears heavily on the housewife". Residents of Carder Crescent, Bradley, could attest to that: they recalled the thick brown dust from Bradley & Foster's works and the occasional piece of flying shrapnel from Perry's rolling mill, which meant that washing often came in dirtier than it went out.[177]

The advent of the 1956 Clean Air Act prompted a wave of debate about the unhealthiness of the Black Country atmosphere. The *Dudley Herald* was convinced that the Act was essential, and that "town and city dwellers of the next century will obviously not be prepared to tolerate the unhealthy conditions that have applied through the last hundred years".[178] Gerald Nabarro, then MP for Kidderminster and a leading proponent of the Act, toured the Black Country opening Clean Air exhibitions before the Act came into force. It went some way to remedying the toxic atmosphere, but was slow to have effect. Tipton still suffered from 15 tons of dust in the atmosphere per square mile in 1962, though this was down from 26 tons in 1950. David Smith recalled frequent, choking fogs well into the 1960s but besides this, the stamping works opposite his school still sprayed iron filings and dust into the playground. The Act legislated against "dark smoke emissions from certain industries" but did not account for local effects like this, or the effects of workplace pollution on workers' health.[179]

Road and Rail

Where canals offered a case study of official decline and amateur revitalisation, the Black Country's road and rail presented contrasting pictures. In 1945, the traveller could reach almost anywhere in the Black Country by rail. From Dudley station, for example, in the centre of the Black Country, passengers could head north to Tipton and Wolverhampton; south to Halesowen and Longbridge; west to Brierley Hill and Stourbridge; and east to

Ned Williams / Black Country Living Museum

Featured in Flanders & Swann's 1963 song "Slow Train", Windmill End Halt was on the Bumble Hole Line between Dudley and Old Hill. This photograph dates from 1964, the year of the station's closure.

FIGURE 19

PROPOSALS FOR NEW TRUNK ROADS

These suggestions for a trunk road system to link the Conurbation with the principal ports and to keep through traffic away from the built-up areas are based upon proposals outlined by the County Surveyors' Society.

Existing roads are shown in red, proposed new roads in black.

Bournville Village Trust

Suggestions for a new trunk road system based on pre-war plans by the County Surveyors' Society, published in *Conurbation* in 1948.

Wednesbury and Walsall. Kingswinford, Oldbury and the Cape Hill Brewery in Smethwick had their own branch lines, and Wolverhampton alone was home to over a dozen local stations. The network was creaking, though, for lack of investment. Passenger traffic was declining, and even after nationalisation in 1948 it proved a struggle to revitalise the railways. In 1962, the BTC appointed the now-infamous Dr Richard Beeching as head of the British Railways Board, and for many local lines in the Black Country, this sounded a death knell. Beeching's controversial programme of closures coincided with the last days of steam travel: by the end of the 1960s, lines from Dudley to Wolverhampton and Old Hill, from Old Hill to Longbridge, and from Wolverhampton to Walsall, Smethwick and Wombourne had all been closed, and the remaining services converted to diesel.

As canal and rail networks declined, the road system came under increasing pressure. Compared to the major radial routes which punctuated Birmingham, the only significant measure to improve road transport in the Black Country had been the Birmingham to Wolverhampton road, opened in 1927. The planners behind *Conurbation* were enthusiastic about this road: "Its extensive use has proved the wisdom of bold and energetic planning."[180] Various proposals were made, from a swiftly-rejected 'Northern and Western Motorway' via the western fringe of the Black Country, cutting through Stourbridge and Wolverhampton, to a 'Bilston Link Motorway' connecting the Birmingham New Road to the proposed London-Lancashire motorway. In the event, two routes were chosen that eventually became the M5 and M6, although these were not completed through the Black Country until the 1970s.[181]

Car ownership in Britain leapt from 2 million in 1950 to 4.9 million in 1960, and doubled again in the next decade. The newly affluent Black Country had car ownership rates above the national average, and with trunk routes still running through town centres, was suffering accordingly from congestion. Plans for ring roads and bypasses were drawn up, often adapting existing roads. Stourbridge completed one of the most radical new schemes, a three-lane 'concrete collar' in 1969, but Wolverhampton's expanded ring road eventually took 25 years to complete. Both required the demolition of swathes of older housing, factories, even churches – all part of the march of progress.[182]

Progress and Nostalgia

Planners became bogeymen for nostalgists like Phil Drabble, but were symbolic of the progressive thinking of the post-war era. In this brave new world of social democracy, the existence of lost worlds amidst hills and hollows was evidence of the social, political and environmental failures of the past. For many the Black Country landscape was "a lasting memorial to the greedy, selfish coalmasters who cared only for maximum returns".[183] In its place, many dreamed of a modern, efficient, forward-looking region. The resultant Black Country bore the marks of both romantic historians and idealistic planners – a landscape of half-completed utopian schemes and half-remedied dereliction. The planners' work did much to save the Black Country from its own legacy, but perhaps unwittingly also began to erode its uniqueness.

Chapter 6

"Different people have different needs"

Housing in the Black Country

Courtesy of Black Country Living Museum

Victoria Street, Cradley, in the late 1950s.

Perhaps the most lasting change in the Black Country landscape has been its shift from an industrial to a residential region, and this change too had its roots in the years around the Second World War. Black Country people's relationships with their homes also reveal much about the cultural and political landscapes of the era. In the preceding century, the national debate over housing had shifted. Mid-Victorian Britain had no housing policy: building was seen as a matter for private enterprise only, and no matter how much the population grew, governments would not intervene. It was only when poverty was 'rediscovered' in the latter part of the nineteenth century by social investigators like Charles Booth and Seebohm Rowntree that the first tentative steps were taken towards council housing. In the Black Country, population had been growing for decades, and inter-war housing estates had been built so unevenly that many Black Country folk still lived in inadequate homes that would soon be labelled as slums. Unlike its near-neighbours Birmingham and Coventry, the Black Country did not suffer huge amounts of damage from enemy action during the war, yet it still faced a stark shortage of places to live at the war's end. How this shortage was met – and the successes and failures along the way – is a story which broaches many of the social, political and cultural themes of the period, from poverty to pragmatism, from utopian dreams to racial tension. It highlights too how individuals and local conditions affected the bigger picture, from the innovation of some individuals and towns, to reactionary discrimination elsewhere – the Black Country was never a cohesive entity in this era, as approaches to housing demonstrated.

The Problem

The Black Country had been short of housing since the earliest days of the Industrial Revolution, so that overcrowding and insanitary conditions were common. Cheap 'jerry-built' terraces, and courts behind older houses, sprang up all over the region. Councils rarely considered building housing before the First World War, viewing it as a hindrance to private enterprise, rather than a necessary solution. Up to 1915, for instance, Wolverhampton had been proud of its exhibition housing on the Old Fallings Estate – privately-built solutions for a problem still seen as one the market could solve. The war changed public opinion somewhat: Liberal Prime Minister David Lloyd George announced in Wolverhampton, in 1918, that decent homes were needed "to make Britain a fit country for heroes to live in". But a faltering economy was followed by a faltering construction industry.[184]

Although Wolverhampton's first council houses date from 1919, most of the Black Country's inter-war buildings date from the economic recovery of the later 1930s. Councils on the periphery of the region began to expand into greenfield and former agricultural areas on the fringes of the region, and central boroughs such as Tipton, Wednesbury and Bilston expanded into former mining areas. Between the wars, the built-up area of the Black Country duly increased by two thirds. Reclaiming land was difficult, and only councils had the capacity to clear the ground for housing. The dereliction and unsuitability of building land meant that many developers and potential residents still considered the Black Country an unattractive place to live.[185]

By the time house-building resumed in the 1940s, most Black Country towns therefore retained an older core of commercial and residential housing, with large estates of inter-war housing beginning to bridge the gaps between towns – "sometimes," it was acknowledged, "with elegant layouts which are prettier on the drawing board than in bricks and mortar"[186]. This situation meant that though the lives of thousands of families had improved greatly, thousands more differed little from their Victorian forebears: close-knit communities around a central yard, water from a standpipe, and outside toilets were all too common.[187]

A resident of Hatton Street, Bradley, in June 1955, using a wash-house shared by seven families. The photograph was taken as part of a campaign by residents for re-housing, and shows a wall that had collapsed after a thunderstorm.

The Solution

Clearing these so-called 'slums' (the term was widely-used in this period, but has a long history as a derogatory expression not just for the environment but the inhabitants) had been hindered by the slowness of building replacements, and was then interrupted by the outbreak of war. The post-war Labour government prioritised repairs of older houses on grounds of cost, but it was soon forced to acknowledge that these poor older buildings were a problem. The 1947 Town & Country Planning Act gave unprecedented powers to planning authorities to buy up and knock down, and many councils set about restarting pre-war programmes of clearance and rebuilding. "Everyone is agreed that the slums should go," noted Phil Drabble, labelling them "the remnants of the plague-spots of last century."[188] Drabble's observation was accurate. Some houses in a 1949 survey of Wolverhampton had been condemned in a sanitary survey in 1873: out of 101 houses in the Charles Street area only one had a fixed bath, 63 had no internal water supply, and only three had internal lavatories. Around a third of Coseley residents in the same year lived in back-to-back houses with communal lavatories and wash-houses. Housing fell under the remit of the Ministry of Health and although the Secretary of State, Aneurin Bevan, was preoccupied with forming the NHS, over half a million houses were built nationally during Labour's first term – no small achievement when both labour and building materials were in scant supply.[189]

In 1954 the Conservative Minister of Housing, Harold Macmillan, announced a national programme of slum clearance, including the 'sweeping away' – councils always used these grandiose metaphors to imply the cleansing and renewing of their towns – of 6,000 houses in Wolverhampton and 3,000 in Dudley. Demolition and rebuilding was a slow and uneven process, and some took the campaign for a decent home into their own hands: residents of Hatton Street in Bradley had to petition Bilston Council to be re-housed, and even undertook a photographic campaign to demonstrate their need.[190]

By the late 1960s, thousands upon thousands of new homes had been built, replacing huge areas demarcated as slum. Homes lacking inside toilets and bathrooms, running water or mains electricity were targeted, but a persistent stigma surrounded some areas too, as the author John Petty described in Walsall:

> *The road had for long been the worst part of the town. Once it had festered with life, but slum clearance schemes had flattened the black banks and buttressed cliffs, the crouching hovels and cracking cenotaphs of*

> *Victorianism, had demolished the terraces and tenements, taken away the black-shawled grannies, the doss-houses and loungers and knots of slatterns, the yelping dogs and mangy cats and mobs of children, the rag-yards and hawkers, the drunks and didicais* (sic).[191]

Councils were uniformly proud of their achievements, with every borough handbook featuring pages and pages of pictures and descriptions of their brand-new municipal housing. Yet even then the problem had not been solved: in 1965 substantial parts of Black Country towns were still considered "actual or potential slums", and the persistence of such poverty amidst the growing prosperity of the region remained jarring.[192]

Lye's Mud Houses

Express & Star

One of the last of Lye's famous mud houses in the 1950s.

The Black Country was famous for its roughly-built squatters' settlements, thrown up quickly and cheaply in the throes of the Industrial Revolution. Rough Hills in Wolverhampton, the Delph in Brierley Hill and Dudley's notorious Low Town were all examples that were knocked down after the war, but none were quite as unusual as Lye's mud houses. Lye had developed as a nail-making hamlet in the late eighteenth century, when the 'Lye Wasters' were infamous for their poverty, violence and insularity. Many homes were hand-built from the plentiful clay which earned the town the nickname 'Mud City.' By the end of the war, most had gone. The last inhabited mud house was 33 Cross Walks, home to William and Elsie Mobberley: it had walls of foot-thick mud and marl supported by crude beams, with four rooms connected by tunnels. It was condemned by Stourbridge council in 1948 and thought to be the last – until Howard Hill, a local antique dealer who had lived in a mud house on Bott Lane in his childhood, discovered one on his land at Meers Coppice in 1956.[193]

West Bromwich Manor House

South Staffordshire Archaeological and Historical Society

West Bromwich Manor House prior to its restoration.

One of the more unusual 'slums' was in Hall Green, West Bromwich. The Corporation purchased a group of ramshackle houses in 1950, believing them to be nineteenth-century tenements built on the site of the old West Bromwich Manor House. When they began excavations, they soon found a moat and older foundations – in fact, this slum *was* the manor house. Built in the thirteenth century, it had once been a grand home with figs, peaches and vines in extensive kitchen gardens, occupied by aristocratic families like Charles I's Solicitor-General Richard Shelton. As the town developed industrially, the manor house was sub-let and became overcrowded and dilapidated, and bricked around to provide dwellings for rent. When West Bromwich Corporation took it over they soon declared it unfit for human habitation: in 1950 "it seemed as if it was about to fall down," said one onlooker; "the windows were in a shocking condition." Experts from the University of Birmingham were called in to conduct an archaeological dig, uncovering fine glass, Elizabethan shoes and medieval tiles. "Beauty is emerging from behind its brick curtain," wrote the *Birmingham Weekly Post*; "History is being hacked out of latter-day bad taste." Eventually the building was restored and let to Ansell's Brewery as a public house and restaurant, and is now a museum.[194]

In the immediate aftermath of the war some families in the Black Country, desperate for somewhere to live, followed the example of others across the country and began moving into abandoned army camps. On 16 August 1946, the families of thirteen ex-servicemen and one disabled man moved into Nissen huts on the former American army base at Burton Road, Dudley. Mr Jackson, who had been living with his family in cramped conditions on Maple Road when he was demobilised from the Fleet Air Arm, explained that the huts were "well appointed", with water, light, sanitary facilities and space for "three good rooms". This was an exercise in

Dudley Archives and Local History Centre (ref Pst/3152)

Families moving into the former American army camp on Burton Road, Dudley, August 1946.
The camp was given the nickname 'Rosemary Crescent'.

communal living as much as it was pragmatic: residents all chipped in for a new water connection and worked with the council to supply other amenities and welfare services. As well as the Dudley camp – nicknamed 'Rosemary Crescent' – other 'squatters' moved into the anti-aircraft base on Walsall Road, Stone Cross, and others took over a Ministry of Health hostel on Church Lane, Tipton. Much of the organisation for this movement came from the local Communist Party who, in the immediate wake of Stalin's victory over Nazi Germany, were becoming increasingly popular. This was true in Tipton, where the local Party took on a second hostel near Locarno Road, but less so in Dudley, where the residents complained about Communist literature being circulated. The national movement caused a media stir that passed in weeks, but it is likely that these camps stayed occupied for some time after 1946.[195]

Perhaps the most famous proposal to solve the housing crisis was to introduce prefabricated homes. The wartime government began research on the potential for prefabricated building in 1943 and between 1945 and 1949, 156,623 of these were built across the country. Wolverhampton was one of the largest early recipients of 'prefabs', more because its site on the periphery of the Black Country meant there was plenty of land available rather than because its need was greater than other parts of the region. Much of the ground preparation was done by German POWs, and the council built large estates near East Park, in Compton, and in Bushbury. The latter was a huge estate, with single-storey temporary prefabs alongside two-storey 'BISF' and 'Orlit' permanent prefabs.[196]

Prefab estates sprang up elsewhere too: 440 houses at Alumwell Road in Walsall, 490 at Dudley Fields, Bloxwich, and scores at Roebuck Lane, Smethwick, Factory Road, Tipton and Lodge Farm, Netherton, among others. While they were popular with residents, and have become iconic for their design and durability, they were not without their detractors. Drabble characteristically described Dudley Fields as "row upon row of Bevan's hutches – 'preconfabulated 'ouses' they call them round here".[197] Despite this, many have stood the test of time: Lincoln Green in Wolverhampton and Henwood Road in Compton are still happily occupied today.

Garden Villages and Happy Towns

It was soon clear, though, that municipal intervention would need to extend to permanent housing to provide a good home for all. In the 20 years following the war, therefore, the biggest single providers of new housing were local authorities. War and austerity, labour shortages and land reclamation put off so many private builders that during Labour's tenure (1945-1951), four-fifths of all new houses in the West Midlands were council houses. In Dudley, for instance, the first permanent post-war council house was completed on Wood Street, Woodside, in July 1946; nine years later, 2,545 homes had been built by the Corporation and just 473 by private enterprise. Proportions were similar elsewhere: a selection of figures published in the *Dudley Herald* in 1954 shows that at

Norman Bridgewater (Cradley Heath)

Drainage being installed at Orchard Road, in the new Dudley Wood estate, 1950s.

least 70 per cent of houses built in the Black Country were council houses, with as many as 92 per cent in Darlaston.[198]

Following the economic revival of the mid-1950s the pace of private building did pick up, and by 1961 fewer than half the new homes in the Black Country were built by councils. Local developers like A & J Mucklow, based at Haden Cross, built swathes of homes in the 1950s and 1960s in suburban areas like Pedmore and Tettenhall. Both authorities and developers were frustrated by the physical challenges they faced, however. Bulldozers were lost down abandoned mine workings, underground fires hindered engineers, and poisoned soil had to be replaced with healthy soil. The age-old problems of mining and dereliction remained tremendously costly to rectify, and it was often only local authorities that could afford this.[199]

The Bentley estate, near Darlaston, represents a unique amalgamation of private and municipal enterprise. At the end of the war, Bentley Common was a derelict landscape: a "rough and tumble area of broken land with its spoil banks and shallow sinkings", home to the ruins of Bentley Hall – once a refuge of Charles II, now more likely to be picked over by 'tatters', rag-and-bone men like the writer John Petty or the Italian POWs he worked with. Its transformation was the vision of Rubery Owen's director, Alfred Owen. Large-scale company housing was unusual in the Black Country: there were no equivalents to developments elsewhere like Bournville in Birmingham, built by the Cadbury family, or Lever Brothers' Port Sunlight on Merseyside. Owen nevertheless proposed a development of 2,257 houses on a 354-acre plot to help house the firm's huge workforce. Although plans took time to mature, the firm stood strongly behind them as an example of doing, in Owen's own words, "what it should have done by those who helped to build it," to create "the garden city of the Black Country".[200]

Plans began to coalesce in 1943 when Owen, and other members of the family, put forward money for a centrepiece church. The changing spirit of the times is evident in the approach to building. Darlaston's Borough Surveyor HN Hughes convened a "council of experts, whose responsibility it is to study the future planning of the whole region". The *Walsall Observer*'s comment that "many mistakes [were] made when men were too exclusively self-centred" also demonstrates this post-war moment: an era in which capitalism was to be constrained by care for its workers, and not left unfettered. Initial work was undertaken by the offshoot Rubery Owen Housing Association Ltd, though in the end Darlaston UDC compulsorily-purchased the site and completed the building. However, this was unlikely to have been an acrimonious arrangement: though: Owen was chairman of both.[201]

Alfred Owen placed a ceremonial pound note under the first brick laid on York Avenue on 22 October 1945, marking the commencement of building. The architect, William Haywood of Birmingham, laid out a design and a model was placed in Darlaston Town Hall of the new Garden Village, scheduled to cost £3-4m and take five years to complete. It provided for 37 acres of industrial development and 9 acres for a traffic route to the east (later superseded by the M6). There were also (at least plans for) 37 acres of public parks, and public amenities, including a British Restaurant, community centre (featuring theatre, club rooms, swimming pool and sunbathing terrace), health centre, library, Sons of Rest clubroom, cinema and three pubs. Richard Twentyman's Emmanuel Church sat proudly at its centre, dedicated to Owen's father, and the site included at least two prototype prefabricated homes manufactured by Rubery Owen.[202]

This utopian thinking was also echoed in Bilston. In 1945, the town clerk invited the Austrian philosopher Otto Neurath – best known for designing revolutionary working-class homes during Austria's inter-war 'Red Vienna' period – to help design the new Stowlawn Estate. He advocated the radical idea of consulting residents themselves, and his conclusions matched those promoted by the Housing Minister, Aneurin Bevan: the new estate ought to "mix up individuals: married and unmarried, old and young". Anticipating later criticism of slum clearance programmes, he urged Bilston to:

> *Study the existing community structure in the slums you are re-housing, and ensure these connections are not broken upon the new estate. Bear in mind that different people have different needs, and do not plan housing on a 'one size fits all' basis. You have to work out what sorts of houses and flats to build and who to put in them.*

Neurath's work was based on extensive research undertaken by the town clerk AV Williams and the chairman of Bilston's Health Committee, Dr Robert Abbott, and as at Bentley, construction was preceded by an exhibition in a disused shop in Oxford Street. Neurath became known as the "sociologist of happiness", advocating a holistic, consultative approach to planning compared to the invasive, bureaucratic attitude that many people ascribed to planners. His ideas were implemented by two well-known architects: Sir Charles Reilly, famous for the village green style of Stowlawn, Bilston and the Old Park Farm Estate, Dudley; and latterly Ella Briggs, who had worked with Neurath in Vienna.[203]

Bilston was particularly progressive in this respect. Its 'castletops' – two pairs of

Used with the permission of Wolverhampton Archives

Bilston's Civic Survey Exhibition, 1944.

modernist semi-detached houses on Lawley Road, Ettingshall, dating from the same period as Stowlawn – are probably the most distinctive council dwellings built in the Black Country of the 1940s. This bottom-up consultative process was not widely taken up, however. In most places, councils were more paternal. Tenants in Rowley Regis, for example, were encouraged to get to know the public health inspector, who "deals with the comfort and well-being of each of you at home, at work and during recreation… he is interested in your housing standards and will do all in his power to improve them".[204] Some – including, of course, Phil Drabble – resented this interference. He referred to housing officers as the "dwarf Paul Prys of the council," and regretted the "tragedy that men have sunk so low as to submit to such dictatorship".[205] But there was at least a new recognition that the working class was worth a home in more than a slum, or a bland "red brick box", and deserved looking after.[206]

Running out of Space?

When the Gipsy Lane Estate – now Beechdale, former home to Walsall's most famous son, Noddy Holder – was built in the 1950s, even its Chief Architect admitted that it was a "large and isolated estate, and a very long journey for the housewife whenever there is shopping to be done".[207] Peripheral boroughs like Wolverhampton and Walsall had the luxury of such space, although Walsall still had to remove half a million cubic yards of waste material from the site of Gipsy Lane. But other authorities struggled, and some even had to build

Used with the permission of Wolverhampton Archives

A Wolverhampton Co-operative Society float delivering milk to the town's Dale Street Estate, completed in 1958.

outside their boundaries: Smethwick, for instance built the Kingsway Estate in the adjoining borough of Oldbury. Others embraced high-rise building techniques and subsidies in order to meet their housing shortage. West Bromwich built the first six-storey blocks in the Black Country on the Yew Tree Estate in 1953, and others soon followed suit. Despite all modern conveniences like electric heating (not always standard – new flats in Smethwick at this time still had coal fires), they were not immediately popular. Only 40 families applied for Wolverhampton's central Dale Street Estate in 1958, and concerns were expressed about the absence of amenities like drying rooms and shops, and the lack of a traditional "little backyard and a little garden". However, once established, they proved popular, far from the stigmatised estates they later became.[208]

Although council-funded, these new estates were a boon for large-scale building contractors like Wolverhampton's Tarmac, who built high-rise blocks in Darlaston and Bentley, and Wates, whose Midland operation was responsible for more Black Country high-rises than any other firm. Wates pioneered the 'system-built' tower block, where panels were fabricated on site and erected by tower crane at top speed. 1964 marked the high-water mark of high-rise building: a fifth of all housing nationally, and no fewer than 28 blocks in the Black Country. By this time most boroughs had high-rises, from the string of mixed-size blocks overlooking the canal in Brierley Hill, to the sprawling

Lion Farm Estate on the old Churchbridge colliery, Oldbury, to the isolated Firmstone Court in Wollaston, near Stourbridge. The latter was one of three built by Stourbridge County Borough, the others revealing much about their time and context: Baylie Court, on the site of the closed Baylie chainworks; and Kennedy Court, named during construction after the recently-assassinated US President. Such blocks fell from favour following the end of subsidies in 1967 and the disaster at Ronan Point in East London the following year, where a gas explosion caused a partial collapse of a newly-built block, though that did not stop the trend entirely: the huge 24-storey blocks at Cape Hill, Smethwick, and Wolverhampton's sprawling Heath Town Estate were still to come.[209]

Despite John Petty's assertion that "nearly everyone lived in a municipally-owned house" by the 1950s, the Black Country was not as socially homogenous as it first appeared. The tradition of managers and owners living close to their works was almost extinct, though with exceptions: JH Lavender kept his family's home in the Georgian Hall Green House – adjacent to West Bromwich Manor House – directly backing on to his modern aluminium foundry. Frequently though, such large houses were demolished, or vacated for shared or even multi-family occupancy. Those who could afford it moved to the outskirts of the Black Country – Kinver, Pedmore or Tettenhall.[210]

Love Lane

In some areas, the clustering of wealth was very noticeable indeed. A walk along Love Lane in Oldswinford, Stourbridge, would have revealed the family and commercial connections of the Black Country's wealthy elites. George Simmons of the Hingley affiliate Hartshorne's lived at The Farlands, and opposite him were Park Hill and Thornhill, home of Edward Webb (of Webb's seed merchants) and later the Elmfield Rudolf Steiner School; and Ronald Pearson, director of the Harris & Pearson firebrick works, respectively. CW Thomas of EJ & J Pearson lived at Clifton House, major coal merchant Ernest Lunt at Swinford House, and Harry Green, director of the Eliza Tinsley chain works, at Oak Leigh. Richard Threlfall, a director of Albright & Wilson, lived at The Quarry, and clustered around Racecourse Lane was another collection of directors and managers: Guy Evers and CAG Thomas of EJ & J Pearson; JE Perry and RE Davenhill of Hinton, Davenhill & Perry's brickworks; William Penn of Penn Bros., Cradley Heath; the well-known local architect Tom Grazebrooke (from the ironmaster family of Netherton); and Bryan Colyer of Staffordshire Edge Tools.[211]

Mirrorpix/Reach Licensing

Sardar and Razina Mohammed with their daughter Sandra, outside their home in Lower Cross Street, Smethwick, July 1961. The Mohammeds' home had been designated 'slum' by Smethwick council and the family were thus entitled to be re-homed in the town.

"Build the Houses for the People"

These were not homes for typical Black Country folk though. Echoing Lloyd George's sentiments, Prime Minister Winston Churchill encouraged Macmillan to "build the houses for the people" as a political expedient.[212] But as the 1950s marched on, what was meant by "the people" came to mean different things to different people. Sardar Mohammed, for example, had moved from Pakistan to Smethwick's Lower Cross Street in 1951, to work as a moulder at Tangye's. He was later joined by his wife Razina, who made the local news in early 1961 when her second baby Azim was delivered by two neighbours. The Mohammeds' home was designated as a slum and scheduled for demolition in July that year, and in accordance with council policy they were re-homed in a brand-new council maisonette on Price Street. The family came with high recommendations from their neighbours, but some residents in Price Street were not happy. One, Norman Butler, led a delegation of 96 (out of 610 residents on Price Street) to the council announcing a rent strike, saying: "This is not a racial question: we just do not want a coloured man here… Their whole way of life is different, and we feel if they must have flats they should all be put in a block of their own."[213] The Labour-led council responded swiftly with threats of eviction and the strikers soon gave way, but the situation brought a particular strain of thought in Smethwick into national view for the first time.[214]

In Smethwick the council was concerned to show itself to be rigidly opposed to housing discrimination, and politicians at higher levels agreed: Dudley's MP, George Wigg, downplayed fears over immigration in the lead-up to 1962's Commonwealth Immigration Act – the problem was bad housing, he said, a problem long before immigration. But the distinction was not so clear-cut in practice. Immigrants living in rented homes were subjected to regular intrusive surveys into 'coloured homes' and were frequently accused of overcrowding. Many who moved to the Black Country in this period recall having to live in overcrowded conditions, in old, inadequate houses, having to share beds as well as rooms; but the reluctance of both private and municipal landlords to let to them left little choice. Advertisements stating "No blacks, no dogs, no Irish" were not unheard of, or vacancies would mysteriously be filled when an applicant arrived who was not white.[215] Some landlords who did let to immigrants were accused of "bleeding coloured tenants to death" by charging over the odds. Many immigrants were left with little choice, however: it was either rent or buy poor 'slum' housing on the private market. One Wolverhampton resident, Dayabhai Patel, put it succinctly in 1968: "The only property we can buy is a slum house. Then the whites turn around and say we're creating slums."[216] Evidence of discrimination was displayed in 1965 as well, when a Wolverhampton Corporation bus conductor named Balwant Singh found himself barred from buying a new house on the Lyndale Estate, Wednesfield. The estate's builders, William Whittington Ltd, had colluded with their estate agents, Skelding and Boucher of Waterloo Road, who commented: "We do and have sold to coloured people, but we have been instructed by our clients not to sell any houses on this estate to coloured people."[217]

Inevitably, then, immigrants were pushed to the least-desirable parts of towns, followed by that persistent accusation that they were responsible for those conditions. These accusations were raised – not without resistance – week after week by a small number of correspondents to local newspapers. Although such prejudices were not limited by political party, the *Smethwick Telephone*, for instance, supported the hostile line on immigration presented by the constituency Conservative Party, and frequently printed letters viciously condemning the town's immigrants for their living habits, health, even their cooking smells. Such persistent reporting ensured that these marginal complaints were represented as a 'colour problem', and soon whole districts of towns were being referred to as Little Punjab, Little Harlem, or in Dudley, a "Negro quarter".[218]

In fact, surveys showed that far from being insanitary or squalid, immigrants' homes were no different from any others. "The coloured folks' accommodation," confirmed one report, "is thought to be capable of favourable comparison with some English homes."[219] Similarly, the size of the 'problem' was always over-estimated. A survey in Coseley in 1958 was undertaken on the suggestion "that there were about 500 coloured homes in the town". In fact, the council spokesman noted, "the figure is considerably less than 100".[220] The majority of the Black Country's residents based their experiences of immigrants on their colleagues or neighbours, and quickly established that whatever cultural differences may have existed, they had much more in common than anything that separated them. Nevertheless, the 1960s brought renewed racial tensions in the Black Country, and housing became the battleground.

Families in Marshall Street, Smethwick, 1964.

Perhaps the most symbolic outburst came in late 1964. The *Birmingham Post* described Marshall Street in Smethwick as full of "terraced houses glowing with fresh paint, windows neatly screened by curtains of net or chintz and tiny, walled front gardens, many of them with a proud privet hedge". But for a handful of residents, it was something else: a representation of all that was wrong with immigration. Emboldened by Peter Griffiths' racist electioneering in 1964, "twelve angry housewives" from the street petitioned the new Conservative-led council to buy up any houses on that street that came onto the market, and to select who was permitted to move there on the basis of skin colour. Their argument was simple, and revealing of their underlying assumption of white superiority: half the street was now "occupied by coloured people," they said, and "if we let any more coloured people move into the street, it will become a coloured community. Immigrant standards will prevail and there will be no chance of teaching them our standards."[221] Conservative council leader Alderman Niven agreed that the action was necessary "to prevent the street from becoming a 'colour segregated place'", adding that if the scheme was rejected, the Spon Lane area "will be known as a coloured quarter… a twilight area".[222]

Unfounded rumours abounded about elderly ladies "worried to death by Indians" and daughters "accosted by coloured people", and the housewives complained about the habits and "social standards" of their neighbours. These neighbours, for their part, were saddened: a Jamaican resident named Charles Downer told the *Post* that he had expected an English Christmas to be characterised by cheer and goodwill but, he said: "I wished one of my English neighbours a merry Christmas and she just pretended not to have heard me… how can you ask anyone to come and share Christmas with you if they won't even speak to you?"[223] In the event, the plan was rejected out of hand by the Labour Housing Minister, Richard Crossman, after a meeting between the "angry housewives" and Crossman's colleague Bob Mellish descended into a shouting match. Nevertheless, housing was still cited as a reason for racial tension: when Enoch Powell conjured up images of women besieged in their homes, surrounded by immigrants, he was using emotive language pioneered in the streets of Smethwick.[224]

From Slums to Utopias?

Housing policy provided one of the most fertile and controversial national debates throughout this period, and the Black Country epitomised all of these tensions. It was home to some of the most innovative solutions to the housing shortage: whole estates were built with the health and happiness of the ordinary working class in mind, tower blocks grew from former collieries, and the poor housing that had blighted the lives of the working classes for years was finally 'swept away'. But housing policy also became a battleground: in particular, it became another tool for racial discrimination, exploited and exacerbated by politicians and the press. Everyone involved in this argument used housing to make political capital, often forgetting just what the disputed buildings really were: not just a house, but a home. The housing debate had come a long way. Just half a century before Marshall Street, the idea that councils might build houses for their residents had barely been broached. Even at the start of the Second World War, council estates were suburban affairs, still not solving the housing difficulties of the poor. But by 1965, even the most reactionary, racially motivated groups had accepted that the private housing market had failed to provide the world they wanted, and that petitioning the council was the way to claim and control urban space. The provision of council housing was by now as much part of the unwritten contract between local authority and local resident as street lighting, school places and bin collections.

Chapter 7

"Life in the kitchen takes on a new cheerfulness"

Domestic life in the Black Country

Used with the permission of Wolverhampton Archives

Washing Day, King Edward's Row – an entry in the Wolverhampton Photographic Society exhibition, 1952.

Many of the changes that the Black Country witnessed in the post-war period were driven from above: industrial demands from government, immigration policy, municipal housebuilding and so on. But despite huge changes, these years remained a socially and culturally conservative time, and the home was a direct reflection of this. The bold styles of the 1951 Festival of Britain, the shining Formica in *Ideal Home* magazines, or the new gadgets filling the pages of Kay's catalogues, envisage colourful homes taking long, confident strides into the space age. But this would have seemed unimaginable for the average Black Country family in this period. Modernity took time to filter through to everyday life, and it did so unevenly. This chapter draws on the experiences of Black Country domestic and family life, particularly the lives of women, on whom so many of the domestic duties fell. The march of modernity in the Black Country depended on gender, origin, location, social class, family patterns of work and many other factors; not least, long-established domestic traditions.

Cynthia Harper was born in Best Street, Old Hill, in 1943. Hers was a classic Black Country upbringing: her home was a Victorian terraced house with black-leaded grate, brew'us, outdoor toilets, chickens in the yard, leftovers and peelings boiled up on a coke-fired stove in the shed for the pigs. Best Street was full of relatives, many of whom – like Cynthia's father and grandfather – walked to work at Stewart's & Lloyd's Coombeswood works each day, just as

Used with the permission of Wolverhampton Archives

New council tenants' home lives on display in Bilston, 1947: all items of furniture from houses scheduled for slum clearance were disinfested in the council's mobile disinfestation unit.

the next generation was expected to. Sundays were sacrosanct: the television was covered with a cloth, and the family attended Ebenezer Strict Baptist Church in the morning, evening and for Sunday School. Cynthia's upbringing would not have been unusual in the nineteenth century and was still common after the Second World War.[225]

Life was not expected to change. Women – working or not – were still expected to look after the home budget, to manage the cooking and shopping, and to provide for the main, male breadwinner. Nellie Coleman, who worked long days in the heavy, dirty brickmaking industry in Brierley Hill, was still expected to have dinner on the table at the end of the day. This was often with little thanks, as the following recollection demonstrates:

> *…her husband had returned home drunk one day and dropped off to sleep straight away while she had her dinner. He slept for several hours and Nellie kept his dinner warm in the oven. She became hungry again and fancied some more of the dinner. She fetched her husband's plate from the oven, got a crust and dipped it in the gravy and wiped it around her sleeping husband's lips before clearing his plate herself. When he eventually woke up and demanded his dinner Nellie said, "You've already had it, you've left some of it around your lips." Satisfied with this explanation he resumed his drunken doze.*[226]

The burden of old housing stock and post-war austerity fell heavily on women. Jo Mary Stafford's description of her Walsall home in the 1940s sums up the experience of many:

> *The living room was sparsely furnished with an old three-piece suite, a square table in the centre of the room and cheap lino on the floor. A sideboard and two dining chairs stood against the far wall. No pictures or photographs decorated the bare walls. The sofa, where we sat, was pulled up in front of the fireplace: a huge, black-leaded affair which occupied most of one wall. On the big hob plate a kettle would be singing while below, in the oven, a large bread-pudding slowly cooked. Above the actual fire was an iron rack for airing clothes. A huge brass-rimmed fireguard was securely hooked to the wall on either side, its Brasso'd goldness mirroring us in miniature. A brightly coloured hand-pegged rug lay before the fireplace. This was home.*[227]

When Dr John Lester visited homes in Walsall in 1954, modern conveniences and housing improvements had yet to make much difference to everyday life. His complaints could have been written a century earlier: "A roaring fire simply created a howling draught so that when people huddled round the hearth their backs remained cold."[228] Some of these hardships were met with local and family support. Couples often lived at one or

Courtesy of Black Country Living Museum

Advertisement for the Dudley Port-based Grovewood Co's 'Daintymaid' fitted kitchens, 1966.

other parental home, and when they moved it was rarely far: Tipton's Betty Tolley's recollection that "I lived at gran's as much as I lived at our house" was far from rare. Women's lives were closely entwined – support for one another was informal, but vital.[22]

"Housewives as Mothers have Vital Work to do..."

Things were changing, however. The NHS, founded in 1948, had a huge impact on women's lives – it increased their own chances of survival in childbirth, and those of their children; it eventually gave them a degree of choice when the contraceptive pill was permitted on prescription by the Minister of Health (and Wolverhampton MP) Enoch Powell in 1961. Yet the NHS was built on the social values of the 1940s: in the report which inspired the welfare state, William Beveridge suggested: "Housewives as mothers have vital work to do in ensuring the adequate continuance of the British Race and of British ideals in the world."[230] Much of the practical operation of the welfare state – and thus society in general throughout the 1950s and into the 1960s – was based on a model of bread-winning husband, and home-making wife.

But for those whose relationships fell outside these norms, life could be hard. Birth control was hard to access, yet childbirth out of wedlock was viewed with such dismay that, for example, any unmarried women who visited one of Wolverhampton's Infant Welfare Centres were interviewed by the doctor there and could be sent to a religious or charitable hostel. In Wolverhampton, 'Mrs Legge's Memorial Home For Unmarried Mothers of Previously Good Character' and 'Mrs Hay's Memorial Home For Friendless Girls' – where residents had to do chores to earn their keep, and were not allowed out alone – catered for this group. Although the welfare state had finally laid the workhouse to rest, it remained reliant on some of society's more damaging attitudes towards women.[231]

Phil Lynott

If single mothers were stigmatised, those who associated with immigrants – and particularly black men – were treated with horror. Inter-racial relationships were certainly not unheard of – in fact, several sources suggest that many male immigrants from South Asia had white girlfriends. Cecil Parris, from British Guiana, and Philomena Lynott, from Dublin met at a Displaced Persons hostel in Birmingham in 1948, when Parris asked Lynott to dance. Their relationship lasted only a few months before Parris was transferred to London. Lynott had become pregnant, however. As an Irish girl with a mixed-race baby, there was significant stigma attached to her son's birth, and Lynott tried several times to terminate her pregnancy. Although in regular work at the Austin plant in Longbridge, she was expelled from the hostel and gave birth at Hallam Hospital, West Bromwich, on 20 August 1949. After the birth she moved to a home for unwed mothers in Selly Oak, but was eventually tracked down by Parris – they settled together in Blackheath before Lynott moved back to Ireland. Her son, Philip, went on to become one of the Black Country's most famous exports as the frontman of the 1970s rock group Thin Lizzy.[232]

Austerity and Thrift

After motherhood, the other key role of the idealised housewife was to put food on the table. This was not always straightforward. Until the early 1950s, the shopping trip was an endless parade of queues, ration books and coupons, often to buy items that were a poor substitute for what the family had been used to before the war. Supplies fluctuated too. An average family ration for a week in 1947 was 13 ounces of meat, 1½ ounces of cheese, six ounces of butter or margarine, one ounce of cooking fat, eight ounces of sugar, two pints of milk, and an egg, perhaps supplemented by the mysterious dried egg, though that came and went too. Rations were significantly more stringent than during the war: in 1946, even bread – made from the hated National Flour, something akin to a fortified wholemeal flour – was rationed for the first time following bad harvests worldwide. The next winter was the most brutal in living memory. Potatoes were rationed for the first time in December 1947 and even coal was limited – wives joined their husbands on abandoned collieries like Saltwells, digging through the snow and picking out discarded pieces of the precious material. Experiments including whalemeat and the dreaded tinned snoek (a bony fish from the South Atlantic) were met with resignation as much as disbelief. Clothes rationing, in place since the war, was abandoned amidst a widespread black market personified by the 'spiv'. It was not until 4 July 1954 that the last rationing ended, but it took some time for anything approaching prosperity to be felt – it had been a long, hard, grey era.[233]

Cynthia Harper's family were not alone in keeping pigs to help the rations go further, and many families 'self-provisioned' during the lean years following the war, and afterwards. Pigs, hens, and even cows were not uncommon in the Black Country, well into the 1960s – Marianne Monro even recalls her friend's father leading goats down Corbett Street in Smethwick to graze, destined for his menu at the Caribbean Club. Allotments and gardens were an essential part of Black Country life too. While gardens seem to have been a mixed responsibility, the allotment was very definitely a masculine space, good for a couple of hours of fresh air and 'a crafty fag' after a day in a dusty factory. It also brought out the competitive spirit in the Black Countryman. Nowhere was this more on display than the Harvest Festival, as essential a part of the church calendar as Christmas or Easter, and almost as important as the children's inescapable Sunday School Anniversary. Even for the irreligious, the opportunity to show off produce was irresistible, and Black Country chapels and churches would assume the character of "greengrocers' shops gone wild" for several Sundays at the beginning of

Festival Fare

The 1951 Festival of Britain was, in hindsight, the swansong of Clement Attlee's Labour government, a national celebration to commemorate Britain's expertise, industry and culture. It was a huge success. Millions visited the exhibition on London's South Bank (the eagle-eyed would have spotted Revo electric fires and Salter's scales amongst the exhibits under the Dome of Discovery: the largest self-supporting dome in the world, manufactured by Tipton's Horseley Bridge company), and events were held across Britain. The Women's Gas Council ran the 'Festival Fare' competition to promote both gas and "the honest and straightforward British tradition – not disguised with garlic or spices, but good, wholesome cooking, uncamouflaged – and with the rations which are available". Betty Morris of Gladys Road, Smethwick, entered on the off-chance after seeing the contest advertised in Smethwick gas showroom, on her way back from the clinic with her new baby. She dropped off a 'county fruit cake' on 1 May 1951, and proceeded to win through to the national final, via awards ceremonies in Walsall and a semi-final in Birmingham in which she cooked a fish pie and meringue fruit flan. Sadly, Mrs Morris didn't make the top four at the final in London, but she did meet Princess Elizabeth – the future queen – and the television chef, Philip Harben, who was judging the competition. The challenge – roast chicken followed by apple pie – sums up British cuisine at the time: spices and garlic forbidden, only the simplest food was allowed to represent the nation.[234]

Courtesy of Black Country Living Museum

Victoria Road allotments in Darlaston, facing Slater Street School.

autumn.[235] At one of the Gornal chapels:

"... you get people who never come to church bring a cartload of onions or a bag of potatoes... You get somebody come in that you've never seen before with a great big bunch of flowers, chrysanths."[236] The journalist Jack Shaw described the loving attention – and secret concoctions – given to potential prize-winners:

> *The amount of care lavished on the plants until the fateful day for picking is astonishing. Long and heated arguments are held in the "local" on the respective merits of stout to give the marrows a "bloom", and the golden rich tan that comes from a diet of "old" or "bitter"; ordinary mild is despised as merely promoting growth.*[237]

Despite the rapid de-rationing of food under the new Conservative government of 1951, British food in the 1950s remained traditional, and Black Country favourites like faggots were still normal fare. Black Country cuisine was characterised by thrift, stemming from a long history of poverty and making do. Even when ordinary meat was available again, offal and cheap cuts were the most popular, supplemented by regional dishes like groaty pudding, or grey peas and bacon. Beer was still brewed at home, onions were still pickled, scratchings were still made locally, and tastes ran to the savoury: one report suggested that sales of cakes and jams were lower in the Midlands than elsewhere but that:

Courtesy of Black Country Living Museum

"The cooker that every woman wants" – the Cannon A125, advertised in a Cannon cookery book in 1957.

> *The acidity of pickles in the Black Country is said to be twice as high as is standard in London… [and] spending on vinegar is the highest in the country… Even the Midland "mild" is a noticeably more bitter beer than what passes under this name further south.*[238]

This deficiency in sweetness was made up for with "ridiculous amounts of [sugar] in their tea and coffee". The Gas Council recognised this heritage in its 1951 *Mr Therm Goes County* cookbook from which the Festival Fare recipes were taken, which included faggots for Staffordshire alongside rabbit pie and, more tenuously, syllabub.[239]

As the Black Country became affluent, some of these older recipes fell from favour. When the Coseley-based Cannon Iron Foundries issued a recipe book in 1957 to accompany their pioneering new A125 model ("the cooker that every woman wants", notable for its novel new high-level grill), no faggots were to be found. Nevertheless, despite more sophisticated leftovers recipes like 'Fish Réchauffé ' or 'Curry of Cold Meat', much of the book featured offal, cheap cuts and vegetable dishes that would have been familiar to generations of Black Country cooks. This worked to the advantage of some Black Country businesses, like Marsh & Baxter – famous for their cured hams and tomato-flavoured red sausages: they in fact manufactured every kind of pork product and marketed it through their dozens of local outlets, and even via the new medium of television. Yet they retained a Black Country thriftiness: their factory claimed to use everything from the pig "but the squale".[240]

The "New Elizabethan" Age

After the rationing and shortages of the age of austerity, the revitalisation of older homes with time-saving devices or modern materials was incremental. Win Downing recalls that her small courtyard house in Woodside, Dudley, had outdoor toilets, with running water only fitted after the war, but they did have a Servis washing machine, a Dansette record player and a large television in the living room. Janet Thomson's family in Amblecote acquired a grand fridge on legs in their glass veranda

Dansette Major Deluxe, 1958 – the automatic changer system was built in the Black Country by BSR.

Courtesy of Black Country Living Museum

that reminded her of a Dalek, while a similar veranda behind Burgins' newsagent in Dudley was home to an electric cooker and a tall Vono kitchenette unit. The Burgins were always keen to stay in fashion. The wallpaper was changed frequently, the old range was replaced by a new tiled fireplace, and a G-Plan sideboard stood in the sitting room alongside a portable television.[241]

Black Country manufacturers were at the forefront of this push for modernisation. Cannon made gas cookers, Revo made electric ones, the Rubery Owen subsidiary Easiclene made refrigerators and dishwashers. Plastics like melamine (manufactured in Oldbury and Streetly by British Industrial Plastics) started to appear too, on Formica tabletops. Even saucepans switched from heavy cast-iron to lighter stainless steel or aluminium, all advertised to promote not just the products themselves but the easing of domestic chores and promotion of happy home lives: "Life in the kitchen," quoted one famous Quarry Bank hollowware manufacturer, "takes on a new cheerfulness when you cook with Jury Jetware."[242]

As usual, not everyone approved. Phil Drabble again bemoaned the passing of old ways:

> *Attempts have been made to popularize or enforce central heating, but a home without a fire becomes no more than a house. Welcomes fade and notions of hospitality by a radiator become as desiccated as the theorists who urged its installation.*[243]

Drabble's rose-tinted view of the traditional way of life was unlikely to be echoed by many Black Country housewives, who for years had struggled with the hard work, dirt and sweat of a coal fire. For them, gas and electrical appliances saved time, money and energy.

Courtesy of Black Country Living Museum

Selection of mid-20th-century Black Country design from the Black Country Living Museum collections.

A Golden Age of Design

The Black Country played its part in defining the look of the home in the 1950s and 1960s. The Design Council began its annual award scheme in 1957, and this became the pinnacle of mid-century taste. In that year, the Black Country was represented by an unusual substance for the region, but one redolent of the era: Melmex melamine produced by British Industrial Plastics' Aldridge works in the classic 'Midwinter' design well-known from Staffordshire pottery. 1958 saw a return to metal: a toast rack designed by Robert Welch at his workshop in the Cotswolds and inspired by Welch's tour of Scandinavia, a seedbed of mid-century modern design. Welch's designs were commissioned and produced by the stainless-steel pioneers J & J Wiggins of Bloxwich, as the Campden range of their 'Old Hall' brand. Old Hall went on to win further awards in 1962 and 1965 for Welch's 'Alveston' cutlery – another unusual manufacture for the Black Country. Brands like Ernest Steven's Judgeware had always played with novel designs, like their 'Jazzy' range in the 1930s, and they continued to inspire. Both they and their competitor from West Bromwich, Izons & Co., won awards in 1960 for their tableware: Judge stewpans and Izons' 'Anniversary Ware' cooking dishes, designed by John and Sylvia Reid. The Black Country had long been associated with heavier and more prosaic production, but these awards recognised a tradition of artistic design that had long been present in the region.[244]

Two Places, Two Cultures

Thrift characterised the domestic lives of those raised in the Black Country during austerity, but as wages rose, so too did living standards. For those moving to the Black Country for work though, thrift remained essential. Many early migrants were men on their own, some of whom had to navigate this kind of domestic life for the first time. Take Dev Raj Sirpal, who moved from Pasla, near Jalandhar, to Smethwick in 1954. From his £12.10s wages for a 72-hour week, £3 went on rent and food, and the rest towards repaying the loan for his journey and remittances for his family. Sirpal could afford mostly masoor dal (lentils) with bread, occasionally supplementing it with tinned spinach, baked beans or a chicken at the weekend.[245]

For immigrants, domestic life could be harsh. Finding a job could be as easy as turning up to the factory gates, but finding a home could be much harder. This was true for everyone: there were huge shortages of both workers and homes; but for many new immigrants, finding a home also depended on the prejudices of landlords. The culture shock on arriving was tremendous too. Many expected the mother country to be wealthy, comfortable

Black Country Visual Arts - Apna Heritage Archive,1960s-1980s Punjabi Migration: a Photographic Journey

Joginder Phokela at his home in Summer Street, Wolverhampton, in 1966.

and luxurious, so seeing white workers cleaning streets came as a shock; so too did the rows of terraced houses – something unheard of in India or Jamaica. Bill Orgill, who emigrated from Jamaica in 1960, thought at first they were factories – why else would they have smoky chimneys? Alone in a strange country, many new migrants took the first accommodation they came across, and not only were rents high but conditions could be very unpleasant. Orgill had to share not only a bedroom but a bed in a Tipton lodging-house, with the bedding changed little or never.[246]

South Asian workers had similar experiences. Whereas migrants from the Caribbean or Ireland tended to be single and to come under their own steam, those from the newly independent India and Pakistan remained connected to a global network of family and geographic links. Labourers at the Birmid, often from the Doaba region of Punjab, acted as recruiters for the extended family networks, so much so that the Punjabi Sikhs who settled in streets like Oxford Road and Cambridge Road, near the works, often came from just a handful of villages. Parveen Akhtar recounts her Pakistani father's tale of arriving at Snow Hill station in Birmingham and immediately meeting a member of his 'biraderi' – an extended, and geographically distinct, family network traditional in Pakistan – who brought him home to Tipton and helped him find work. Such close relations meant that migrants relied heavily on one another. One Indian man remembers arriving at the door of someone from his home village, in Smethwick: "Not only did he give me shelter, he also took me the very next morning to the nearby foundry and I was working where the melted iron was flowing like canal water in our Punjabi farms."[247]

When more female family members began to arrive in the 1960s, cultural differences were still a shock for many. Some things were familiar, though. At first, most Sikh women were expected to stay at home, and socialise only amongst themselves, but this did not last long. Avtar Singh Jouhl remembers the disapproval from his community when his wife started work at a nearby launderette, but she was more than capable of defending herself: "I am working hard," she told a group of male elders. "It's of no disgrace… I'm going to work! Wait ten years and more women will also be working."[248] Despite the physical shortcomings of housing in the Black Country, home could be a sanctuary too. Lenny Henry recalls his childhood in Dudley – in houses later condemned as 'slum' – as one of conviviality with family and the wider Caribbean community in Dudley, of good food on a shoestring budget, and of memorable Christmas celebrations. Steve Pope, later editor of British-Caribbean newspaper *The Voice*, moved as a child from Barbados in 1961, and only felt physically safe at home during the turbulent 1960s in Wolverhampton – at home he could not be spat on, physically abused or called "black bastard".[249]

To begin with, immigrants had to make do with what they could get. Some rural Punjabi migrants, for instance, had to learn to use the gas cooker in their new home; some had to adapt their traditional wood-fire cooking to a Black Country coal fire. Just as Black Country families had experienced during rationing, finding food they were used to was not easy.

Black Country Visual Arts - Apna Heritage Archive, 1960s-1980s Punjabi Migration: a Photographic Journey

Perminder Hayre as a child at home on the Willenhall Road, 1962.

Wolverhampton's diverse workforce was lucky in one respect: from 1956 they could find familiar food. The Anglo-Continental Delicatessen in Wolverhampton opened to sell food from across the world. The manager Margaret Konczyk told the *Birmingham Post* that her key customers were "Continentals" from Poland, Ukraine and Germany, but that she also served "Malays, Chinese, Dutch, French, West Indians, some Americans" and even some English customers "of the old school" who requested foods they had eaten on imperial service in China and elsewhere. In other towns shopping could be more difficult. In Smethwick, long queues formed on a Friday night when the only shop to sell okra, aubergine and Indian spices made them available. Cooking occasionally drew some complaints from neighbours unused to spicy food, although this was often simply thinly veiled racism. In fact, many Punjabi women in particular remember food as an important way of making friends with neighbours curious to try novelties like curries and samosas at home or work.[250]

Those moving to the Black Country in the 1950s and early 1960s remember the cramped, shared living arrangements and cold, draughty houses – more than any other object, the paraffin heater is remembered as ubiquitous in Caribbean households. As the region became more prosperous though, immigrants too began to share in the growth in material comforts. By 1965, the doctor and writer Dhani Prem noted that:

> *The home life of Indians has considerably improved. In an average home, we can see better furniture, television set, radio, sometimes tape-recorder. Some homes have fitted-in carpets and gay coloured curtains. Walls are decorated with pictures of Gandhi, Nehru, or religious saints. Young people will, naturally, have pictures of film stars or even 'Beatles'.*[251]

The homes of immigrants were, in the cultural critic Stuart Hall's words, "the result of movement between two places, two cultures". The mixture of television set, radiogram and pictures of saints on the wall might be just as true in an Irish or Polish household. In Caribbean immigrants' homes, the front room was strictly separated and only used on high days and holidays, decorated with dark paintings, Bible verses in ornaments – in fact, much like the front room in Cynthia Harper's Old Hill home of the 1940s. The Victorian roots of so many working-class traditions had been absorbed by Black Country industrial workers and Caribbean colonial workers alike.[252]

For all the comforting, old-fashioned images of the traditional Black Country way of life that Phil Drabble called up, the reality was that working-class lives in the region had often been hard, cold and hungry, with the burden of domestic labour falling on the women of the house. Although full employment and the new welfare state removed some of the old, pre-war uncertainties, and despite wide-ranging technological revolutions, change did not always come easily. This was a period when the ideal of the nuclear family was at its pinnacle: men were expected to be out at work, women at home with the children, and those who fell outside this standard were, to a greater or lesser degree, treated differently. The 1960s was the decade in which some of these older boundaries began to crumble; but as the experience of immigrant families shows, even as new people and new cultures entered the Black Country scene, that same domestic hardship could still be found. 'Traditional' attitudes to money, domesticity and gender roles persisted, and change came slowly, and unevenly.

Chapter 8

Market towns and "local Gothams"

Everyday urban culture in the Black Country

Courtesy of Black Country Living Museum

Darlington Street, Wolverhampton, in the late 1940s.

This chapter broadens the lens from the home to the community to examine the effects of the shift from austerity to prosperity in the post-war period on the distinctive urban and local cultures of the Black Country. As in industrial and domestic life, the Black Country's cultural and social experience was a negotiation between older traditions and the sweeping changes of the modern world, played out against the urban settings of the Black Country. New communities, from religious groups, to gays and lesbians, to new ethnic groups, became a visible part of life in this industrial region, and the famous working-class cultures of the Black Country came to embrace all of this.

For well over a century, working people in the Black Country had been stereotyped as "violent or apathetic".[253] Memoirs such as Archie Hill's from the 1930s, first published in 1972, perpetuated this sense of a hard-drinking, hard-living, Black Country culture typical across the region. This had never been accurate across the board: middle-class life was very different from that of the working class, for instance, and the experience of a new arrival from the countryside or Ireland was different from that of a well-established family, even in the nineteenth century. The post-war years demonstrate how that 'culture' remained more localised than homogeneous: each town and village maintained its own traditions, and embraced new trends in different ways, and this chapter highlights the importance of differences as well as similarities in the composition of the post-war Black Country.

The Austerity Years

In 1946, the literary critic Walter Allen toured the Black Country, discovering the distinctiveness and character of its towns. "Despite its antiquity as an industrial town," he noted, "Dudley remains a pleasant place" – a sentiment echoed by a surprised British Pathé announcer, who described its approaches as "almost sylvan". Allen damned other places with faint praise: "There are far worse places than Wolverhampton, even outside the Black Country." Eliciting similar surprise in 1953, *John Bull* magazine described Wolverhampton as "unexpectedly clean" – some buildings were even "whitish". Market towns on the edge of the Black Country were also pleasant: Halesowen "still retains something of the atmosphere of a country market town" and Stourbridge "bustles, but not aggressively". He was less impressed with the more industrial towns. Oldbury, for instance, was "attractive because it has remained sturdily of its time, the first half of the last century. Its only concession to modernity is the crimson and gilt facade of a nothing-over-sixpence store." Tipton was "frankly an industrial town" with "no foolish claim to be an ideal residential centre," and Allen recognised West Bromwich's impressive "Municipal Gothic" architecture only after satirising its self-description as the "Chicago of the Midlands". Most baffling to him was Gornal, a "local Gotham" – he was fascinated by the characterisation of its residents as door-to-door salt-sellers in Birmingham.[254]

Allen's pleasant descriptions contrast with the more common view of the Black Country as dirty and poor. In fact, with the exception of the industry in their midst which still made "the taste of the air… that of soot," most Black Country towns were not that unusual. Butchers, bakers, grocers, confectioners and drapers proliferated on every shopping street, with chemists, solicitors, coffee houses and cinemas in every town. Chain shops were already common: 'national multiples' like Home & Colonial, British Home Stores and Burton's, the 'ten-shilling tailor', took their place alongside regional chains like George Mason grocers, Firkin's bakers, and Palethorpe's or Marsh & Baxter's butchers' shops. Most people could do the majority of their shopping within half a mile of home, although social scientists recorded that an 'outing to town' was still something to look forward to. Shopping was a personal experience, conducted entirely over the counter, though this was becoming less popular. Housewives frequently complained at the lack of counter space in the crowded, inefficient shops, "having to grovel on the floor among fellow-shoppers' feet in order to rearrange wet or fragile foods". Given the relative luxury of refrigeration in the 1940s, chilled and frozen food was rare, and shopping therefore a more regular chore.[255]

Shortages and queues were ubiquitous. 1946's wet summer affected global grain production, leading to bread rationing and panic-buying for the first time. But as the 1940s drew to a close, both food supplies and inflation crept up. Rationing became an ideological

Used with the permission of Wolverhampton Archives

'Waiting, taken at Wolverhampton's Wholesale Market on Cheapside, for the Wolverhampton Photographic Society.

battleground between political parties: Labour wanted to retain rationing to combat inflation and create a more equal society; the Conservatives in turn blamed Labour for price rises and argued for a return to a free market. Although Labour managed to hold on in the 1950 election, they had to acknowledge that rationing was unpopular and unsustainable. Bread and petrol came off in 1948, clothing in 1949; but it was not until 1954 that confectionery, sugar and finally meat became available to buy without a ration book.[256]

"Supermarket Hypnosis": the Advent of Self-service

In 1948, Jim Green, a manager in the Halesowen & Hasbury Industrial Co-operative Society (HHICS) visited a Birmingham Co-operative Society store to view its conversion to a new kind of retail experience. Reporting back to his colleagues, "he referred to the move towards self-service grocery shops and said he thought we should be trying something in that direction". Green was so impressed that the Society authorised its first conversion to experimental self-service at the Wollescote branch, which re-opened in the new format in March 1949. HHICS was typical of the many small co-operative societies in the Black Country. Founded in 1871 it had grown from one shop on Peckingham Street, Halesowen, to 20, from Quinton to Kinver. It was small enough that everyone was on familiar terms – all staff knew the general manager 'AJ' Hayward – but also so small that only after the war was it able to upgrade from horse and cart to motorised delivery.[257]

For the Co-op, self-service was "a form of rationalisation, which must be applied in the public interest to the chaotic retail trade".[258] "People complained about the loss of personal contact," recalled the manager of the Hasbury branch, "but they soon got used to it."[259] Counter service was personal and community-minded, but increasingly frustrating for many customers who enjoyed the novel experience of self-service, "provided it is introduced to them properly and provided the shop is laid out so as to prevent any confusion in their minds".[260] In early conversions, counters were simply removed and signs and baskets provided – it took some time for customers to become accustomed. The Co-operative movement was in the vanguard of changing retail practice in the 1940s but by the 1960s, competition from new supermarkets like Tesco, Price Right and Fine Fare threatened its position, including in the Black Country. Big stores like these had grown by more than a fifth in the previous three years, but Co-operatives only by four per cent. The little HHICS struggled and was eventually swallowed by the larger BCS in an attempt to counter this "epidemic of supermarket hypnosis".[261]

"Pat Collins' Dodgems" – an image from the 1952/3 Wolverhampton Exhibition of Photography. The location of this photograph is unknown, but Pat Collins' fairs were a staple of Black Country life ever since the original Collins set up in business in Walsall in 1882.

"Never had it so Good"

As the economy grew after post-war austerity, so did disposable income – the Black Country, with its highly-skilled workforce, came to typify that new invention of the era, the affluent working class. In the new Prime Minister Harold Macmillan's famous words: "Most of our people have never had it so good." Wolverhampton boasted that the area around it was "one of the most prosperous in the country". People simply bought more: whereas across Britain consumer spending grew by 48 per cent between 1947 and 1951, in the Midlands it grew by 55 per cent; local spending on clothes and household goods like televisions and washing machines grew by 79 per cent, well above the national average. Wolverhampton boasted of its

> *...department stores selling literally everything likely to warm a woman's heart, most of them with restaurants or serve-yourself cafeterias, provision shops, furniture shops, tailors, 'madame shops' and haberdashers. Whether preference is for intimate shopping or the hustle and bustle and friendliness of the store, then either want is satisfied.*[262]

Town centres began to reflect this consumer confidence and changing demographic. Dudley's tall art deco shops overlooked a bustling market and busy side streets, but as car ownership increased and the town became correspondingly congested, the council needed to modernise the medieval street layout. The Georgian townhouses of Castle Street – including the well-known Stanton's music shop – were among those making way for wider roads and modern buildings. Stanton's was the main source of 45rpm singles and tickets to Town Hall dances, and became the meeting point for Dudley teenagers in the 1950s. With an upturn in trade and improvements in the townscape, Stanton's needed to update too. The store manager Jimmy Nash was amongst those pushing for the old shop to be demolished, and eventually it was; the singer Frankie Vaughan opened Stanton's brand-new flagship store on the widened Castle Street in 1961, full of everything the modern affluent teenager could aspire to, but what the cultural critic Richard Hoggart acerbically described as "shiny barbarism": record players and records, televisions and radios, pianos, guitars and amplifiers for the rock 'n' roll groups springing up across the region. The result was that people were genuinely proud of their town, and identified more with it than with the Black Country as a region. Cynthia Burgin, who helped run a newsagent's shop on Wolverhampton Street, Dudley, remembers her town as "remarkable": full of grand buildings and every type of shop, names like Hill & Steel, Bunce's drapery and Cohen's men's outfitters still memorable 60 years later. Even former mining hamlets thrived: residents recall that Woodside, near Dudley, was virtually self-sufficient, with shops for almost every need and civic buildings like the library providing space for dances, clubs, galas and wedding receptions as well as lending books.[263]

The changes in the townscapes of the Black Country were analysed in a series of articles in the *Birmingham Daily Post* in 1962-3. They reported development ranging from the dramatic – like the vast swathes of land recently cleared in West Bromwich – to the minimal. The *Post* was unsure, for example, whether Walsall's comparative inaction was "merciful" or simply "tedious". In Smethwick, the issue that generated most comment was not the demolition of older buildings – that came later – but the changing nature of the High Street. Where once a "forbidding" green and brown Congregational church overlooked traditional butchers, bakers and grocers, the *Post* was fascinated to see that "mangoes, sweet potatoes, yams and goat meat are in much demand" near the new Sikh gurdwara.[264]

Courtesy of Black Country Living Museum

Whippet racing at Hayseech, Halesowen, in 1963.

Crossing Cultures: Leisure Time in the Black Country

Leisure time in the Black Country – where it could be had – had long been focused on two iconic institutions: the pub and the chapel. The development of other forms of mass entertainment before the war – cinema, dancing, spectator sports – took on new life after it, and the consumption of diversions such as these became part of a national growth in leisure activities, particularly amongst the young. Nevertheless, there were elements of local Black Country cultures that remained distinctive even during the age of affluence.

Despite the soot, sweat and toil of life in the Black Country, most residents would not have dreamed of moving. The sociologist Doris Rich interviewed a large number of families in Coseley in 1949, about their feelings towards the town and their leisure time. Most liked Coseley and spent their spare time locally. "Coseley is alright for Coseley folk," one declared; although his wife grumbled about never going on holiday, he was content on the local bowling green. One couple spent almost all of their time within the village, never venturing further than Bilston for shopping, while another thought Coseley a "dead hole" with people who are "not intellectual". Those with wider horizons visited Wolverhampton or Sedgley – but only very rarely ventured into Birmingham.[265]

Rich's survey also demonstrated an age and gender divide in leisure time. Married women expected their leisure activities to centre on home and husband: visiting, hobbies, sewing and reading featured, although many included housework in their leisure time. If they went to the pub or the cinema, it was with their husbands. The divide appeared to blur in younger generations though. In one multi-generational home, the father spent every evening in the local pub, while the mother mostly stayed in: her typical Tuesday evening was spent "doing the ironing with daughter". This daughter still spent time at home mending and doing housework, but had a more sociable life too. She accompanied her husband in most of their leisure time, whether pub, cinema, or at home reading. The *Daily Herald* reported Rich's survey as "Modern Wife Gets Best Deal". [266]

Rich had much less to say about single women's lives – her assumption in 1953, like her subjects', was of the inevitability of marriage. By the 1960s, this was beginning to change. With greater spending power and growing cultural influence, the teenager had been on the rise, and unmarried girls in particular were spending more than they ever had. The social scientist Mark Abrams' study of the teenager as a consumer summarised how the young spent their money: on fashion (clothing, footwear and cosmetics); consumables (soft and alcoholic drinks, sweets, cigarettes); music (records and record players); reading material (particularly, romantic magazines and fiction paperbacks); and going out, primarily to the cinema or the dance hall. Milk bars and coffee bars began to appear in the Black Country, first in the larger towns, then more widespread: the Galleon or Milan's in Wolverhampton, the Del Rio in Walsall, the Ravello in Stourbridge. Music and fashion became ways that teenage girls could express themselves both in public and at home, as consumers of records, magazines and clothes. The Teddy style was followed by rock 'n' roll and Mod fashions, for instance: Milan's rebranded itself Milano to reflect the Italian influences of the latter. Nevertheless, as historian Rosalind Watkiss Singleton has shown for the Black Country, all of these influences still pointed to the primacy of romance and marriage as the ultimate goal of the teenage Black Country girl.[267]

To the Pub

The pub had been the centre of social life for centuries in the Black Country. Many clung to an old-fashioned world, where flat-capped men drank mild from dimpled mugs and talked of pigeons, dominoes or cribbage. There were pigeon-fanciers' pubs, gardeners' pubs, trade unionists' pubs, or dog pubs like the Cross Guns in Cradley Heath, run by the legendary breeder of

Staffordshire Bull Terriers, Joe Mallen – or more accurately, his wife Lil who did most of the work. Few new pubs were built until the late 1960s, though a few social clubs joined the scene; most pubs were old, and thus retained a degree of separation between the working-class, masculine space of the public bar, and the middle-class or feminine space of the smoking room. Doris Rich summed up a typical weekday evening in 1953. The family sat down to tea when the man of the house returned from work, then following a period of washing, resting and reading the evening newspapers, the man would go to his local – likely just yards from the home – while his wife put the children to bed. Sometimes women would sit with the publican's wife in the back room, or get a bottle of stout from the 'outdoor' and take it home with fish and chips, but this was more likely in the older generation – the younger would be at the cinema or visiting friends.[268]

But times were beginning to change and by the 1960s pubs were becoming more diverse places. Not all, of course: in 1961 local councillor Donald Finney founded a branch of the far-right Birmingham Immigration Control Association at Smethwick's Red Cow. This pub – like at least ten others in Smethwick alone – maintained a 'colour bar', excluding drinkers by skin colour even when this was made illegal in 1965. But many pubs embraced this new diversity. Wolverhampton's Elephant & Castle is a

Patrons outside the Elephant & Castle, at the corner of Stafford Street and Cannock Road, Wolverhampton, in the 1960s.

Black Country Visual Arts - Apna Heritage Archive, 1960s-1980s
Punjabi Migration: a Photographic Journey

Anoop Grewal with friends, in a pub in Wolverhampton, 1969.

good demonstration of how the Red Cow was the exception rather than the norm. Although its history was never written as the Red Cow's has been, this landmark pub had served Irish immigrants since the 1830s. After the war it remained a meeting point for cultures from all over the world as old and new Irish emigrants were joined by drinkers from the Caribbean, many of whom worked from the bus garage in Fallings Park and who participated in its popular dominoes club, and South Asian workers from nearby factories too. And while most of these pubs remained adult masculine spaces, Lenny Henry recalls walking to the Bush on Blackacre Road in Dudley to fetch a jug of stout for his parents; and Shendo Jassal similarly remembers waiting in the yard of the Elephant & Castle to collect her father after he had met with old friends from India.[269]

For Punjabi immigrants who formed a large proportion of the incoming workforce, the pub became a vital coping mechanism for single men missing home and family. Some found solace in the Black Country's pubs. A remarkable poem written in Punjabi by one immigrant to Wolverhampton gives an insight into the feelings of upheaval, loss, and community experienced by the migrant labourer. Madho Ram Mahimi composed a poem in Punjabi entitled *Mera England da safr*, or 'My passage to England', to share his experiences of leaving India and finding work in the Black Country. Here he finds his compatriots sharing experiences of their past and boasting of their importance in India:

When Sachurda [Saturday] came, I was in the pub. I saw countless India-men,
Drinking full glasses there, drinking and drinking as if there's no tomorrow...
As one, they were all in England and were just fools who were full of pride.
When pub closing time came they all got up and went home.
They would all spend a comfortable night and tomorrow they would get up in the morning and go to work.
Oh, Madho Ram, they all forgot their troubles, those that had made their own troubles with the pass [emigration].[270]

Auntie's Bar

Other Black Country pubs welcomed another marginalised group. Male homosexual acts were illegal in Britain until 1967, and gay men were actively pursued by the police for breaching the boundaries of what this morally conservative society still considered indecent. A string of very public prosecutions, including Alan Turing, Sir John Gielgud and Lord Montagu, meant that public paranoia about homosexuality was high, with over a thousand men in prison for homosexual acts by 1954. In 1957, the Wolfenden Commission (which included Walsall MP William Wells) recommended de-criminalising homosexuality – nevertheless, public attitudes were hard to shift until the Sexual Offences Act 1967, in which Wolfenden's proposals were accepted. This public fear about the "homosexual 'underground' in most of our large provincial cities... a continuous menace to youth" forced gay and lesbian culture underground, and this was as true in the industrial towns of the Black Country as elsewhere.[271]

Courtesy of Walsall Archives from the Alan Price Collection

The Fountain Inn, otherwise known as Auntie's Bar, Walsall.

Most meeting points for gay men were clandestine, sometimes in public lavatories known as 'cottages', including at Lightwoods Park in Bearwood, on Dudley Road and in Victoria Park, Smethwick. But some pubs and clubs also adapted to this need. Wolverhampton's Gay Flamingo was probably the first gay nightclub in the Black Country, in a building "like an asbestos roofed tin hut". This was followed by the Silver Web, above the

Wolverhampton Co-operative Society headquarters in Stafford Street, opened by Norman and Betty Webb around 1965, and famous for its kitsch décor and the Webbs' Boxer dogs. In 1968, a young gay rights campaigner named John Holland described the Flamingo as "the best social club for homosexuals in Europe" – not long after, it was raided by police and investigated for "obscene and indecent acts" – that is, allowing men to dance together. The Fountain Inn in Bott Lane, Walsall, was taken over by a Walsall-born former music hall artist, Alice Cronin, in 1940 and became known as 'Auntie's'. By the 1960s, it was a small, unassuming pub, but a popular venue for Birmingham's gay and lesbian communities, who visited on the Midland Red bus from the time Cronin took it on. One visitor in 1963 recalled it as a "real fun place" where "lesbians dressed in suits". Nevertheless, the life of a gay man in the West Midlands of the 1960s was still dangerous. One regular at Auntie's was 21-year-old David Palmer, nicknamed 'Welsh Wendy'. Cronin described him as a "good-class boy… I would sooner have their type of customers than the 'Mods' and 'Rockers'. They caused us no trouble." Palmer, though, made the news in tragic fashion – he was murdered in Cofton Park, Birmingham, his lifestyle picked over in the press, his murderer never identified. The killing provoked terror amongst the local gay community: at a time when homosexual activity was still illegal, both the unidentified murderer and the presence of plain-clothes police visiting pubs asking questions were deeply threatening, and many gay men chose to stay away from Birmingham altogether.[272]

Pubs and Heritage

One Tipton pub stands out in the history of the formation of a Black Country identity: the Noah's Ark on Wood Street, where the Black Country Society (BCS) was founded in 1967. "As the social life of the Black Country has always revolved round its local pubs, the Society have found that by holding its meetings in public houses, this congenial atmosphere has been retained." In its first year, the BCS visited the Dudley Canal Tunnel, factories in Coseley, Tipton and Wednesbury, Galton Bridge in Smethwick and the Gornals. It also published the first issue of its journal, *The Blackcountryman*, which featured articles about Wednesbury, Baggeridge, Coseley, Walsall, Sandwell, Dudley Port and Withymoor. The BCS would do more to present the Black Country as a cohesive whole than any other group. Although most people still considered themselves as being from their town rather than from their region, when the shock of de-industrialisation hit in the later 1970s, the BCS's hard work was already there to give pride to an afflicted Black Country.[273]

To the Dance

If the pub was a regular event, going out dancing was the highlight of the week. This might have been the big dance at Dudley Town Hall, or the upstairs room at the library, boarded-over swimming baths or the Adelphi ballroom in West Bromwich. Even a local branch library like Woodside, near Dudley, held regular dances in the 1940s and 1950s, where Horace Robinson presided over the library's upper room, and partners danced the Veleta or the Military Two-Step to records of jazz standards like 'It's Only A Paper Moon'. Dances were the key place for young people to court their partners, as Doris Rich identified – they were where social groups formed in school began to separate as young men and women paired off to eventually get married. Settings like this also provided a first glimpse of stardom for many young rock 'n' roll groups. Danny Cannon & the Ramrods, from Bilston, or Steve Brett & the Mavericks from Wolverhampton (featuring a young Noddy Holder) could

Hal Hall/Stourbridge Library (ref 1235)

Teenagers at the Corbett Hospital fête, Amblecote, in 1957, taken by 'Hal' from Market Street, Stourbridge (Christopher Hall).

be found every weekend at pubs and halls in the Black Country. Eventually, bigger stars began to tour too: in 1957 and 1958 Bill Haley and the Comets, Buddy Holly and Gene Vincent all played the Gaumont cinema in Wolverhampton. In 1962, Smethwick's Thimblemill Baths hosted an up-and-coming new band named The Beatles: they had driven down after an afternoon show at Liverpool's Cavern Club and went on to the Adelphi in West Bromwich in the evening.[274] The Black Country's place in rock 'n' roll history was further secured in the mid-1960s when a young West Bromwich-born construction worker named Robert Plant joined a local group named Band of Joy. He soon recruited his friend from Redditch, John Bonham, who moved to Butterfield Court, a high-rise in Eve Hill, Dudley, in order to be closer for concerts at venues like Dudley Zoo's Queen Mary Ballroom. The pair became better known in the 1970s as half of Led Zeppelin.[275]

Wolverhampton Scala

One Wolverhampton nightclub became the centre of national attention in 1958. Shortly after opening, the Scala on Victoria Street turned away a student draughtsman from Wolverhampton, Udit Kumar Das Gupta – known to his friends as Robin – because of his skin colour. His complaint became a major news story when Wolverhampton's licensing authorities renewed the Scala's licence against fierce opposition from the town's Labour council, the Musicians' Union and local MP John Baird. *The Observer*'s George Clay interviewed the manager, Michael Wade, who claimed that his colour bar made economic and practical sense: "Other dance halls have let them in and look what has happened... [but] the trouble would never have started if they hadn't been there." He claimed people had told him: "We have to work with them; some of us even have to live next to them. We want to get away from them sometimes." Wade's claims contradicted a Gallup poll conducted following the news stories, in which only 22 per cent of the population supported a colour bar, but he clung on to his admission policy. The Musicians' Union blacklisted the Scala – its first intervention in the so-called 'race question' in post-war Britain – and the famous jazz musician Johnny Dankworth even sued a newspaper for suggesting he had agreed to cross the picket – he donated the proceeds to his charity, the Stars Campaign for Inter-Racial Friendship. Despite this public backlash, other clubs were influenced by Wade's stand: some began to suggest only admitting people of colour if they brought their own partner. Clay described "the unmistakeable scent of prejudice... in Wolverhampton's smoky air," and in Wolverhampton – and the rest of the Black Country – colour bars such as this were to become a persistent problem. [276]

Courtesy of Black Country Living Museum

Doorman Tommy Stanford stands outside the Clifton Cinema, Castle Street, Coseley, decorated to commemorate the coronation of Queen Elizabeth II in 1953. The cinema was opened in 1939, and closed in 1963 – the last showing was *Nurse on Wheels* starring Juliet Mills.

To the Pictures

As in most working-class regions, a trip to the cinema was a regular outing, particularly for the young. The Black Country's first cinema opened in West Bromwich in 1910, but by the 1950s, resident Marjorie Dunn remembered:"We had about seven cinemas in West Bromwich and they were cheap enough for you to go two or three times a week."[277] Saturday mornings in the cinema were essential for Black Country children. Jo Mary Stafford recalled her weekly visits to the Forum at Caldmore Green, Walsall. There would be "a queue of urchins stretching right around The Green" to watch Tarzan, Old Mother Riley or Lassie:

> *A crone of an usherette, "Passing Cloud" cigarette dangling from slack bottom lip, snatched the tickets and pointed the beam of her torch wordlessly to four vacant, up-tipped seats on the back row downstairs… The whirr of the projector could be clearly heard above the soundtrack. My eyes followed the beam of light from the screen to high up above the balcony, reflecting particles of dust and gobs of spit aimed at us from the posher kids lording it over us in The Gods.*[278]

The release of rock 'n' roll films like *Blackboard Jungle* and *Rock Around The Clock* was met with near-riots, sparking national panics about Teddy Boys and juvenile delinquents. This was certainly the case at Dudley's Gaumont Cinema where "jive-crazy youths ripped off their jackets and stepped into the gangway ready to jive and shout". Cinema manager Mr Jones blamed out-of-town youngsters "prepared to work themselves up into a frantic state before they even stepped into the theatre".[279]

A number of cinemas began to show Asian films during this period with comparatively little backlash. One of the first was Darlaston Picturedrome. Repeated requests for special showings by Satya Goel of the Indian Filmgoers' Association had been denied by Darlaston Council on the grounds that there were "only 74 resident Indians" in the town. When the request was finally approved, 316 members of the Society came to watch the Hindi-language film *Ladki*, and the cinema manager Leslie Taff noted that "their attention and behaviour was much better than the average British audience".[280] West Bromwich followed suit, and St George's Cinema converted to the Krishna for a few months in 1955 before closing. But the town's South Asian population was persistent and formed an Eastern Film Society in 1956, hiring films from the Indian Film Society in London, and negotiating the lending and purchase of equipment and Linguaphone records for Indian and Pakistani children in the town. This was a golden age of Indian 'Bollywood' cinema too, and other cinemas – Wolverhampton's Coliseum, Bilston's Alhambra, Smethwick's Beacon – all began to show Indian films.[281]

Out for Tea

The post-war years were also when eating out first became a possibility for many in the Black Country. With its strongly working-class demographic, the Lyon's Corner House or the Civic Restaurant was always more popular than fine dining, and that continued into the 1960s with the emergence of chain restaurants like Wimpy bars and Berni Inns. Most meteoric though was the growth in 'foreign' cuisine. As the Festival Fare competition had demonstrated, Britain had long been infamous for its resistance to anything spicy or highly-flavoured, but this was beginning to change. The first Chinese restaurant in the Black Country, Chu Kong, opened in 1958 in Castle Street, Dudley, and was swiftly followed by others like San Chun in Wolverhampton and Star of China in West Bromwich. The first Indian restaurants are harder to trace. The earliest were probably cafés catering for Indian workers in towns like Smethwick, offering simple, authentic Indian food. By contrast, the first Indian restaurants catering to English customers served something that would have been completely unfamiliar to the Punjabi or Pakistani immigrants in the region. Mostly run by Sylheti families (a region of Bangladesh, then East Pakistan), restaurants like the Kohinor in Wolverhampton (opened 1961) served a range of curries heavily adapted to English tastes. Their growth was dramatic. From just a handful in the 1940s, by 1970 there were 2,000 Indian and 4,000 Chinese restaurants in Britain. These were typically in larger towns: by 1968 there were eight Indian restaurants in the Black Country, five of which were in Wolverhampton. They were often treated with less respect than their due, ranging from the comical – such as Dennis Scrivens who accidentally swallowed a fork while balancing it on his nose at the Omar-e-Khayam in Wolverhampton – to the more serious, like the vandalism of the China Light in Great Bridge, and the assault of its owner Mr Chung, and a waiter Chow Kwok Chun, by a group of drunken men in 1963 – one of whom had just served time for his part in the Dudley race riots.[282]

To Church

The main competitor to the pub in Black Country history had always been church or chapel. There was not necessarily a stark divide: Phil Drabble recalled returning home from "a Sunday morning ferreting" and meeting churchgoers in Wednesfield in the pub "to celebrate a good sermon… or to wash down the dust of a bad one".[283] In the main, Britain remained a socially conservative, religious nation throughout the 1940s and 1950s, evidenced by a peak in church attendance: three-quarters of the population described themselves as "being of a religion or denomination" in 1951, particularly women, the young, and the working classes; although attendance at all churches in Coseley in 1949 was only about 14 per cent of the population, and that mostly women. Anglicanism still competed with Methodist and other nonconformist chapels, particularly amongst the young. Sunday School was, for most, compulsory. Whole communities came together for Sunday School anniversaries, with processions and packed halls each year – some clergymen in Dudley even fretted that these services were much better attended than traditional church festivals. Residents of Lower Gornal, for instance, attended as many local anniversary services as they could: Five Ways Chapel, Zoar Methodist, Ruiton Congregational and St James's Anglican Church all competed for the grandest occasion, just as they competed for children, the length of the procession and the cleanliness of the scrubbed gravestones.

The Black Country tradition of industrial patronage persisted too. JH Lavender, director of a West Bromwich foundry, held daily prayer meetings for his workers and served them hot cross buns at Easter, was a lay preacher at the Spring Head Mission in Wednesbury, and welcomed Sunday School classes to his large Georgian house – with swimming pool – adjacent to the foundry. Participation was not only limited to children but included teenagers too: members of the Hasbury Methodist Guild remember turkey suppers and salad teas, old-time dances and devotional meetings for teenagers, all of which were full to the rafters. Other denominations had long Black Country histories too: Roman Catholic churches, for instance, often built to accommodate an earlier wave of migration when the Irish arrived in the nineteenth century, grew again with new worshippers from Ireland, Poland and elsewhere. At the Ross, near Blackheath, Walter Darby created a whole new 'undenominational' church, the 'Church in the Garden', in 1944. Based in Darby's garden shed, he also produced tracts and posters on a hand-operated printing press.[284]

Rev John Hencher

The local vicar played a huge role in local life, and perhaps none was better-known than the vicar of Amblecote, John Hencher. A former actor, Hencher became instantly famous in 1966, when a church newsletter reporter asked him whether he did not want a wife for his 15-room Georgian rectory in Amblecote. His tongue-in-cheek response – that he would like a "nice cosy wife; she must adore Shakespeare and be prepared to sleep in a four-poster bed" was picked up in the national tabloid press and Hencher ended up in hiding from reporters. The irony was that Hencher was just as well-known locally for his openly gay relationship with a long-term partner, John Cupper. He was a tremendously popular local figure, often seen with his Boxer dog Jessica or in his sports car, or appearing in full powdered wig as George III at Bank Holiday events. Though discrimination and prejudice remained, 'The Johns' proved that gay couples could, and did, live happily in the Black Country.[285]

New Religions

Part of this religious upsurge was due to diversification. Other Christian denominations became established during this period, from the esoteric (like the Christian Community in Stourbridge, based on the principles of the philosopher Rudolf Steiner) to the specific (like the Ukrainian Orthodox Church in Wolverhampton, which served the needs of its new migrant community). The Pentecostal movement grew too, and churches were formed to serve new immigrant communities. After facing discrimination at local churches, the Jamaican Dr Oliver Lyseight founded the first New Testament Church of God in Britain. He rented rooms above the Stafford Street YMCA in Wolverhampton for a while before taking a dedicated building on Nursery Street, Wolverhampton, on 27 January 1962. Chief Constable Goodchild of the town's police opened the new church "on

Courtesy of Black Country Living Museum

Ocker Hill Methodist Church and the Three Horseshoes pub on Ocker Hill Road, Tipton, 1968. The pub was a newly-built replacement of an older one, but the chapel was nearing the end of its life - it was demolished in 1970.

behalf of all the Christians of every creed and every colour in Wolverhampton".[286]

Wolverhampton's synagogue on Fryer Street also experienced a revival during this period, as Jewish servicemen stationed at RAF Cosford and in the resettlement camps near the town boosted the congregation to 150. Other ancient religions were new to the Black Country, however. Sikh migrants in Smethwick met in a school hall in Brasshouse Lane from at least 1958, but they found acquiring accommodation for a permanent gurdwara challenging. Smethwick's disused Congregational church was for sale for £5,000, but when one of the group's leaders, Buta Singh, approached the estate agents to enquire about the building, he found counter-offers coming in from groups unhappy with a "heritage building" being used by such a group. Eventually, Smethwick's Sikhs had to pay £11,600 for the church, though as Piara Singh Purewal remembers, they had help:

> *As we gathered the money to buy the property, the West Indians who live in the flat below us handed over an unopened pay packet. So this gurdwara was bought by all communities, and we are grateful to all of them.*[287]

The Guru Nanak gurdwara opened in 1961, attended by Smethwick's MP Patrick Gordon Walker and the Mayor, Councillor Richard Pritchard, who "addressed the gathering wearing a bowler hat, a dark suit, his mayoral chain, a garland of flowers, and no shoes". Peter Griffiths, the controversial Conservative councillor, stayed away, disingenuously suggesting that "integration insults the ancient culture of the Sikhs… They should be allowed to keep their identity just as we wish to keep ours." Nevertheless it became, and has remained, a focal point in Smethwick: the first dedicated gurdwara in Europe, and still the largest.[288]

Other towns followed suit: Sikh worshippers acquired permanent homes in Wolverhampton in 1962 and Walsall in 1963. In Walsall, with its larger Pakistani population, a Muslim Welfare Association was founded in 1958, with a mosque following in 1966. In 1964, Bhagat Jaspal Bhatti emigrated from the Punjab to England and settled in Walsall. He quickly founded a temple in his home where Hindus in the town worshipped until a suitable building was found for conversion into a dedicated temple in 1983. The post-war period was one of tremendous growth and diversification in religious practice and culture.[289]

To the Match

The other mass-participation leisure pursuit in the Black Country was sport. This was extremely varied, of course: Stourbridge's War Memorial Ground hosted first-class cricket until 1961; Wolverhampton's Dunstall Park hosted the Queen's first winning racehorse, Menai, in 1964; Tipton Harriers athletics club soared in popularity due to their national champion marathon runner, Jack Holden; and Cradley Heathens built an impressive legacy at their Dudley Wood speedway stadium. Some much older Black Country traditions continued too: the 'tumbling and tippling' of pigeon racing; national greyhound racing at Monmore Green and local whippet racing at Hayseech Road, Halesowen; and even the persistence of much older Black Country bloodsports. Joe Mallen, the first breeder to win Crufts with a 'Staffie' (Staffordshire Bull Terrier, a breed originating in the Black Country), was the subject of a BBC documentary in 1958 – his dog Gentleman Jim had won in 1939 despite missing a tooth from fighting. One of the most widespread participation sports was crown green bowls, characterised less by gentility and white uniforms than a flowing bar and flat caps. Works and amateur leagues flourished, and top players were in heavy demand from company teams: when Colin Reed won the 1955 Staffordshire championship, he so impressed Willenhall's Union Locks that they awarded him a silver tea service and offered him a job. A good sportsman rarely found himself out of work.[290]

On 9 September 1954 Chief Amri Dodo, with other visitors from Tanganyika as guests of Dudley Council, visited the Molineux to watch Wolverhampton Wanderers beat Sunderland 2-0. Dodo recorded the "astonishingly skilful" players and a crowd of 45,000: "There were more people there than anywhere else in the country." They were baffled to find newspapers already reporting that match as they left: "How was this? When were these newspapers being printed? This remains a

Mirrorpix/Reach Licensing

The Black Country derby has always been the region's biggest match. Here West Bromwich Albion host Wolves at the Hawthorns in April 1951. From left to right: Billy Elliott, Bert Williams, Ray Barlow, Bill Shorthouse and Billy Wright.

great mystery."[291] Professional football was big business in the Black Country. Under Stan Cullis' coaching and Billy Wright's captaincy, Wolves won the FA Cup in 1949 and 1960, and the league championship in 1954, 1958 and 1959. They also famously played the first FA-sanctioned matches under floodlight in 1954, beating Maccabi Tel Aviv 10-0 as well as Celtic, Racing Club Avellaneda, South Africa and Spartak Moscow. The *Daily Record* suggested that the Russians had been "hammered and sickled"; Russian newspapers omitted the result entirely. In December came the achievement which crowned Wolves "champions of the world" – after some tactical extra watering of an already sodden pitch, they defeated the greatest club side in the world, Budapest Honvéd, by three goals to two.[292]

Several of Wolves' stars had been recruited from Walsall FC, but the latter's luck was out in 1954 – they finished bottom of the league. Wolves' biggest rivals were in fact another Black Country team, West Bromwich Albion. Originally formed by a works team from Salter's spring factory, they finished runners-up to Wolves in 1954 and beat Preston North End to win the FA Cup that year – a Black Country double. Elsewhere, Dudley's Duncan Edwards was signed by Manchester United in 1952, becoming one of the fêted 'Busby Babes' – the youngest player ever in the First

Division, and the youngest England player since the war. His career was tragically cut short before his expected star performance in the 1958 World Cup, when the United team plane crashed outside Munich, killing 21 people. Edwards survived for two weeks, and was reported to have been most concerned about missing kick-off against the club he grew up following, Wolverhampton Wanderers. It was not to be though: Edwards died of his injuries on 21 February 1958.[293]

Austerity to Prosperity in Black Country Culture

The tribalism of Black Country football is a convenient place to end a chapter in which the individuality of different local experiences is evident. The post-war Black Country was a microcosm of British society in this respect. It suffered national shortages and austerity, it embraced nationwide growth and prosperity and it experienced the same social trends. But all of these were filtered through local experience, tradition and tastes. For a start, it was better-off: well-paid work stimulated consumption, shops were full of people, and homes were full of things. Larger towns boomed in particular. Wolverhampton, Dudley or Walsall were certainly not in the shadow of Birmingham as regional shopping centres – they were confident, attractive towns where every need could be met. This post-war period was when these large towns began to eclipse some of the smaller centres in the Black Country which, while most were growing, could not offer the cultural diversity or excitement of a Dudley or a Wolverhampton, with their record shops, supermarkets, foreign foods and eclectic nightlife.

These local differences meant the region's new diversity was highlighted in different ways. Pubs in smaller towns, Smethwick for instance, were easily able to operate colour bars; in Wolverhampton, where both the night-time economy and immigrant society were more in evidence, it made headline news. Likewise, gay nightlife was usually limited to the larger towns, despite clear evidence that homosexuality was by no means uncommon in the smaller Black Country villages. Nevertheless, progress could often just be the result of individual choices: self-service shopping came to the industrial suburb of Wollescote before the market towns of Halesowen or Stourbridge. Whether taken as a whole or as a group of distinct communities, however, the Black Country was evidently not a region on the margins of society. It was not an indistinct region or a suburb of Birmingham, but a thriving, diverse set of interweaving communities. Whether it was industry or immigration, self-service or Staffies, new restaurants or old pastimes, the Black Country grew in confidence, and retained a unique blend of cultures of its own.

Chapter 9

Local patriotisms

Public and civic life in the Black Country

Black Country feelings, whether of pride in a craft or loyalty to a place, are intensely local.[294]

Courtesy of Black Country Living Museum

Bilston Town Hall seen from Lichfield Street in the 1950s.

The individuality of the Black Country's towns was also echoed in its intricate political geography. The long-debated reorganisation of the local authorities in 1966 had stimulated conversation and controversy since before the Second World War. It spoke to deeply-held feelings of local identity within the Black Country. The relationship between state and individual was especially local in post-war Britain: town councils dealt with everything from speeding fines to maternity care, and when some authorities looked after fewer than 3,000 people, these issues were more than local: they were personal. Both town elders and the population had pride in their towns, expressed through civic monuments, town handbooks with fulsome histories, even pageants and processions. This chapter describes the complex patchwork of councils, utilities, boards and services which served the Black Country, and their roles in creating those local identities. It also introduces the fierce battles over political autonomy that characterised the period. By the mid-1960s, the practical arguments for modernising and centralising many of these amenities, and amalgamating most of the local authorities, had won out. Local loyalties remained firm, but this decoupling of local cultures and local politics left space for a stronger pride in the Black Country as a region to emerge.

Urban and Municipal Politics

The political map of the Black Country in 1945 was the result of centuries of industrial, urban, and social change. The Black Country traditionally straddled the ancient counties of Staffordshire and Worcestershire (with small exclaves of Shropshire), creating what one Victorian writer called an "interminable village".[295] Scattered houses formed into villages, villages grew into towns, towns sprawled, and concerted efforts began to attempt to bring order to the chaos. From the mid-nineteenth century, towns began to take on different responsibilities, so that the picture in 1945 was a patchwork of statuses: County Boroughs (CB) like Wolverhampton or Walsall, Municipal Boroughs (MB) like Wednesbury or Stourbridge, Urban District Councils (UDC) like Rowley Regis or Sedgley, and Rural District Councils, like Kingswinford (see Appendix 3). As it had been a century earlier, the Black Country was still "a congeries of small industrial towns, running indiscriminately together", each with its own local authority; nothing like the huge, nucleic structure of neighbouring Birmingham. The 21 local authorities looked after populations ranging from 2,836 in Amblecote – the smallest UDC in the country – to Wolverhampton at nearly 150,000. Their roles differed substantially: each had to look after housing, refuse,

Conurbation, 1948, p.48.redrawn by Sophie Lamb

Map of the West Midlands conurbation in 1948, showing the complex patchwork of boundaries and jurisdictions that made up the Black Country.

utilities, parks and sanitary inspection; larger MBs added child welfare, weights and measures, and a borough magistracy; and CBs were almost entirely independent of the County Council, assuming responsibility for everything from police, to hospitals, to protection of wild birds.[296]

The divisions reflected historically distinct identities, geology and industry, and each fought fiercely for its independence and civic pride. Something of this can be seen in the range of promotional handbooks printed by local councils, setting out their town's civic history to demonstrate

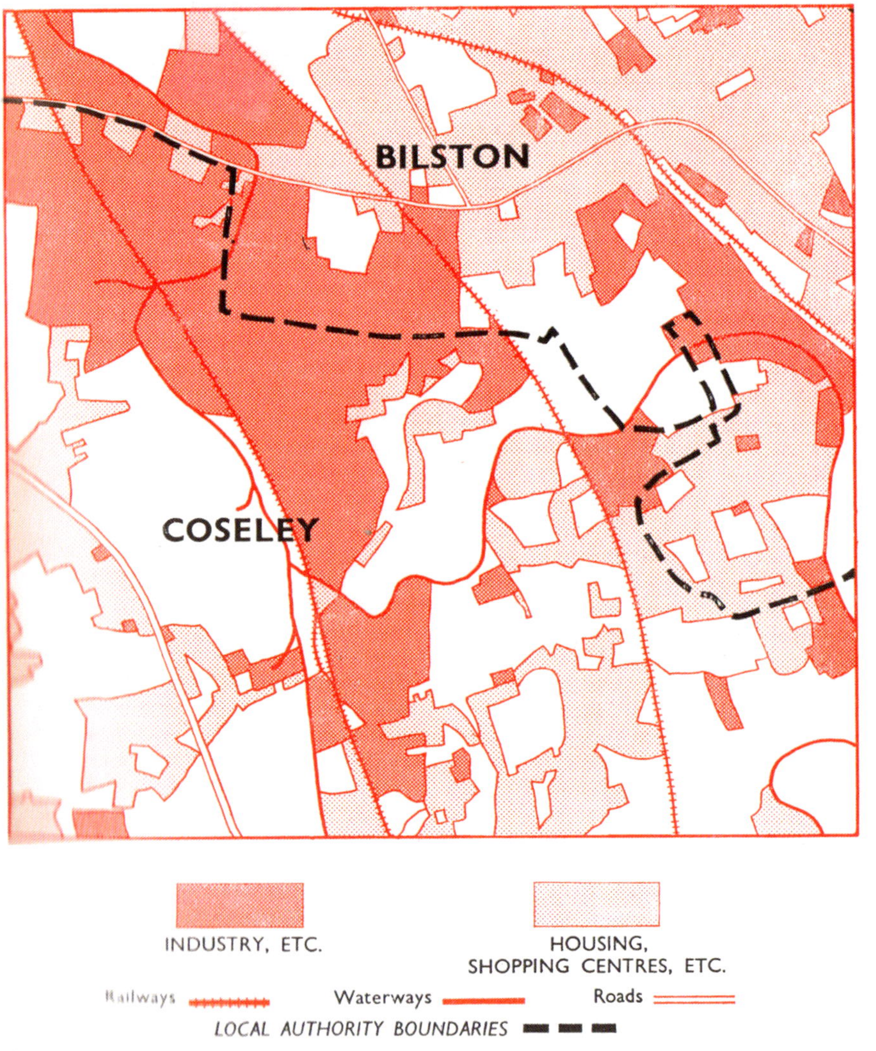

Bournville Village Trust

The boundary between Coseley UDC and Bilston MB in 1948, running through the middle of Bilston Steelworks and creating a ‘pan-handle’ at the Bankfield Works .

its place at the vanguard of the onward march of progress. Wolverhampton suggested that “without a shadow of a doubt Local Government must be the best bargain in the world to-day”. It organised a centenary exhibition in 1948 explicitly to show its townspeople the “virility” of their Council. For 4s per week, they argued, the “equivalent of one packet of cigarettes and half a pint of beer, you obtain the whole of your services in this town”: cradle to grave care, a full education, municipal amenities like parks and sewerage, and “if at any time during his lifetime this Wulfrunian falls on bad times, the welfare services are there to assist him and his children". Willenhall included a map showing its exports all over the globe in its handbook; Sedgley, notably, claimed to be a "well-defined and separate town, [which] has not lost its own individuality amid a crowd of larger neighbours". Each presented its local healthcare, slum clearance, civic amenities, industry and shopping as essentially modern and driven by expertise and care for the local people.[297]

Nevertheless, this was an incredibly complex way of organising space. Dudley remained an exclave of Worcestershire, completely surrounded by Staffordshire, and the boundaries between districts continued to vex planners. Coseley, for instance, was a sprawling collection of villages with a serpentine border featuring a 'pan-handle' seemingly established to embrace the long-gone Bankfield Ironworks; it also ran through the middle of the Spring Vale steelworks so that one set of blast furnaces fell in Coseley, another set in Bilston. Planning was undertaken by district groupings; education was an equally tortuous mixture of County Boroughs, joint educational authorities and counties; and parliamentary representation was a completely separate arrangement again. The West Midlands Group – modernisers to the core – bemoaned the "arbitrary and illogical" divisions as a fatal hindrance to development.[298]

Such civic independence resulted in a patchwork of local authorities and municipal buildings. Each authority needed somewhere for the council to meet, so there were town halls scattered across the region, from large Victorian halls like Stourbridge and Darlaston, to grand inter-war buildings as in Dudley. These were hubs for all kinds of functions, and attracted other municipal facilities: libraries, magistrates' courts, police and fire stations. Many of these clusters still survive. In West Bromwich, the town hall on the High Street is next to the grand, Carnegie-funded central library; but close by are the former magistrates' court, Edward Street Hospital, art school and grammar school; the Gas Department showroom and workshop, clinic, public baths and technical college have been demolished. Even the former restaurant on the corner of Lombard Street West was converted into council offices, backing onto the 'Corporation yard' at the rear of the town hall. Some Districts had less impressive public offices. Amblecote UDC conducted its business from three terraced houses on the High Street, but the only room big enough for the council to meet as a whole was upstairs at the Fish Inn. Where some authorities stamped their civic identity with grand town halls, little Amblecote had to make do with a clock attached to the pub, unveiled to commemorate the Festival of Britain in 1951.[299]

The Pageant of Dudley

Courtesy Black County Living Museum

One of the many dramatic moments of the 1951 Pageant of Dudley. Here, Rev. EAD Naylor of St Augustine's, Holly Hall, meets his doom as the Prior of Wenlock. The swords with which Naylor was being wounded were made specially for the performance at Round Oak steelworks.

The Festival of Britain in 1951 provided an opportunity to display this civic pride to the nation. Towns around the Black Country held fetes, processions and parties, but perhaps none were as grand as the Pageant of Dudley. Historical pageants were a national craze between the world wars and experienced a resurgence in popularity during the Festival. Dudley's was a huge affair, staged in the dramatic setting of Dudley Castle across ten nights in June, and depicted scenes from the town's history ranging from the Norman conquest to the town's Victorian fetes, via Queen Elizabeth's visit to the town and Dud Dudley's Civil War experiences. The stories were to represent "the story of you of Dudley town; they are the story, too, of the proud 'Black Country', of the Midlands and of England, for so interwoven were the threads that fashioned the tapestry of history". The cast of hundreds were all local: the Earl of Dudley (played by Robert Pine) was present in each scene but so too, the organisers were keen to point out, was The Smith – a representation of the ordinary working man played by the conveniently-named John Smith. He represented "the townsman, quiet, industrious yet sometimes rebellious, who provides the continuity and upon whose labours and skill the industrial wealth of the town has been created". The pageant was organised by the experienced Pageant Master Gwen Lally, affectionately known as 'The Lally' – ever-present with megaphone in hand to shout "instruction, threat, advice, and (sometimes) praise". She was instrumental in choosing the script, the cast, the production team, and for roping in Joyce Naylor, wife of the vicar of St Augustine's. Naylor's role eventually included stage-managing an entire episode; ordering mild steel so that the Earl of Dudley could ask his workers at Round Oak to make 60 swords; and writing to numerous Roman Catholic scholars to find the correct setting for the Te Deum. Unfortunately, the weather made a major dent in visitor numbers and the pageant made a £3,000 loss – enough to make local councils think twice about staging such an extravaganza again.[300]

A similarly tangled political geography was found in the provision of services and utilities in the region. Compared to Birmingham's history of 'municipal socialism', the Black Country's mixture of statutory and private utilities presented a bewildering mixture of jurisdictions. Most local authorities had their own gas undertaking, while others relied on private companies, meaning the region was dotted with gas showrooms, offices and gasworks large and small. Electricity was equally confusing. Wolverhampton, West Bromwich and Walsall had municipal providers; the Staffordshire Urban Districts were supplied by the Midland Electric Corporation (from their power station at Ocker Hill); and the southern Black Country by the Shropshire, Worcestershire and Staffordshire Electric Power Co. Such complexity was an obvious target for rationalisation, which was swift in coming. The post-war Labour government swept to power on a manifesto of nationalisations, and soon these utilities joined other publicly-owned industries. The only utility that retained its historical complexity was water. Here, the South Staffordshire Water Works Co. dominated, having just completed a vast new reservoir at Blithfield, near Rugeley (built during the war by Polish refugees). Some of the historical anomalies remained: Bilston's tiny municipal supply, fed by the Victorian Bratch pumping station at Wombourne, lasted until 1959 when it was absorbed by Wolverhampton, which in turn lasted until the nationalisation of the industry in 1973.[301]

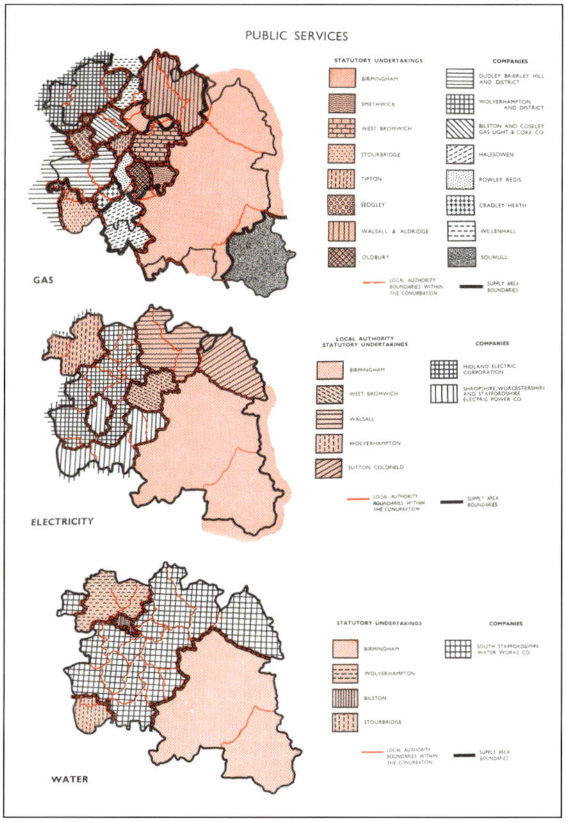

Bournville Village Trust

Maps of utility provision in the West Midlands prior to nationalisation and reorganisation, from *Conurbation*.

Municipal Services

National changes also had a local impact on services like education. The 1944 Education Act, introduced by the Conservative Education Minister 'Rab' Butler, defined the shape of post-war schooling, introducing the

Eating out at the Civic

One marker of how closely councils paid attention to the welfare of their community was the Civic Restaurant, found in many towns in the Black Country. These facilities traced their roots to public canteens sanctioned in 1940 by the wartime coalition government as a means of providing subsidised hot meals to a population struggling with rationing. Originally known as Community Kitchens, the name was considered too "redolent of Communism and the workhouse" by Winston Churchill and they were rebranded British Restaurants. They were typically housed in repurposed public buildings, such as the West Bromwich Drill Hall at Carter's Green or the Primrose League Hall in Darlaston. The Ministry of Food helped out with expenses and the Women's Voluntary Service often provided workers, meaning that the cost of a three-course meal could be kept as low as 9d. Opinions were divided about their place in society: when the Wren's Nest restaurant was opened in 1943 it was criticised for undercutting local restaurants, but this was swiftly rebutted by Dudley's Mayor on the basis that "good food makes sound, healthy bodies". Jennie Lee, MP for Cannock, also praised them for their vision "of how life can have more grace and more comfort than at any time in the past" for women.[302]

British Restaurants proliferated in the Black Country, providing a welcome service in a region where most works had no canteen facilities. With rationing ever more stringent after the war, many remained popular and in 1947, the government permitted those making a profit to stay open as Civic Restaurants. This fitted squarely within Labour's egalitarian, redistributive principles. Minister of Food, John Strachey, noted that "private enterprise in the catering trade has, on the whole and by and large, catered for the middle class and not for the working class" and Civic Restaurants – by now essentially a nationalised hot dinner – were one way of improving matters. Some towns even built new Civic Restaurants. Dudley's Central Restaurant, a long, low, prefabricated concrete building on the corner of Fisher Street and Birmingham Street, was just such a case. Designed for efficiency and speed, it could serve up to 600 people in a two-hour dinnertime, with a large cafeteria-style dining hall, coffee lounge and terrace, when it opened on 29 July 1948. Despite its Modernist design, most diners remembered it as somewhat austere, and its food was not much more exotic: on its last day of opening in 1956 customers could choose fish and chips, cottage pie, or rice pudding, amongst other hearty but very traditional foods. The Restaurant – by this time known as the Ednam – closed on 29 September 1956, its hearty but basic wartime fare a victim of the region's prosperity.[303]

Held by Dudley Archives and Local History Centre (ref DH/1/9/7)

Dudley Central Civic Restaurant, seen from Fisher Street, Dudley in 1954.

so-called 'tripartite system' of free grammar schools, secondary moderns and secondary technical schools, streamed by the 11-plus examination. Labour adopted the Act because it promised free schooling for all, despite its potential to entrench existing class divides on subtle lines, from the cost of grammar school uniforms, to the kinds of jobs available to those leaving the different streams. Black Country schools produced many famous names during this period, from footballers like Duncan Edwards to writers like Allan Ahlberg and musicians like Robert Plant. Some Labour politicians had argued for more radical reform in the 1940s, and when the party returned to power in the 1960s it began to convert the tripartite scheme into a national comprehensive education programme. This coincided with a substantial school-building programme: future England manager Sam Allardyce's school, Wren's Nest Secondary Modern in Dudley, was typical of this, opened in 1965 to replace the ageing Wolverhampton Street Secondary, where Duncan Edwards had studied.[304]

Some schools found themselves embroiled in much broader political questions, in particular that of immigration. Education became a contested issue during Peter Griffiths' tenure as Conservative leader on Smethwick Council. Griffiths – a schoolteacher himself – and other Conservative councillors developed proposals to segregate schooling in Smethwick, blaming children of Indian immigrants for lowering standards and decreasing white children's chances. This fitted Griffiths' overall approach towards Smethwick's immigrant families, but it was an extreme proposal in an era of civil rights movements. Indeed, he was accused of advocating "educational apartheid", leading one councillor to exclaim: "This is Staffordshire not Alabama!"[305]

Later on, Wolverhampton's West Park Primary School found itself the centre of global attention after Enoch Powell's incendiary 1968 speech, when he cited an anonymous school having just one white child. West Park, brand

Bettmann/contributor/Getty Images

Lessons in the playground at West Park Primary, Wolverhampton, in 1968.

new the previous term, was held up as a symbol of Wolverhampton's immigration problem – in fact, the claim was altogether false. Much more common was the experience of students like Wolverhampton residents Shendo Jassal and Desmond Cox, both the only non-white children in their whole schools. Some areas of the Black Country did see large numbers of immigrant children in their schools, and it inspired some unusual responses. In West Bromwich, Walsall and Wolverhampton the town councils resorted to dispersal: bussing immigrant children around the borough to spread the responsibility for their teaching. Although this was often done in the spirit of improvement, it certainly increased the stigma faced by immigrant children in the Black Country.[306]

Alongside schools were a large number of municipal libraries, ranging from grand edifices such as Tipton or West Bromwich, to smaller branch libraries across the region. In 1941, the Library Association commissioned Lionel McColvin to report on the condition of libraries across Britain. Those in the Black Country were considered well below national standards. Dudley was just "close to tolerable" and only in Smethwick and Wednesbury was borrowing higher than the national average. McColvin's bold recommendations included "de-Victorianizing" library buildings, which were too often "unsuitable, inappropriate, inadequate, expensive and ill-sited", and converting inefficient, parochial library services into a new, comprehensive, national one.[307]

Not all of McColvin's suggestions were taken up, but many library services did seek to modernise as a result of the report. By the 1960s these changes were starting to show. In Dudley, much of this was due to the pioneering Borough Librarian Alexander Wilson. Upon appointment in 1952, he immediately introduced a 'Parents' Corner' with picture books like *Muffin the Mule* for under-fives, a scheme so successful that Dudley soon employed a Children's Librarian, MT Tarry. Tarry extended the scheme into a wider Library Circle for children up to age 13, and in 1963 introduced a further innovation: a badge featuring a Buddhist deity, referred to in newspaper reports as "Weit'o, the Chinese god of books". A badge was available for anyone who kept library rules, visited regularly and reported back to Tarry. Such a one was 10-year-old Owen Lawson of Saltwells, who claimed to one reporter that he read 30-40 books per month and was currently reading *Peter Pan* and a book that taught him how to make a breech-loading pea shooter. This was not Dudley's only innovation. Wilson also introduced gramophone records in 1961, and later paperbacks – "the sort with the flamboyant covers". He responded to local needs in other ways too, providing books in Polish in 1958, and in Punjabi and Urdu in 1967. In fact, Dudley's improved library service was so popular that the Central Library was

Birmingham Mail/Dudley Archives and Local History Centre (ref PRO/622)

Library Circle in the Children's Library at Woodside Library, Dudley, February 1963.

completely refurbished in 1966, transforming it from a "gloomy monument to Edwardian solidity into a brilliantly-lit building incorporating all modern comforts". One of the features of its redecorated lobby was a Victorian post box, cast at Cochrane's foundry, Woodside, in the 1870s and rescued from its London home as part of plans by librarians to inaugurate a new museum of the Black Country.[308]

This modernising spirit was echoed in other local authority functions. Urban Districts and above took responsibility for ambulance services; County Boroughs also ran fire services, the police, and the new Civil Defence Corps which existed between 1949 and 1968, when Cold War fears were at their height. The 999 emergency service was introduced in the late 1940s, but it took time for both the public and services to adapt to it. Sometimes it worked well, as when Sergeant Wright received a call at All Saints police station, West Bromwich, at 3:20pm, cycled furiously to Friar Park, and apprehended his man at 3:25pm. At other times it did not, with tragic results. When John Hickinbottom broke his neck in a marlhole in Tividale in 1953, his schoolfriend Robert Lowe was told by the operator: "Shut up, don't be foolish." Hickinbottom later died of his injuries.[309]

Policing was a face-to-face service. Most families knew their local beat officer by name and number, and the officers knew them, sometimes leading to an uneven enforcement of the law. John Petty, for instance, wrote about those who worked salvaging scrap from the railway tip in Bentley – the police frequently patrolled these areas looking for easy pickings for arrests. Other officers, though, overlooked petty offences. The shortages of the 1940s, in particular, meant that small crimes like ration coupon exchanges and black-market trading were frowned upon officially, but tolerated in practice.[310]

As austerity turned to prosperity, the police became concerned with other issues. The Teddy Boys were the emblematic youth movement of the 1950s. For some, it was simply about the look: "tails down the back… DA [hairstyle]… brothel-creepers" was how Norman Raybould of Pensnett described his style. But Teddy Boys also became infamous for the 'mob hooliganism' and 'juvenile delinquency' that seemed to characterise them. Nationally, convictions of 14- to 17 year-old boys more than doubled between 1938 and 1959; and despite National Service, for 17- to 21-year-old young men it nearly tripled. As historians have shown, the measurement of crime is less a reliable measure of actual crime rates than a reflection of what was making society anxious – the Teddy Boys were comparatively few in number but their distinctive look, disrespectful attitude and threat of violence (often racially motivated) made them targets of moral outrage.[311]

Black Country newspapers were therefore full of Teddy Boys and hooligans in the 1950s and early 1960s, whether disrupting an old people's gala in Netherton, assaulting a police officer in Wednesbury, or firing air rifles to shatter the window of St Christopher's on the Wren's Nest Estate. The vicar despaired, describing them – in JD Salinger's famous phrase – as "crazy, mixed-up kids".[312] Venues like the Dorchester and the Gaumont in Wolverhampton became the destination for Teddy Boys. Willenhall's Civic Restaurant found its "weekly Teddy Boy hops" banned by the town council after violent incidents; one councillor suggested that "these alleged specimens of humanity" were in danger of turning Willenhall into "a Paris of the Midlands".[313]

Teddy Boys were blamed for racist violence in Nottingham and Notting Hill in the late 1950s, and were held responsible too for Dudley's 'race riots' in 1962, when homes and individuals in North Street, Wellington Road, and other parts of town where immigrants had settled, were attacked. This made national news, and much praise was awarded to Dudley's police, who responded swiftly by arresting the rioters; and to magistrates, who sat late into night to process the charges. Superintendent Hullah and Sergeant Robert Allardyce, for example, testified to being in charge of the North Street cordon when a lorry had

Graham Gough/Dudley Archives and Local History Centre (ref p/3484)

Police and rioters at the corner of Castle Street and Hall Street, Dudley, during the so-called 'race riots' of 1962. Dudley Police were praised for their quick response, and especially their use of police dogs.

approached at high speed full of men throwing sticks, stones and bottles at the police at around 11:45pm on Monday 31 July, and the following night the police were prepared with more officers and Alsatian dogs. Over 50 arrests were made and nearly 20 people were given exemplary sentences. In the final analysis, few were really Teddy Boys. Alongside a handful of older ringleaders, most were in their early twenties, in low-skilled but decently-paid jobs, living on council estates like the Priory and Old Park Farm – where they would have been neighbours with Sergeant Allardyce and his son Sam.[314]

Introducing the Welfare State

Perhaps the most substantial – and most lasting – change in the relationship between the individual and the state in post-war Britain was Labour's creation of a 'cradle to grave' welfare state. The idea of state pensions for all, free healthcare, and security during unemployment was not new. From the late nineteenth century trade unions and some politicians had been arguing that the free market had not met the needs of many of the population for whom poverty and precarity were an everyday experience. The industrial unrest of Edwardian Britain – like the famous women chainmakers' strike in Cradley Heath in 1910 – alongside political pressure from the new Labour Party, and the cataclysms of the First World War had convinced Liberal leaders to introduce national insurance, labour exchanges and opt-in pensions. Nevertheless, when Labour embraced Sir William Beveridge's report recommending the introduction of a comprehensive programme of insurance, assistance and healthcare for all – not just the poor – it was a dramatic change. On 5 July 1948, not just a National Health Service, but a complete system of social provision was inaugurated.[315]

Although the NHS immediately became the third-biggest employer in Britain, its organisation was complex. General Practitioners became the Primary Care strand, and Hospital Services a second strand under the administration of fourteen Regional Hospital Boards (the Black Country fell under Birmingham). The final strand was Community Services, which remained under local authority control. By 1961, the NHS was the largest employer in Britain and was drawing new recruits from around the world to staff its services. Its administration was in the hands of a Minster for Health from the Black Country, Enoch Powell, who – in addition to continuing recruitment from Ireland – championed recruitment from around the Commonwealth to meet the need for junior doctors, nurses and other staff.[316]

Local authorities retained their influence in community services and also made tremendous strides in advancing local healthcare according to local needs. This

Used with the permission of Wolverhampton Archives

Lea Road Infant Welfare Centre, Wolverhampton, 1953. Centres such as this acted as both medical and social hubs for new mothers, providing welfare foods, vaccinations, infant weighing, classes in 'mothercraft', and most importantly, many cups of tea.

strand was made up of what had been the traditional functions of Council sanitary committees: health education, child welfare, prevention of disease, and other public health concerns. The Medical Officer of Health (MOH) was a familiar sight in the streets: Wolverhampton's James Forbes Galloway was even featured in a long newspaper profile in 1963, crediting him with a major improvement in the town's health over his nearly two decades in the position. Galloway stressed that the welfare state had dealt with many of Beveridge's five evils – "want, idleness, disease, ignorance, squalor" – but that new ones had risen. "Now the problems are four," he said: "birth, growing up, getting old, and mental stress."[317]

Galloway's assessment was widely shared. Full employment, national insurance, clean air acts and slum clearances had dealt with many of the social conditions that caused many diseases, and scientific advances enabled treatment of those diseases. Infant vaccination, in particular, was putting paid to many of the diseases which had once been rife in the Black Country: smallpox, diphtheria, measles, tuberculosis and more.

Nevertheless, outbreaks still occurred to keep minds focused. Occasional outbreaks of smallpox were linked to the new age of global mobility – one in 1947 started with a soldier on leave, for example. Diphtheria was rare except, it seemed, in Coseley, where in 1951 one-third of all cases in the country fell within the urban district – all on the western side of the Birmingham New Road. Two years later another outbreak occurred – this time on the eastern side of the road, mystifying local health inspectors. Despite advances in vaccination, some diseases still caused major public concern. There were calls to screen new migrants for tuberculosis – firstly Irish and later Caribbean and South Asian – and in some areas, it became popular as an anti-immigrant trope. In fact, the advice given to Powell was that most tuberculosis was in fact contracted in Britain. The disease remained, as it always had been, a disease of poverty and overcrowding – not of race.[318]

Perhaps the most feared disease of the period, however, was poliomyelitis, and "the feeling that polio lurks round every corner", in the words of the Rev Crawshaw of Smethwick, was common. This debilitating, and sometimes fatal, epidemic disease made frequent post-war appearances, affecting the Black Country throughout the 1950s. Any reported cases rapidly stimulated demand for vaccination, in particular the death of Birmingham City and England defender Jeff Hall in 1959.

Learning to peg rugs at Bilston Occupation Centre, Bradley, in 1952. The Centre provided work and social programmes for those with mental illnesses.

Vaccination programmes made a tremendous difference although outbreaks such as that in 1961, when the Black Country heard reports of victims being rushed to hospital under police escort, affected the whole region. "Life to our children," suggested Oldbury's MOH, "must seem to be an endless series of pin-pricks" – but mass vaccination programmes made a huge impact on everyday life in the Black Country.[319]

Several councils also attempted to treat Dr Galloway's last "evil", that of "mental stress". Bilston's MOH, JP Neylon, estimated that 40 per cent of patients at an average GP surgery experienced "some sort of mental or psychological disturbance", although understanding of what that might mean was still very limited. Bilston also owned an Occupation Centre on King Street, Bradley, managed by the former mayor, Audrey Chettle-Hartill, which provided work schemes and care for those diagnosed medically as "sub-normal", "mentally defective" or "mentally retarded". Nevertheless, tremendous stigma remained (Neylon himself suggested "that those who are mentally retarded should be castrated") – as with unmarried mothers, there were still many issues society preferred to hide away.[320]

Proposals for Change

One July evening in 1961, 150 people turned out for an unusual meeting at Bilston Town Hall. It was called by Walter Hughes, chairman of the Bilston Defence Committee, in protest at the proposed merger of Bilston into an expanded Wolverhampton CB. Hughes announced a sticker and poster campaign for the town declaring 'Bilston for Bilstonians!', a picket of the Minister for Housing's London home, and a referendum on the town's future. When results came in, 11 per cent voted to merge with an adjoining borough; three per cent voted for the merger with Wolverhampton; and no less than 86 per cent voted for Bilston to remain as it was. Amalgamation into fewer, larger County Boroughs had been proposed since before the war. The idea preoccupied local reconstruction talk and prompted the existing CBs (Dudley, Smethwick, Walsall, West Bromwich and Wolverhampton) to propose taking over other, smaller authorities. In 1954 fierce battles ensued between the Black Country local authorities and Staffordshire County Council, whose boundary committee chair warned of "a number of Hitlers in the south of the County" who "would spend their last penny to snatch territory from the county". Those plans, proposing to make seven new boroughs out of eleven existing districts, met fierce opposition. A fresh boundary commission made new proposals in 1960, again triggering protests in towns like Bilston and Oldbury, where it was suggested the town should be merged with Smethwick and Rowley Regis. Coseley householders voted by 7,525 to 297 against proposals which would see "the dismemberment and death of the urban district". Tipton, which had been a Borough only since 1938 and was threatened with takeover from several directions, claimed that "as a unit in the Black Country [Tipton] is not dead, its pulse is still beating and its blood, albeit black blood, is still coursing in its veins". The plans even renewed the old debate as to where the Black Country started and stopped. Patrick Brown QC, arguing for Halesowen against the movement of Hill and Cakemore into the new Warley Borough, said that Halesowen "regarded itself as being part of Worcestershire on the edge of the Black Country, and most emphatically not as being part of the Black Country in Worcestershire".[321]

In the end, there was no triumph for those campaigning against change. The Housing and Local Government Minister, Sir Keith Joseph, accepted only minor amendments to the 1960 proposals and rubber-stamped the plans to allow the extinction of Amblecote, Bilston, Brierley Hill, Coseley, Darlaston, Sedgley, Tettenhall, Tipton, Wednesbury, Wednesfield and Willenhall as political

Courtesy of Black Country Living Museum

Council chambers at Darlaston Town Hall.

entities. Instead, the Black Country faced the future in 1966 with five enlarged County Boroughs: Wolverhampton, Walsall, Dudley, West Bromwich and the new Warley, formed from Rowley Regis, Oldbury and Smethwick, and slivers of six other districts. It was a bitter blow. While earlier plans had suggested forming authorities "capable of a comprehensive outlook yet with sufficient discernment to retain those local interests and characteristics whose preservation is important," Joseph's plan treated the Black Country as though it was simply a collection of "residential suburbs". His solution lasted just eight years, before further amalgamations produced the four modern Black Country boroughs as they now stand.[322]

The attempts and failures to re-draw the boundaries of the Black Country are an appropriate place to conclude this chapter. The local patriotisms that some onlookers referred to were probably the strongest they ever had been, or ever would be, in the prosperous, confident 1950s and 1960s. Although these boundaries hampered all kinds of things that modern urban areas need – effective public transport, coordinated amenities – the idea of letting one's urban identity decline seemed to be impossible to embrace. As the 1960s drew to a close, and these hyper-local authorities passed into history, the intimacy of post-war politics seemed to some to have been taken away forever. These changes pre-empted the massive industrial upheavals of the 1970s and 1980s – with both political and industrial distinctiveness stripped from individual towns, pride in the Black Country region finally began to replace pride in individual towns. Popular organisations like the Black Country Society and civic ones like the proposed Black Country museum – both founded in the fertile urban and civic life of the post-war era – were able to fill this gap when they were needed in the 1970s.

Chapter 10

"Never had it so good"

The brief life of social democracy in the Black Country

DJ Norton

Taken from the tower of St John the Baptist, these markings show the site of the new Queensway shopping area in Halesowen in July 1956.

...a satisfactory solution of these problems will involve the almost total re-planning and redevelopment of the whole 200 square miles. Such a plan should aim at the rehabilitation of the environment of two million people and the readjustment of the urban units with each other, with the region, and with the country as a whole. Radical physical re-planning of the whole area of the Conurbation and of the surrounding countryside is required.[323]

There is a very strong movement afoot to combine – centralize – all the Black Country local authorities into a single big township, which would aim at killing their individuality at one fell swoop. There are those who would prostitute their skill for wealth and go into mass-production markets where we are not built to compete. Some would send away our industries and leave us. To hell with all of them. Instead, let us strive for what they would destroy: for a reverence of tradition and consciousness of craft. Let us not be ashamed of a nostalgia for the skill of our forebears and their love of sport and food and drink. Do not despise these 'little men', the chaps who own no man as gaffer. It was men like them who raised us to the pinnacle of our fame... If we can only breed more of their kind, the future may not be worse than the past, but infinitely better.[324]

Tradition and Modernity

As the 1960s drew to a close, the debate between tradition and modernity was still unresolved. Despite the best efforts of planners and politicians, writers and romantics, the Black Country was still a complicated mixture of the old-fashioned and the new-fangled. Whatever the national picture might have looked like, at a local level it would have been hard to see this period as revolutionary – but it would also have been impossible to deny the fundamental shifts in society that were in evidence all around. Most Black Country people would have recognised that both perspectives were true at once.

Some argued that modernity had won outright. 1945 had been a real turning point. Economically, the Second World War turned the Black Country from just another industrial region dealing with inequalities and neglect, into the engine room of a new world. Over the course of the following two decades, a region which had been famous earlier in the century for its poverty and exploitation became one of the most prosperous, best-paid working-class regions in Britain. From this perspective, the 'white heat' of technology was more and more coming to replace the old industrial structures of the Black Country: foundries and steelworks mechanised, businesses conglomerated into vast corporations or nationalised, and skilled engineering work became more common than the region's traditional, artisanal industries. Modern technology applied to housing had met the housing shortage and replaced the slums with utopian schemes for high-rise and communal living. Outdated town centres had been drastically altered for the benefit of traffic, shopper and trade. Boundaries had been redrawn rationally and unemotionally into a region ready for the modern world.

Yet tradition clung on. For all of the talk of a new world, the Black Country's history as a metalworking region was what placed it so centrally in the post-war economy. This clinging to tradition in the face of change was what inspired the Black Country Society (BCS) to to define a historic Black Country, and to fight for the preservation of its industries, buildings and customs. It advertised a traditional "grorty puddin' supper" at the Pear Tree in Blackheath and a night of Black Country folk songs in Wolverhampton, and helped members of the Ruiton Congregational Church scrub their gravestones. It supported Dudley librarians in setting up a museum for the region – like other industrial museums set up in the post-war period it was to be an open-air, living museum, celebrating the region's architecture and industry, but also the everyday lives of the Black Country's working men and women. The BCS even proposed a unifying Black Country local authority, trading off Drabble's fear of the

Courtesy of Black Country Living Museum

An outing of the newly-formed Black Country Society through the Dudley Tunnel, itself recently taken on by the Dudley Canal Trust.

loss of individuality against the fear of being overshadowed by their big brother in the West Midlands conurbation, Birmingham. In the end, the four large boroughs swallowed up the older districts, improving efficiency but draining some of the local identity from the smaller Black Country villages. Those communities could be fiercely local – occasionally to a fault, as immigrants to the Black Country sometimes found. This sense of preservation of past glories, combined with pragmatism in the face of a changing world, gave birth to a greater sense of regional identity which would grow during the following decades: proud of the Black Country as a whole, rather than ashamed of the dirt and soot and poverty of the past.[325]

Either of these narratives would make a good story. In fact, in the Black Country at least, the reality was that tradition and modernity existed alongside one another, often uncomfortably. This can be seen across all of the themes covered by *Forging Ahead*, but perhaps most notably in industry, housing, and local politics. The changing nature of industry was an economic boon for the Black Country, but it hastened the demise of many traditional industries, along with the skill and craftsman's pride that went into them. Some echoes of the past – like GKN's dog cart deliveries – were done away with swiftly; others – the crumbling Victorian factories in which this new world took shape, for instance – persisted. Some canals were filled in; others clung on as coal routes; some were reinvented as spaces of leisure. Distinctive Black Country characteristics like the local specialisation of industry even thrived amidst a world of mergers and globalisation: Willenhall was still synonymous with locks at the end of 1960s, Darlaston with nuts and bolts, Stourbridge with glass.

Although a new political consensus emerged, placing the needs of the working class at its heart, bringing higher wages and workplace benefits, other political choices entrenched its stratification. Those who had to leave school at 15 and go straight into unskilled labour had a very different experience from those whose parents could afford for them to enter an apprenticeship. This was cemented by modernising education reforms which did just the same, and was reinforced in the changing social geography of the Black Country: despite a fierce attachment to place, many of those who could moved away from the region's tough, smoky heart, to its more desirable suburbs. That meant that no one type of home typified the Black Country working class as it once might have, and affluence could be experienced in different ways. For some that meant a new home provided by the council, at ground level or twelve stories up, some with high-tech shared amenities, some requiring coal to be brought up in the lift. For others, home meant a cramped courtyard house with shared facilities as previous generations had lived in – but perhaps with the addition of a television, melamine on the table, or a family car outside.

Gender and race also provide what the historian Joan Scott termed "useful categories of analysis".[326] For women, the years immediately *before* 1945 may have appeared the most revolutionary: war and work provided many with more autonomy than before. For some, leaving the workplace and returning to domestic duties at the end of the war must have seemed a step backward, rather than a leap forward. The following decades saw the encapsulation of the nuclear family, with an increasingly restrictive role for women as wives, mothers and homemakers. For people outside this narrow definition of sexuality, too, the post-war years brought persecution rather than progress. Adding 'race' into the equation also demonstrates how social change could appear shocking, or prompt people into reactionary prejudice. The increase in immigration from outside Britain, into the Black Country, was closely related to the boom in industry and the growth of working-class affluence. Responses to this played out across many arenas: in the workplace, in churches, and notably in housing, where many immigrants were forced to endure the worst of the conditions – the same conditions experienced by the working-class forefathers of those espousing the worst racism. For women and immigrants, homes and workplaces were certainly the site of a struggle between old and new.

The final key battleground was in the local political sphere. This was more than just boundary commissions: local attachments can be felt behind all of the debates over landscape, services and civic identity. Understandably in a rapidly globalising Britain, there was ongoing attachment to the municipal structures of the previous generation, in which personal and territorial matters were at the fore. The resistance to the distant, bureaucratic planners can be understood in the same terms: to some extent the Black Country towns felt themselves too distinctive, too idiosyncratic to be properly managed by outsiders, even if that outsider was just the next-door council. Without wider planning, it can be argued that the region's housing shortage would not have been solved, that its roads would have been even more congested, and that its landscape would still be littered with dangerous relics of an industrial past. The conflict between the two perspectives left a legacy of half-measures, uncompleted projects, and improvements which took decades to enact, and which perhaps hindered the development of the Black Country in later years. The same conflict might also explain the slow decline in attachment to town, and the consequent rise in attachment to region that has characterised the Black Country in recent years.

The term 'Black Country' has always been one of convenience, covering a disparate geography, population and society, and this remained true after the war. The historian Linda Colley wrote: "Identities are not like hats. Human beings can and do put on several at the same time."[327] So it was, and is, with the Black Country. Local pride certainly interacted with loyalty to an employer: even when a Darlaston worker was employed elsewhere, he could still be proud of his town's connection to the country's largest family-owned business, Rubery Owen. Work loyalty overlapped with religion, as those seeking a job at Gibbon's in Gornal knew. Class identity interacted with housing tenure, particularly so when 'race' was brought into the equation. Racial or ethnic identity overlapped with local pride, as immigrants to Smethwick found out, or with work and leisure, as in Madho Ram Mahimi's poetry about Wolverhampton pubs. Gender and sexuality interacted in the pub too, as Alice Cronin might have told you. All of these complexities are Black Country stories; but the Black Country is also as complex as each individual story.

De-industrialisation and Nostalgia

The Black Country ended the 1960s under full steam, but new problems were emerging. Rubery Owen was the perfect example. In 1969, Sir Alfred Owen was on the board of 99 different companies, chairman of over 80, most particularly of the £100m Rubery Owen empire, with huge works in Darlaston, Yorkshire, Wales, Scotland, South Africa and Australia. Yet financial pressures were already coming to bear. A huge inheritance tax bill led to pressure to make major structural adjustments. *The Times* reported that "Sir Alfred refused to part with any of his beloved empire," but in the end the firm was forced to close its famous structural fabrications division, and begin selling subsidiary companies, making redundancies (and facing strikes), and relying on extended credit to make ends meet.[328]

The 1970s saw Britain's share of global industrial output fall as manufacturing boomed in competitor economies, including West Germany and Japan. Edward Heath's Conservative government (1970-1974) was beset by economic crises globally and at home, with international oil embargoes and miners' strikes, and entry into the European Economic Community – long promoted by Black Country business leaders – seen as the only way to prevent this terminal decline. Some exploited this anxiety to push a political agenda that then, as now, was extreme. Enoch Powell remained Wolverhampton's MP until 1974, still claiming that areas of Wolverhampton "have ceased to be part of England".[329] Race relations became increasingly fraught as economic fears were stoked by racist groups like the National Front. Harold Wilson's second Labour government (1974-1976) implemented some drastic measures – including nationalisation of the car industry – but eventually had to limp to the International Monetary Fund for a £2.3bn bailout in 1976. Britain had become the 'sick man of Europe'. By the 'winter of discontent' in 1978-9, 1.5 million people were unemployed, public sector strikes rocked the country, and Wilson's successor James Callaghan (1976-1979) looked increasingly vulnerable.[330]

These were the headlines, at least. The other story is that the 1970s saw working-class wages at their highest point and income inequality at its lowest.[331] Industrial workers in the Black Country were better-paid and better-protected in their work than ever, the post-war housing shortage was almost completely met, and personal consumption was at a peak. In April 1979,

Courtesy of Black Country Living Museum

'Hell of a job' – a photograph of a steelworks in Wednesbury taken by G Bowater of the Wednesbury Photographic Society in 1967.

Steven Cartwright for Creative Black Country's Desi Pubs Landmark Project

Stained glass windows at the Red Lion, West Bromwich, designed by Steven Cartwright to represent the story of migration from South Asia into the Black Country.

Bilston Steelworks became a victim of structural reorganisation within the nationalised steel industry and closed, with almost 3,000 redundancies, even though it was still in profit. At the front line of protests was the Bradley-born steelworker, market trader, bingo caller, and Wolverhampton's youngest councillor, elected in 1964 aged 22, Dennis Turner, later MP for Wolverhampton South-East and Baron Bilston. The steelworkers showed how reliant the Black Country was on a diverse workforce by the end of the 1970s: almost a quarter of employees were from minority ethnic backgrounds, including those listed as "African, Dutch, German, Hungarian, Indian, Irish, Kenyan, Lithuanian, Pakistani, West Indian [and] Yugoslavian".[332]

Despite continuing, often violent racism during the 1970s and 1980s, there was strong evidence of genuine cultural exchange. Emblematic of this are the Black Country desi pubs, which began to appear in the late 1970s – old pubs taken over by South Asian landlords to serve local beer and Punjabi food. Symbolic of this change was Smethwick's Red Cow: once home to a colour bar and anti-immigration organisations, in the twenty-first century it serves curries and grills to a diverse clientele.[333]

Three weeks after Bilston's closure, Margaret Thatcher's Conservatives won a convincing general election victory and set about radically restructuring the economy away from industry and towards financial services, resulting in recessions, strikes, and a substantial reduction of the role of manufacturing in the British economy. The Black Country was an exemplar of this de-industrialisation. Rubery Owen was a notable casualty of the restructuring of the British car industry, shedding hundreds of Black Country jobs before its Darlaston works closed in 1981. 1,500 people lost their jobs when Wednesbury's Patent Shaft steelworks closed in 1980, and 1,300 when Round Oak followed suit in 1982. These closures heralded a bleak period in the Black Country's illustrious industrial history. Most of the Birmid's Smethwick foundries, Chance's glassworks in Smethwick, Sankey's in Bilston, FH Lloyd's Wednesbury works, Guy Motors' Fallings Park factory, Noah Hingley in Netherton, John Thompson, many of GKN's subsidiaries, and scores of other firms closed in the early 1980s, leaving a landscape pitted with derelict factories and a population scarred by employment rates sometimes approaching 40 per cent. Between 1978 and 1983, employment in manufacturing in the wider region fell by a third – significantly more than the 20 per cent fall seen nationally – and relative earnings fell from being the highest of any region in 1970, to almost the lowest. Although the Black Country is an industrial region still, it never returned – and likely never will – to the position it held in the 1960s.[334]

The history of the Black Country is inevitably viewed from this perspective of a post-industrial society. The post-war period appears to mark the climax of an industrial society that had been in the making since Lord Dudley's illegitimate son Dud recorded 20,000 metalworkers in the Black Country in 1665. Three centuries later, the Black Country was still an essential part of the British economy, making everything that the country required to run, and it was not expected to slow down. Within just two decades though, Black Country industry was a shadow of its former self.[335]

However, there is another interpretation, according to which the post-war period appears as an aberration in a long social history. Since industrialisation began in the Black Country, the needs of its working people had always taken second place behind the needs of capital: most of the time, the quest for profit trumped workers' rights. After the Second World War, serious attempts were made for the first time to reverse this. Never before had the Black Country experienced full employment: gone were the insecurity and exploitation of the workers, replaced by a safety net of health care, pensions, and social security. It seemed that the "great recasting of values" promised by William Beveridge had come to pass, and that the ordinary working people of the Black Country and Britain were truly to have a say in the way the economy, the country was run. In this more pessimistic view, the de-industrialisation of the 1980s restored the social relations of an earlier period, where workers were forced to be in thrall to the masters once again.[336]

The historian James Vernon has called this period the "brief life of social democracy".[337] It forms a period to be nostalgic for: bustling high streets and busy factories, local teams winning the league, no queues at the job centre or urban malaise. In reality, of course, life was more complex and variable than this, especially for the more vulnerable: women, immigrants, gay people, the disabled. But when the Black Country was stripped of its industrial economy in the 1980s, this post-war period became something to be proud of. The Black Country Living Museum, the Black Country Development Corporation of the late 1980s and early 1990s, and the Black Country flag of the 2010s, have all employed nostalgia for the Black Country's industrial history to make the region more distinctive, more promotable and more unified than could have been imagined in any period before. The debates about where the Black Country starts and stops rumble on, of course. But at least now local authorities are making sure that they are included in the Black Country's story, rather than being ashamed of its associations.

Nostalgia can have both positive and negative connotations. At its worst, nostalgia imagines a past that never existed, or that glosses over the full picture. The post-war period is ripe for this. This was a time when social democratic politics and increasing affluence sat uncomfortably alongside rigidly conservative morals and widespread prejudice, and it would be easy to pick a grand narrative which highlighted one or the other as 'traditional', or normative, in British culture. The work of history is to puncture such over-simplifications, and the Black Country is a good example of why history is always more complicated than we might imagine. Recent political debates have drawn on imagery of the 1950s as an era before many of the problems of the modern world existed. In 2016 the then Liberal Democrat leader Vince Cable suggested of those voting for Brexit that "too many were driven by nostalgia for a world where passports were blue, faces were white, and the map was coloured imperial pink".[338] This too is an over-simplification, and the complex voting patterns of the Black Country in subsequent general elections stand as evidence of that, but in highlighting this tendency, Cable was aware that nostalgia can misrepresent the past, and that seeking the restoration of an imagined 'Golden Age' comes with its own risks.

There is a positive side to nostalgia, however. Whilst avoiding rose-tinted spectacles, and with careful contextualisation, reflecting on what was good about the post-war Black Country can help us actively engage with the present and the future. If work was such a positive experience in this period, we might ask, why was that? If communities were so strong, what might we learn from the past to improve the present? As I am writing this conclusion, the world looks likely to change once again after the coronavirus pandemic: how might the experiences of a world rebuilding itself help us to imagine the future? [339]

The post-war period is thus a crucial

Express & Star/Wolverhampton Archives

Clocking off at Britool, Wolverhampton, in 1961.

piece of the Black Country's history. By placing the social-democratic context of the 1940s, 1950s and 1960s within the Black Country's long, proud history, we see that prosperity and inequality do not have to go hand in hand, but that an industrial region like the Black Country can still be hugely successful when its wealth is more evenly distributed. This was a period when the Black Country thrived. It retained its distinct character – or rather multiple characters – while embracing modernity, and provided the 'white heat' which fuelled Britain's success at home and abroad. Whether these years are seen as the last hurrah of British industry, or a breathing space for the working class in the long history of British industrial capitalism, the people of the Black Country really "never had it so good".

Appendix 1: Glossary and Acronyms

ACRONYMS

AUFW	Associated Union of Foundry Workers
BCN	Birmingham Canal Navigations
BICA	Birmingham Immigration Control Association (later British Immigration Control Association)
BCLM	Black Country Living Museum (originally Black Country Museum)
BCS	Black Country Society
BMC	British Motor Corporation
BRD	Blade Research & Development (a GKN subsidiary based in Aldridge)
BRM	British Racing Motors
BSC	British Steel Corporation
BTC	British Transport Commission
CB	County Borough
DP	Displaced Person
DCT	Dudley Canal Trust
EVW	European Voluntary Worker
GKN	Guest, Keen & Nettlefold
ICI	Imperial Chemical Industries
IWA	Indian Workers' Association
IWA	Inland Waterways Association
ISC	Iron and Steel Corporation of Great Britain
ISHRA	Iron and Steel Holding and Realisation Agency
LGBT	Lesbian, Gay, Bisexual and Transgender
MB	Municipal Borough
MOH	Medical Officer of Health
NCB	National Coal Board
NHS	National Health Service
MOH	Medical Officer of Health
NALGO	National Association of Local Government Officers, later National and Local Government Officers' Association
NSHC	National Services Hostels Corporation
POW	Prisoner of War
RDC	Rural District Council
STC	Standard-Triumph Company
TGWU	Transport and General Workers' Union
TI	Tube Investments Group
URC	Urban District Council
WHS	William Hunt & Son's, Oldbury
WVS	Women's Voluntary Service
VE	Victory in Europe

GLOSSARY

Arc furnace: an electric-powered industrial furnace used in foundries and steelmaking.

Austerity: a policy of strictly limited government spending during times of economic hardship, usually considered to encompass the Second World War up to 1951 or 1954.

Beveridge Report: *Social Insurance and Allied Services* by William Beveridge, published in 1942, which formed the basis for many of the post-war Labour government's policies. It outlined the biggest problems facing society (the five 'Giant evils:' squalor, ignorance, want, idleness, and disease) and recommended a number of social reforms that collectively became known as a 'welfare state'.

Bevin Boys: a tenth of men conscripted between 1943 and 1948 were employed in British coal mines rather than military service. Most were chosen by lot; some chose this role as an alternative to fighting. The title came from the Minister of Labour and National Service, Ernest Bevin.

Blast furnace: an industrial furnace used in iron and steelmaking, in which air is blasted in to cause chemical reactions to the molten metal inside.

"Blue Billy": calcium sulphate, a blue-grey waste product from the chemical industry. Large heaps were found in areas of the Black Country where this industry was concentrated, particular Oldbury.

Brew'us: a domestic outbuilding traditionally used for washing clothes, bathing and other chores.

British Empire: the collective title for the dominions, colonies, protectorates, mandates and other territories ruled by the United Kingdom. At its peak in the 1920s, the British Empire governed nearly a quarter of the world's land mass, and nearly a quarter of its population.

British Restaurant: a subsidised restaurant run by local authorities during and after the Second World War. From 1947 the profitable British Restaurants converted to Civic Restaurants.

Bull (horn): a siren used to mark shift changeovers in factories.

Casting (metal): the process of delivering molten metal into a mould containing a hollow shape of the intended shape. Casting may also refer to the cast metal product. Pressure casting is a form of metal casting in which air pressure is used rather than gravity to force molten metal into a mould.

Charging car: moving part of a mechanised foundry designed to feed into the furnace.

Civic Restaurant: see British Restaurants.

Civil Defence Corps: a volunteer organisation operated in Britain between 1949 and 1968 to be prepared for dealing with the aftermath of a major national emergency such as a nuclear strike.

Coal-picking: collecting coal from the remains of former colliery workings.

Cold-forming, cold-rolling: processes in which cold metal is worked at high speed and high pressure. Working cold metal can create a more precisely-measured end-product and more consistent finish than hot-forming or hot-rolling.

Colour bar: an unofficial ban preventing access or service to people of colour. No legal colour bar was enforced in the UK (compared to the legal colour segregation in the Southern USA) but people of colour still found that they could be excluded from shops, lodgings, pubs and workplaces because they were not white. Such discrimination was first formally legislated against in the Race Relations Act 1965.

Commonwealth of Nations: a political association, currently including 53 nations that were former territories of the British Empire. The British Commonwealth of Nations was created through the Balfour Declaration of 1926; the organisation as it exists today was constituted via the London Declaration of 1949.

Commonwealth Immigrants Act 1962: Act of Parliament passed by Harold Macmillan's Conservative government, by which all Commonwealth Citizens and Citizens of the UK and its Colonies *not* born in the UK or holding a UK passport were subject to immigration controls. After this, only a tightly-controlled number of 'vouchers' were issued by the government granting the right to settle.

Commonwealth Immigrants Act 1968: Act of Parliament passed by Harold Wilson's Labour government, by which the right of Citizens of the United Kingdom and Colonies to settle in Britain was further restricted. After this Act, only those who had at least one parent or grandparent born in Britain were permitted to settle.

Core (foundry): a device used in casting and moulding processes to produce the cavity into which molten metal is poured to give a casting its shape.

Core binder: a material – often an oil or resin – added to a casting core.

Corporation: the administrative organisation of a local authority.

Court (housing): a development of typically small houses around a courtyard, often to the rear of an older, larger house. This housing was often built quickly and cheaply with little regard for sanitation or living conditions, to house the industrial working classes, and was common in the West Midlands, as well as in other industrial cities in the nineteenth century.

Die: a mould to shape forged metal. Metal is placed onto the die and then struck to fill the shape of the die.

Displaced Person (DP): the official name for those displaced by the Second World War, including those in Nazi camps and refugees from war-torn areas.

Dominion: a semi-independent political entity forming a tier within the British Empire. The Dominions recognised as autonomous by the 1926 Balfour Declaration were Australia, South Africa, Canada, Newfoundland and the Irish Free State; from the late 1940s India, Pakistan and Ceylon (Sri Lanka) joined them until they gained their full independence.

Drop hammers: equipment used in the metal forging process, involving a heavy weight raised by a powered mechanism, and dropped onto a die to strike the metal. Drop forging was common in the Black Country from around the First World War, and gives great strength and consistency to the product.

Education Act 1944: Act of Parliament passed by Winston Churchill's wartime National Government, creating a tripartite education system of Grammar Schools, Technical Schools and Secondary Modern Schools.

European Voluntary Worker (EVW): workers recruited from Eastern Europe and the Baltic states under a number of schemes in the late 1940s and early 1950s.

HMT *Empire Windrush:* a ship famously associated with the arrival of the first generation of Caribbean migrants to the UK. It was launched as the cruise ship MV *Monte Rosa* in Hamburg, Germany in 1930, but was appropriated by Britain as a prize of war after the Second World War and renamed. It docked in Kingston, Jamaica in 1948 to pick up servicemen on leave but was also joined by around 800 Caribbean residents and 66 Polish exiles who had been living in Mexico, in anticipation of the passing of the British Nationality Act and the Polish Resettlement Act. The *Windrush* arrived at Tilbury Docks in Essex on 21 June 1948 and has come to mark the symbolic beginning of post-war Commonwealth migration to Britain.

Fabrication (metalwork): the process of cutting, bending and assembling (typically welding) metal into structures, known as fabrications.

Faggots: a traditional working-class offal dish, often made from minced pork, liver and heart and wrapped in bacon or pig's caul. As a thrifty but nutritious dish, faggots have a long association with Black Country cooking.

Festival of Britain, 1951: a national exhibition and fair inaugurated by Clement Attlee's Labour government and open between May and October 1951. The Festival centred on the major exhibition on the South Bank of the River Thames in London, but also featured events, parades, competitions, travelling exhibitions and even a Festival ship, HMS *Campania*.

Fireclay: a type of especially heat-resistant clay used for various manufacturing purposes. The characteristics of the fireclay mined in the south-western Black Country made it particularly suitable for industrial uses such as furnace linings and gasworks plant.

Forge, forging (metal): an industrial process in which metal is shaped by striking. Forging can be done with cold, warm or hot metal. In the Black Country, metal forging ranged from hand-forged small metal items like nails or small chains, to mass-produced drop-forged car components, to huge, bespoke forged items made with presses of many tons.

Formica: a laminated composite material made from melamine resin, invented in the USA in 1912. It became increasingly popular in the 1950s for its wipe-clean, heat-resistant properties.

Foundry (metal): an industrial space in which metal castings are produced.

Furnaceman: a job within an iron or steelworks involving maintenance of the furnace and 'tapping' it at the correct moment.

Gas, town/coal and natural: a fuel used for street-lighting, industry and domestic use from the early nineteenth century. One of the first gas light installations was at Smethwick's Soho Foundry in 1803-4, then the manufacturing base of the Boulton & Watt Company. Gas was produced principally from the burning of coal and resulted in large and small gasworks across Britain; its use by municipal authorities gave it the alternative name town gas. By the 1940s, gas was struggling to compete with electricity, and was itself replaced when natural gas deposits were discovered in the North Sea. Natural gas was non-toxic, more efficient and cheaper to produce. The conversion from town gas to natural gas took place between 1967 and 1987, with all gas appliances converted and all town gas works decommissioned.

Glass cone: a conical structure designed to channel air into furnaces and as a workspace for glassmaking. Cones were common in the glassmaking district of Amblecote and Wordsley, near Stourbridge; now, only the Red House Glass Cone, formerly belonging to Stuart Crystal, remains in the Black Country.

Greenfield land: undeveloped or agricultural land which has not been built on previously, as distinct from brownfield or derelict land.

Groaty pudding: also known as grorty pudding or groaty dick, a traditional Black Country dish made from groats (whole grains of various cereals including oats, wheat, rye and barley), leeks, onions and beef.

Gurdwara: a place of worship for Sikhs.

Hollowware: metal table and cookware, excluding cutlery and utensils. Hollowware may be enamelled, and is frequently cast from iron, steel or aluminium.

Hot-forming, hot-rolling: processes in which metal is worked at high temperature. Working hot metal can give a more accurate and cheaper result than cold-formed metal products.

Ironstone: a sedimentary rock once mined extensively in the Black Country, and used as a source of iron. The stone is first fired in a kiln then smelted in a blast furnace to produce raw, or pig, iron. The Black Country's ironstone deposits were largely exhausted by the mid-nineteenth century.

Kiln, beehive kiln, downdraught kiln: an oven used to fire clay products, often bricks. Kilns came in many shapes and sizes, though the most common in the Black Country was the cylindrical, dome-roofed 'beehive' kiln. This was a form of 'downdraught' kiln, in which air is forced down from the domed roof to ensure an even distribution of heat.

Lend-Lease: an American programme to provide Allied powers with aid and military provisions during the Second World War.

Limestone: a carbonate sedimentary rock used in building, concrete, soil conditioner, and in blast furnaces to remove impurities in iron ore. Limestone was mined extensively in the Black Country through to the early twentieth century.

Machining, machine tools (metal): the final stage of the metalworking process to produce the finished product. Machine tools, which can include shears, grinders, cutters, lathes and many more, are used to work cast or forged metal items. In the Black Country, the finishing process is often referred to as "fettling."

Marl hole: a large pit from which clay, or 'marl' is or was dug.

Marshall Aid, Marshall Plan: an American aid programme between 1948 and 1952, officially known as the European Recovery Programme, for European nations affected by war. Britain received the largest share (26% of the total $12 billion, equivalent to $100 billion, or £80 billion, in 2020); other recipients included both Allied and Axis powers, although the Soviet Union refused aid and blocked it to Eastern European nations under its influence.

Medical Officer of Health: a local authority official in charge of the public health of the community.

Melamine resin: a combination of the industrial compounds melamine and formaldehyde, patented in 1936. Melamine resin was used in Formica and the tableware popularised by Oldbury's British Industrial Plastics, who used the trade name Melmex.

Migration, migrant: the movement of people from one place to another, regardless of physical or political boundaries. Emigration is the act of moving *from* a country; immigration is the act of moving *to* a country.

Miscegenation: the mixing of racial groups through marriage or procreation.

Modernism (architecture): a style of architecture developed during the first half of the twentieth century, and the dominant style from the Second World War to the 1980s. Modernist architecture is guided by function, with form following, and is characterised by minimalism and lack of ornament. A derivative of modernism was Brutalism, characterised by stark shapes and exposed concrete finish. Dudley Zoo's "Tecton" structures designed by Berthold Lubetkin (1937) are Black Country examples of Modernism; Wolverhampton School of Art (1968-9) is an example of Brutalism.

Moulding, moulder: the making of a mould to shape metal castings.

Munitions: military equipment and weapons. Many Black Country factories were turned over to military production during both world wars.

National Insurance (NI): a compulsory, contributory tax system paid by workers and employers to fund state benefits. NI was introduced in 1911 by Chancellor of the Exchequer David Lloyd George as a system of health insurance for workers. It was expanded in 1948 by Attlee's Labour government to cover health, pension and unemployment, including the National Health Service.

National Service: a system of peacetime conscription in operation from 1949 to 1963 (the last men to be called up began service in 1960). Healthy males between 17 and 21 were expected to serve 18 months' military service.

Nationalisation: the process of transferring private assets into public ownership. In Britain, means of production such as coal mining, services such as railways or healthcare, and industries such as steel were all nationalised at some point. The opposite process is privatisation.

Nissen hut: a prefabricated steel building designed during the First World War, and used extensively in the Second World War.

Nutty slack: a cheap fuel consisting of small 'nuts' of coal and coal dust known as 'slack'. Nutty slack was not rationed like ordinary coal, and was promoted as an alternative source of fuel.

Outwork: work completed in the home, most often by women. Historical examples include small chainmaking and nailing, carding items such as hair grips, or taking in laundry.

Partition of India: the division of British India into two autonomous dominions, India and Pakistan, in 1947. Two states – Punjab in the West, and Bengal in the East – were divided by religious majority, prompting mass migrations and widespread violence. The Dominion of India became the secular, independent Republic of India (remaining within the Commonwealth) in 1950; Pakistan became the Islamic Republic of Pakistan in 1956; following civil war, East Pakistan gained independence from Pakistan in 1971, becoming the People's Republic of Bangladesh.

Pig iron: also known as crude iron, made by smelting iron ore into blocks known as 'pigs'.

Plate steel: sheet metal with a thickness greater than 6mm (1/4 inch).

Plating: the process of covering a conductive surface with metal.

Poliomyelitis: a preventable, infectious disease often abbreviated to polio, causing muscle weakness and sometimes resulting in permanent disability or occasionally death. Polio was common in post-war Britain, but has now been eradicated from Europe.

Prefabrication, prefabs: the process of manufacturing parts of a structure in advance and assembling them on-site. 'Prefabs' typically refer to the large number of prefabricated domestic dwellings manufactured immediately after the Second World War to provide temporary housing. Popular prefabs included the Airey house, Taylor-Woodrow's Arcon, Orlit Co.'s two-storey house, Tarran houses, and George Wimpey's 'no-fines' houses. See also, system-building.

Privatisation: the process of transferring publicly owned assets into private hands. Industries such as gas, electricity and rail that were nationalised during the post-war period have since been privatised.

Puddling: the process of stirring molten iron to reduce inconsistencies and brittleness.

Race, racial: a historical concept in the natural and social sciences, used to categorise human beings into types on biological grounds. Today, scholars from disciplines ranging from biology to sociology agree that there is no biological basis for 'race', but that this belief has had, and continues to have, material consequences. For instance, the trade in enslaved people, justified on the grounds that African captives were 'savage' or 'uncivilised'; the eugenics movement pioneered in Britain in the early twentieth century; and racial profiling in late twentieth-century policing have all had racial justifications. 'Race' is not synonymous with 'ethnicity' (a group which identify with each other based on presumed shared characteristics including common language, ancestry, history, society or culture) or 'nationality' (the legal relationship between an individual and a state).

Race Relations Act 1965: Act of Parliament passed by Harold Wilson's Labour government, the first to outlaw discrimination on "grounds of colour, race, or ethnic or national origins".

Racism: the belief that some 'races' are superior or inferior to others. In practice, racism has defined structures of power at least since the period of imperial slavery, and continues to have lasting, material effects on the lives of those racialised as something other than the dominant power in a society.

Rationing: a government scheme to limit the availability of certain goods in a period of economic or political difficulty. In Britain, fuel, clothing, paper and many food and household items were rationed during the Second World War to ensure that enough could be had by all. After the war, economic difficulties and poor weather meant that rationing continued throughout the 1940s, in some cases more stringently than during the war – for instance, bread and potatoes were not rationed until after the war. The last rationed goods became freely available on 4 July 1954.

Rayon: a synthetic fibre manufactured from cellulose. Rayon was manufactured in the Black Country at Courtauld's Wolverhampton works.

Reconstruction: a catch-all term for the spirit of regeneration following the Second World War, particularly focusing on the rebuilding of land and buildings affected by enemy action, and embracing modern planning techniques.

Refractory, refractories: a refractory material is heat-resistant. Refractories usually refers to a ceramic product manufactured to withstand very high temperatures, for example, firebricks used in kilns.

Remittance: a sum of money sent as a gift. Remittances were often sent by migrant workers in Britain to their families in the country they had emigrated from.

Retort: an airtight vessel used for chemical processes. Black Country fireclay was notably used to manufacture retorts for the coal gas industry.

"Rivers of blood": the name given to Enoch Powell's 1968 speech on immigration in Birmingham. Powell did not use this exact expression: the phrase comes from his quotation of Virgil's *Aeneid*: "As I look ahead, I am filled with foreboding; like the Roman, I seem to see 'the River Tiber foaming with much blood'."

Rolling mill: a factory site for the cold or hot rolling of metal, producing metal sections or bars.

Rowley Rag: a volcanic dolerite stone quarried in the Rowley Hills. The stone was particularly used for road surfaces and kerbs.

Section (metal): a length of metal typically produced with a rolling mill for a variety of purposes. These can vary in profile from simple bars, to girders for construction, to complex bespoke profiles.

Sheet steel: metal formed into thin, flat pieces.

Slag, slag heap: waste mineral matter from the iron and steel-making process. Not to be confused with spoil, which is waste matter from the coal-mining process.

Slum, Slum clearance: the demolition of areas of poor-quality housing, with a consequent relocation of residents. The term 'slum' gained popularity in the late nineteenth century to describe insanitary or dangerous areas of urban poverty, often with a moral stigma attached. The process that would later be known as slum clearance began in larger cities in the mid-nineteenth century, but became more common in the inter-war period.

Smelting: the process of extracting metal from its ore by heating and melting.

Smestow Brook: a tributary of the River Stour, rising in Wolverhampton and meeting the Stour at Prestwood, near Stourbridge. Sometimes known as the River Smestow.

Snoek: *Thyrsites atun*, a species of snake mackerel found in the southern Atlantic and Indian oceans. Canned snoek was imported into Britain in an attempt to mitigate rationing in the late 1940s, but was very unpopular.

Social democracy: a political and economic system characterised by a mixed economy embracing both capitalist markets and government intervention. Its aim is typically to achieve social justice within a liberal, democratic framework. Social democratic policies were, to a greater or lesser extent, the defining framework of most post-war Western economies. In Britain, the economic principles of John Maynard Keynes and William Beveridge – high taxes and high public spending – underpinned the welfare state and nationalisation of industry and, arguably, the post-war economic boom.

South Staffordshire coalfield: the region which forms the historic heart of the Black Country's coal industry. Not to be confused with the Cannock Chase coalfield, which is separated from the South Staffordshire field by the Bentley Fault.

Spiv: a slang word for a petty criminal involved in the black market, particularly during and shortly after the Second World War, when rationing was at its height.

Squatting: the occupation of an otherwise-unoccupied building not owned or rented by the squatter. Squatting in the Black Country has a long history dating back to the informal communities developed around coal-mining areas such as Rough Hills or the Black Delph; in the post-war period, the expression was most identified with the squatting movement in 1946, in which large numbers of families occupied abandoned military camps across Britain.

Stamping (metal): the process of manipulating metal sheets into specific shapes.

Steelworks: an industrial plant producing steel. A steelworks may be integrated, in which all steps from smelting to rolling are undertaken; or a site for the production of semi-finished casting products such as ingots or billets.

Superannuation: a pension programme organised by a business for its employees.

System-building: the semi-mechanised production of construction materials, particularly concrete for high-rise buildings. This may include completely prefabricated components of the building, or concrete panels that are poured and set on the building site. See also, prefabrication.

Tannery: a site where skins and hides are cured to produce leather.

Tapping the furnace: a process in iron or steel-making in which a furnaceman strikes the clay plug at the base of the blast furnace to remove it, and allows the molten metal to be poured. The job required significant experience to assess the exact moment to tap.

Tatting, tatters: the collection of scavenged or unwanted items for the purposes of selling on or recycling, otherwise known as the rag-and-bone trade. Tatters remained a common sight on Black Country streets much longer than elsewhere in Britain. The term can also refer to 'scrap pickers' like the writer John Petty, who scavenged industrial waste dumps for small metal items.

Teddy Boys: a British youth subculture of the 1950s. The name originates in the Edwardian fashions worn, such as tapered trousers and long draped jackets. Teddy Boys also became the subject of moral panics after they were blamed for vandalism and violence, particularly targeting immigrant minorities.

Town & Country Planning Act 1947: Act of Parliament passed by Clement Attlee's Labour government. It established the principle of planning permission and required planning authorities to prepare comprehensive development plans.

Transistor radio: a small, portable radio based on transistor technology, which became popular from the late 1950s.

Trolleybus: an electric bus, powered by overhead cables.

Tubes: cylindrical metal sections which were a key Black Country product, used for a wide variety of purposes from golf clubs to bicycles to construction.

Victory in Europe (VE), Victory over Japan (VJ) Days: celebrations of the end of the Second World War in Europe (8 May 1945), and of victory over Imperial Japan (15 August 1945)

Vesting Day: 1 January 1947 was the day on which coalmining in Britain was transferred to public ownership.

Welfare State: a form of government characterised by the universal, unconditional provision of social welfare for those of its citizens who require it, including insurance, healthcare, unemployment support and legal redress.

Appendix 2:
Gazetteer of Black Country industries

This appendix shows the major Black Country manufacturers of the post-war period. It is not exhaustive. Subsidiaries are listed alongside their parent company, rather than by industry. Only Black Country firms and subsidiaries are listed.

Coal (nationalised in 1947)

The British coal industry was nationalised under the Coal Industry Nationalisation Act 1946. The National Coal Board (NCB) was formed to take over all collieries in the country on 'Vesting Day', 1 January 1947. Open-cast mines followed in 1952. The NCB split into regional divisions: West Midlands headquarters was at Himley Hall. Remaining Black Country collieries in 1945 were:

- Baggeridge Colliery, Himley (closed 1968)
- Beech Tree Colliery, Cradley (closed 1958)
- Coombs Wood Colliery, Halesowen (closed 1952)
- Hamstead Colliery, West Bromwich (closed 1960)
- Sandwell Park (Jubilee) Colliery, West Bromwich (closed 1965)

Bricks and firebricks

A number of firebrick manufacturers also operated small collieries, as fireclay is frequently found between coal seams. These were not nationalised in 1947.

- Bromley Brickworks
- Corbyn's Hall Brickworks, Pensnett
- George King Harrison, Brierley Hill
- Harris & Pearson, Brierley Hill
- Himley Bricks, Kingswinford
- Hinton, Perry & Davenhill, Pensnett
    - Dreadnought Tiles
    - Ketley Bricks
- J & S Bagot, Dudley
- J Hall, Amblecote
- King Bros., Stourbridge
- Mobberley & Perry, Cradley
- Oak Farm Brickworks
- Price-Pearson (Refractories), Brierley Hill. Formed in 1957 from:
    - EJ & J Pearson, Amblecote and Brierley Hill
    - JT Price, Brierley Hill
- Rufford, Stourbridge
- Stourbridge Glazed Brick, Dudley
- Stourbridge Refractories, Pensnett
- Timmis & Co., Lye
- Trotter, Haines & Corbett, Stourbridge

Iron and Steel

The Iron and Steel Act 1949 formed the Iron & Steel Corporation of Great Britain (ISC) and nationalised the capital of 92 of the largest iron and steel companies, coming into effect in 1951. The move was opposed by the Conservative opposition who converted the ISC into the Iron and Steel Holding and Realisation Agency (ISHRA) in 1953, to sell the industry back into private hands. The ISHRA sold off all nationalised companies except the largest, Richard Thomas & Baldwins (based in South Wales but with works in the Black Country at Brockmoor). In 1967, Harold Wilson's Labour government nationalised the entire iron and steel industry as the British Steel Corporation (BSC). It should be noted that the complexity of the metalworking industry meant that many firms fell into several of the following categories.

Black Country firms nationalised under the Iron & Steel Corporation of Great Britain (1951)

- Birchley Rolling Mills, Wolverhampton and Oldbury – acquired 1954 by Wolverhampton Steel and Iron Company, forming Wolverhampton and Birchley Rolling Mills in 1955.
- Bradley & Foster's, Darlaston – pig iron. Part of Staveley Coal & Iron Co. in 1951, the parent company was sold by the ISHRA to Stewart's and Lloyd's, who formed a new company, Stanton & Staveley.
    - o Bradley (Concrete) Ltd., Darlaston – concrete
    - o Bradley (Darlaston) Ltd., Coseley – metallic abrasives
    - o Arblaster & Co. Ltd., Darlaston – drop forgings
- District Iron & Steel, Smethwick – re-acquired in 1953 by J Brockhouse & Co.
- John Bagnall & Sons, Tipton – acquired in 1955 by N Hingley & Sons
- Patent Shaft and Axletree Co. – acquired 1956 by Metro Cammell and Cammell-Laird
- Richard Thomas & Baldwin (headquarters in Neath)
    - o Cookley Works, Brockmoor
    - o Swindon Works, Dudley
    - o Netherton Works, Dudley
- Round Oak Steelworks, Brierley Hill – acquired 1953 by Tube Investments
- Stewarts and Lloyds (headquarters in Corby) – re-acquired in 1954 by Stewarts and Lloyds
    - o Spring Vale Steelworks, Bilston
    - o Coombs Wood Tube Works, Halesowen
    - o Crown Tube Works, Wednesbury
    - o Prothero Steel Tube Co., Wednesbury
- Wolverhampton Steel and Iron Company (1946) Ltd., Wolverhampton – acquired in 1954 by Thomas W Ward Ltd.

Black Country firms not nationalised in 1951

- British Rolling Mills, also known as Brymill, Tipton – rolling mills
- Ductile Steels, Willenhall – rolling mills
- FH Lloyd, Wednesbury
    - o EC and J Keay, Darlaston
- Midland Bright Drawn Steel & Engineering, West Bromwich – steel bars
    - o MCL & Repetition, Ltd., Oldbury – machined components
- HF Spencer & Co., Fordhouses, Wolverhampton – steel sheets and sections
- Stourbridge Rolling Mills, Stourbridge – rolling mills

Foundries

- Bilston Foundries, Bilston – sanitary castings
- Birmid Qualcast, Smethwick. Formed in 1967 from:
    - o Birmid Industries, Smethwick – iron, aluminium and magnesium castings
        - – Dartmouth Auto Castings, Smethwick – iron castings
        - – Midland Motor Cylinder, Smethwick – vehicle components: 'Chromidium', 'Honikrom' and 'Cromol'
        - – Pneulec, Smethwick – foundry equipment
    - o Qualcast (Wolverhampton) Ltd, Wolverhampton – engineering castings
        - – Qualcast (Swan Gardens), Wolverhampton – iron castings
- Beans Industries, Tipton – acquired by Standard Motor Company in 1956, British Leyland in 1968 – vehicle components
- Brickhouse Dudley, West Bromwich. Formed in 1967 from:
    - o Brickhouse Foundry, West Bromwich – pipes and drainage products
    - o Dudley & Dowell, Cradley Heath – iron castings
- Brockmoor Foundry, Brockmoor – malleable and grey iron
- Cannon Iron Foundries, Coseley – cookers and iron castings
- Conygre Foundry, Tipton – later incorporated into Birmid Industries – iron castings
- Glynwed Holdings, Bilston
    - o Allied Ironfounders, Bilston
    - o Darlaston Steel Stockholders, Darlaston – stockholders
    - o George Gadd & Co., Netherton – rolling mills
    - o Hipkiss Bros., Blackheath – pipe fittings
        - – Steelway, Wolverhampton - furniture
    - o Normalized Bolts, Darlaston – fastenings
        - – James Wiley & Sons, Darlaston - fastenings
    - o PH Muntz & Barwell, Tipton – non-ferrous and plastic tubes
    - o Steel Parts, West Bromwich – fastenings
    - o Wednesbury Tube Co., Wednesbury – tubes
- HW Lindop, Walsall – iron castings and plastics
- JH Lavender & Sons, West Bromwich – aluminium castings
- John Harper & Co, Willenhall – cast iron, Meehanite and ductile iron
- Phoenix Foundry, Bloxwich – malleable and blackheart castings
- Shotton Bros., Oldbury – blackheart malleable
- Thomas Dudley, Dudley – iron castings including "Dauntless" brand
- Triplex Foundries Group
    - o Churchfields Spring Co., West Bromwich – springs
        - – Walsall Spring & Presswork, Walsall - springs
    - o Dudley Wood Engineering, Netherton – constructional engineering
    - o Eclipse Foundry and Engineering Co., Tipton – iron, aluminium and non-ferrous castings
        - – Eclipse Metal Industries, Tipton - engineering
    - o Great Bridge Foundry, Great Bridge – non-ferrous and iron castings

    – Morris (Engineers) Ltd., Tipton - engineering
  - Henry Harrison & Son, Willenhall – 'Belfry' padlocks
  - Patterncrafts, Tipton – wood and metal patterns
  - Phipps Plastic Products, West Bromwich – plastics
    – Gibson, West Bromwich – plastics and safety glass
  - Sillett & Cooksey, Tipton – metal fabrications
  - Triplex Foundry, Tipton – grey iron castings
  - Vowles Foundries, West Bromwich – aluminium castings
    – Ridgacre Foundry, West Bromwich – sanitary castings
    – Vowles Aluminium Foundry Co., West Bromwich – aluminium castings
    – Vowles Bros., West Bromwich – iron castings
- William Barnsley Ltd., Bilston – non-ferrous castings
- William Mills, Wednesbury – aluminium castings

Manufacturing: metal boilers and pumps

- Baelz Engineering, Wolverhampton
- Cradley Boiler Co., Cradley Heath
- Edwin Danks, Oldbury
- H & T Danks, Netherton
- John Thompson, Ettingshall
  - John Thompson (Dudley), Dudley – boilers
  - John Thompson Water Tube Boilers, Ettingshall – boilers
  - John Thompson Motor Pressings, Ettingshall – vehicle components
  - John Thompson Beacon Windows, Wolverhampton - windows
  - John Thompson Castings, Ettingshall
  - John Thompson-Kennicott, Wolverhampton
  - Thompson Brothers (Bilston) Ltd., Bilston – tankers, acquired 1959
- Jones & Attwood, Stourbridge
- Joseph Evans and Sons, Wolverhampton
- Lee, Howl & Co., Tipton
- Tangye Brothers, Smethwick
- WG Allen & Sons, Tipton

Constructional Engineering

- Braithwaite & Co., West Bromwich
- Coseley Buildings, Ettingshall
- Hill & Smith, Brierley Hill
- Horseley Bridge & Thomas Piggot, Tipton
- Metal Sections, Tividale
- Rubery Owen, Darlaston

Drop forgings

- Burton, Delingpole & Co., Old Hill
- Dudley Drop Forging, Dudley

- Hughes-Johnson Stampings, Oldbury
- Victoria Drop Forgings, Willenhall
- WH Tildesley, Willenhall

Engineering and plant

- Angle Ring, Tipton – steel benders
- Birlec, Aldridge – furnaces
- Birmingham Sound Reproducers, Old Hill and Stourbridge – audio equipment
- British Thomson-Houston, Blackheath (headquarters Rugby, Warwickshire) – electrical engineering
- Contactor Switchgear, Walsall – electrical engineering
- Crabtree, Walsall – electrical engineering
- Daniel Smith Ltd., Wolverhampton – machine tools and engineering plant
- David Etchells & Son, Darlaston – furnaces
- Electric Construction Company, Wolverhampton – electrical engineering
    - ECC (Moulded Breakers), Wolverhampton – electrical engineering
    - Federal Electric, Wolverhampton – electrical engineering
- Ever Ready, Wolverhampton – electrical engineering
- Gibbons (Dudley), Lower Gornal
    - Gibbons Bros. (brickworks), Lower Gornal – bricks and retorts
    - GWB (Furnaces), Dudley – furnaces
    - FJ Ballard & Co., Tipton - furnaces
- Hampton & Beebee, Wednesbury – washers and engineering
- HC Milburn, Wolverhampton – refrigeration engineering and metalwork
- Hipkiss Brothers, Blackheath – steel manufacturing
- John Barnsley & Sons, Netherton – cranes and lifting gear
- John Cashmore, Tipton – machine tools
- Metal Products, Willenhall - alloys
- Metallisation Ltd., Netherton – metal spraying
- Quasi-Arc, Bilston – welding
- Samuel Platt, Wednesbury – machine tools and iron castings
- Simplex Electric Co., Oldbury – electrical engineering
- Siviter Group, Old Hill – engineering plant
- Victoria Engineering, Brierley Hill – engineering plant
- Villiers Engineering (later Norton-Villiers), Wolverhampton – engines
- Walter Somers, Halesowen – heavy forgings
- Wellman Smith Owen Engineering Corporation, Darlaston – furnaces
    - Wellman Smith Owen (Furnaces) Ltd., Darlaston
    - Wellman Incandescent Furnace Co., Smethwick
    - Incandescent Heat Co., Smethwick
- Wilkins & Mitchell, Darlaston – engineering
- Woden Transformer Co., Bilston – electrical engineering

Fastenings

- Charles Richards & Sons, Darlaston
- David Etchells & Sons, Darlaston
- FH Tomkins, Walsall
    - OD Guest, Walsall – fastenings
    - Bromford Iron & Steel Co., West Bromwich – steel manufacturing
- James Wiley & Sons, Darlaston
- Metal Closures, West Bromwich
- Newey Brothers, Tipton
- Steel Nut & Joseph Hampton Co, Darlaston
- Steel Parts, West Bromwich
- Stevens Screw Co., Wolverhampton
- W Martin Winn, Darlaston

Hollowware

- Archibald Kenrick & Sons, West Bromwich
- Bradley Group – acquired by Butterfield Group of Shipley, Yorkshire, 1959
    - Bradley & Co., Bilston – 'Beldray' hollowware
    - General Galvanizers, Wolverhampton – galvanising
    - Globe Tank & Foundry, Wolverhampton – 'Gloco' tanks
- Ernest Stevens, Cradley Heath – 'Judge' brand
- Izons & Co., West Bromwich
- Jury, Quarry Bank

Locks and safes

A very large number of lock manufacturers in Willenhall remained as small workshops rather than major employers. A gazetteer of lock and key manufacturers can be found online.

- Chubb, Wolverhampton
- Josiah Parkes, Willenhall – acquired by Chubb in 1965
- Walsall Locks and Cart Gear, Walsall
- Yale, Willenhall

Other metal manufacturing

- Alfred Allen & Sons, Lower Gornal – chutes and tanks
- Bilston Enamels, Bilston – enamelware
- British Pens, Bearwood – pens
- Fafnir Bearings, Wolverhampton - bearings
    - Fischer Bearings, Wolverhampton – bearings
- Guest, Keen & Nettlefold (GKN), Smethwick
    - Atlas Division (formerly F.W. Cotterill), Darlaston – nuts and bolts
    - Bayliss, Jones & Bayliss, Ettingshall – engineering, other metalwork
    - Birwelco, Wolverhampton - welding
    - Blade Research & Development (BRD), Aldridge – vehicle components

- C & B Smith, Wolverhampton – iron foundry
  - Executors of James Mills Ltd., Wolverhampton – steel manufacturing
  - Garrington's, Darlaston and Bromsgrove – tools
  - GKN Research, Wolverhampton – research and development
  - GKN Screws & Fasteners, Smethwick – fastenings
  - J & J Wiggins, Bloxwich – 'Old Hall' tableware
  - Joseph Sankey & Son, Bilston – hollowware, vehicle components, other metalwork
  - Ionic Plating, Smethwick – electroplating
  - Smethwick Drop Forging, Smethwick – drop forgings
  - Twisteel, Smethwick – reinforced concrete
- Imperial Metal Industries (IMI)
  - Wolverhampton Metal Co., Wednesfield – acquired 1964
    - James Bridge Copper Works, Darlaston – copper refinery
  - Marston Excelsior, Wolverhampton – radiators and machinery
- Henry Hope & Sons, Smethwick – windows
- John Folkes (Lye Forge) Ltd., Lye – heavy forgings
- Rubery Owen, Darlaston
  - Rubery Owen, Darlaston – vehicle components and constructional engineering
  - Bentley Hall Brickworks, Bentley – bricks
  - Charles Clark & Son, Wolverhampton - engineering
  - C & L Hill, Wolverhampton – non-ferrous castings
  - Nuts & Bolts (Darlaston) Ltd., Darlaston – fastenings
- Sidebotham's, Wednesfield – traps
- Skefko/SKF Bearings, Willenhall - bearings
- Star Aluminium, Wolverhampton – aluminium foil
- Taylor Law & Co., Stourbridge – kitchenware

Nails, chains, anchors and lifting gear

- WL Byers & Co., Cradley Heath - chains
- Eliza Tinsley & Co., Old Hill – chains and nails
- Griffin-Woodhouse, Cradley Heath – chains and lifting gear
- Isaiah Preston, Cradley Heath – chains and anchors
- William Hackett, Cradley – chains
- N Hingley & Sons, Netherton – acquired by FH Lloyd in 1966
  - Brierley Hill Colliery – colliery
  - Chain Developments, West Bromwich – chains
  - Brettell Lane Foundry, Brierley Hill – foundry
  - E Baylie & Co., Stourbridge – chains

  British Machine Made Cable Company, Netherton – cables
  - Halesowen Brick & Tile Company, Halesowen – brickworks
  - HP Parkes, Tipton – chains and anchors
  - John Bagnall & Sons, Tipton – iron manufacturing
  - John Bradley & Co., Stourbridge – steel sections

  - M & W Grazebrook, Netherton – heavy engineering
    - Westwood & Wrights, Brierley Hill and Dudley – structural engineering
  - Richard Sykes & Son, Cradley Heath – chains and anchors
  - Samuel Taylor & Sons (later British Tayco), Brierley Hill – chains and anchors
  - Wright's Forge, Tipton – heavy forgings
  - G Hartshorne & Co., Netherton – chains
  - Lloyd's British Testing Co. – chain testing
  - Midland & Coast Canal Carriers, Wolverhampton – canal carrying
  - Midland Research Company, Netherton – technological research
  - Mole & Beddall, Cradley – chains and anchors
  - Netherton Iron, Chain, Cable & Anchor Co., Netherton – chains and anchors
  - B Perkins & Sons, Stourbridge (later Turner's Flanges, Handsworth) – anchors and shackles
  - Joseph Wright & Co., Tipton – chains
  - Thomas Perrins & Co., Wollescote – chains
- Solid Swivel, Cradley Heath

Springs and scales

- W & T Avery, Smethwick
- Hill & Jackson, West Bromwich
- Northern Spring Co., West Bromwich
- George Salter & Co., West Bromwich
- Staffordshire Spring Co., West Bromwich
- West Bromwich Spring Co., West Bromwich

Tools

- Brades and Nash Tyzack Industries, Oldbury – acquired by Spear & Jackson, 1960; later Spearwell, 1967
  - William Hunt & Sons, Oldbury
  - Nash Tyzack Industries, Wollaston, Stourbridge
- Britool, Wolverhampton
- Chillington Tool Co., Wolverhampton
- Helix, Lye – stationery and scientific instruments
- Edward Elwell, Wednesbury Oldbury acquired by Spearwell, 1967
- Smith Edge Tools, Oldbury
- Staffordshire Edge Tools, Dudley
- Swindell & Co., Netherton
- Timmins & Foulkes, Dudley
- Wooldridge, Stourbridge

Tubes

- Allan Everitt, Smethwick
- Ductile Steels, Willenhall and Wednesfield
- Foster Brothers, Wednesbury
- John Knowles, Wednesbury
- Monmore Tubes, Wolverhampton

- Newman Tubes, Wednesbury
- Thomas Pritchard & Co., Wednesbury, formerly Tipper Brothers and John Knowles Ltd.
- Tube Investments (TI), Oldbury
    - o Accles & Pollock, Oldbury – tubes
    - o Helliwell Group, Walsall – vehicle components
    - o Metal Sections (later Metsec), Oldbury – cold rolled steel sections
    - o Pel (Practical Equipment Ltd), Rounds Green – steel furniture
    - o Raleigh Industries – bicycles – acquired 1960
    - o Talbot-Stead, Walsall – steel bars and tubes
    - o Tube Products, Oldbury – tubes
    - o Weldless Steel Tube Co., Wednesfield – tubes
- Wellington Tube Holdings
    - o Wellington Tube Works, Tipton – tubes
    - o Wellington Engineering Works, Tipton – engineering
    - o Gibbons (Dudley), Dudley – acquired 1962, bricks and engineering

See also: Stewart's & Lloyd's

Vehicles and components

- Birmingham Railway Carriage & Wagon Co., Smethwick – railway
- Comrade, Darlaston – bicycles
- Cramic Aircraft Components, Tipton – aviation
- Dowty Boulton Paul, Wolverhampton – aviation
- G Clancey, Halesowen – vehicle components
- Guy Motors, Wolverhampton – buses
- HM Hobson, Wolverhampton – acquired by Lucas Aerospace in 1970 – aviation
- Henry Meadows, Wolverhampton – cars and engineering
- Herman Smith, Netherton – aviation
- Isaiah Oldbury, Wednesbury – vehicle components
    - o Reliance Works, Wednesbury
    - o Britannia, Hill Top
- J Brockhouse & Co., West Bromwich – vehicles and vehicle components
    - o Brockhouse Castings, Wednesfield – steel foundry
    - o Brockhouse Steel Structures – constructional engineering
    - o District Iron & Steel Co. – steel manufacturing
    - o Lones, Vernon and Holden, Smethwick – vehicle components
    - o Richard Berry & Sons, Smethwick – springs
    - o Richard Disturnal & Co., Wednesbury – vehicle components
    - o Warwick Rim & Engineering, West Bromwich – steel sections
    - o WE Cramp & Sons, Tipton – bearings
- JA Phillips, Smethwick – bicycles
- Jensen, West Bromwich – cars
- Nortons-Tividale, Tipton – railway
- Simon Engineering, Dudley – hydraulic lifting vehicles

- Sunbeam, Wolverhampton – cars and buses
- Turner Manufacturing, Wolverhampton – vehicle components
- Viking, Wolverhampton – bicycles
- Wearwell, Wolverhampton – bicycles
- Willenhall Motor Radiator Co., Willenhall – vehicle components

Manufacturing: non-metal

- Albright & Wilson, Oldbury – chemicals
- British Industrial Plastics, Oldbury – plastics
- Carver & Co. – leather whips
- Chance Bros., Smethwick – industrial and domestic glassware
- Courtauld's, Wolverhampton – textiles
- Doulton & Co., Rowley Regis – sanitary earthenware
- Firkin's, West Bromwich – bakery
- Garner Boak, Walsall – leather
- Goodyear, Wolverhampton – tyres
- James Groves & Sons, Halesowen – buttons
- Hickinbottoms, Wednesbury – bakery
- Imperial Chemical Industries (ICI), Oldbury – chemicals
    - Chance & Hunt, Oldbury – chemicals
- Jabez Cliff, Walsall – leather
- Kenrick & Jefferson, West Bromwich – printing
- Mander Bros., Wolverhampton – paint
- Manifoldia, West Bromwich – printing
- Marsh & Baxter, Brierley Hill – pork products
- Midland County Dairies, Wolverhampton – dairy
- Midland Tar Distillers, Oldbury – chemicals
- Mitchell's & Butler, Cape Hill, Smethwick – brewery
    - Davenport, Walsall – brewery
    - Darby's Ales, West Bromwich – brewery
    - William Butler, Wolverhampton – acquired 1959 – brewery
- Palethorpes, Tipton – pork products
- Royal Brierley Crystal, Brierley Hill – domestic glass
- Scribbans-Kemp, Smethwick – bakery
- Stourbridge Glass, Stourbridge (later Tudor Crystal) – domestic glass
- Stuart Crystal, Stourbridge – domestic glass
- Tarmac, Ettingshall – construction materials
- T Mason & Sons, Smethwick – soft drinks
- Thomas Webb & Sons, Stourbridge – domestic glass
- Vono Industrial Products, Tipton
    - Cromwell's, Tipton – plastics
    - Duport Foundries, Tipton – iron foundry
        - Revo Electric, Tipton – acquired in 1956 – electrical engineering

- o Ewarts, Dudley – vehicle components
- o Teledictor, Dudley – electrical engineering
- o Vono Ltd., Tipton – furniture
  - – Grovewood, Tipton – furniture
- • Webb-Corbett, Stourbridge – domestic glass
- • Wolverhampton & Dudley Breweries, Wolverhampton – brewery
  - o Julia Hanson & Sons, Dudley – brewery

The British Motor Industry

By 1968 the British motor industry was dominated by four main manufacturers: British Leyland Motor Corporation (BLMC); Chrysler (UK); Ford; and Vauxhall. Each manufacturer was the product of mergers and acquisitions over many years, making the industry difficult to summarise. The following is a brief overview only.

British Leyland Motor Corporation Ltd. (BLMC)

Formed in 1968 as a merger of:

- • British Motor Holdings (BMH), formed in 1966 as a merger of:
  - o British Motor Corporation (BMC), Birmingham, formed in 1952 from:
    - – Austin Motor Company, Longbridge, Birmingham
    - – Nuffield Organisation formed from:
      - Morris Motors, Oxford
      - Morris Commercial, Oxford
      - Morris Industries Exports, Oxford
      - Wolseley Motors, Birmingham
      - MG Car Co., Oxford
      - Riley, Coventry
      - SU Carburettor Co., Birmingham
      - Nuffield Mechanizations and Aero, Birmingham
    - – Fisher & Ludlow, Birmingham, acquired 1953
    - – Pressed Steel Co., Oxford, acquired 1965
  - o Jaguar Cars renamed from SS Cars in 1945, based at Whitley, Coventry. Subsidiaries included:
    - – Daimler Motor Company, Coventry, acquired 1960
    - – Guy Motors, Wolverhampton, acquired 1962
    - – Coventry Climax, Coventry, acquired 1963
    - – Henry Meadows, Wolverhampton, acquired 1964
- • Leyland Motors founded in 1896, based at Leyland, Lancashire. Subsidiaries included:
  - o Albion Motors, Glasgow, acquired 1951
  - o Scammell Lorries, Watford, acquired 1955
  - o Standard-Triumph, Coventry, acquired 1961, a merger of:
    - – Triumph, Coventry
    - – Standard Motor Company, Coventry
    - – Beans Industries, Tipton, acquired 1956
  - o Associated Commercial Vehicles, London, acquired 1962, a merger of:
    - – Associated Equipment Co. (AEC), London

    – Thornycroft, London
    – Park Royal Vehicles, London
    – Charles H Roe, Leeds
  - Rover, Birmingham, acquired 1966, including subsidiary of:
    – Alvis, Coventry, acquired 1965
  - Aveling-Barford, Grantham, acquired 1967

BLMC was part-nationalised when it went bankrupt in 1975. The state-owned company was renamed Rover Group in 1986 and was re-privatised in 1988. It was bought by British Aerospace, then by BMW, who sold parts of the business off. A new consortium named MG Rover Group purchased the Longbridge plant in 2000, but it was declared insolvent in 2005.

Chrysler (UK)

Chrysler's British holdings were predominantly from its purchase of the large Rootes Group. Rootes was founded in 1913 in Hawkhurst, Kent. The group was built up from a number of subsidiaries, acquired before the Second World War:

- Hillman Motor Car Company, Coventry, acquired 1928
- Commercial Cars, Luton (also known as Commer), acquired 1929
- Humber, Coventry, acquired 1929, including subsidiaries
- Karrier Motors, Huddersfield, acquired 1934
- Sunbeam Motor Company, Wolverhampton, acquired 1934
  - Sunbeam Commercial Vehicles sold to Brockhouse (West Bromwich) in 1946, then to Guy Motors of Wolverhampton in 1948
- Clement Talbot, London, acquired 1934
- British Light Steel Pressings, London, acquired 1937
- Tilling-Stevens acquired 1950, founded 1897 in Maidstone
- Singer Motors acquired 1956, founded 1875 in Coventry

In 1949, Rootes became Rootes Motors, with three factories in Coventry, and others in Luton, Cricklewood and Acton. Chrysler purchased the Rootes Group in stages between 1964 and 1967.

Ford

The American company Ford built cars in the UK from 1911, at Trafford Park, Manchester. It opened a new factory at Dagenham, Essex, in 1931. Ford acquired Briggs Motor Bodies of Dagenham in 1953 and built further plants at Halewood, Merseyside in 1962, Basildon, Essex in 1964, and Swansea in 1965.

Vauxhall Motors

Vauxhall Motors was formed in 1907 in Luton and was bought out by the US company General Motors in 1925. Vauxhall formed Bedford as a commercial motors subsidiary in 1930, and continued to expand its Luton site after the Second World War. A new factory at Ellesmere Port was opened in 1962.

Appendix 3: Development of municipal authorities in the Black Country

The Black Country appeared on an Ordnance Survey map for the first time only in 2009. It has never been a single area for the purposes of local governance – only in recent years have quasi-non-governmental organisations like the Black Country Urban Development Corporation and the Black Country Local Enterprise Partnership taken a wider view of the region. Like many industrial regions, the Black Country has always sat across several administrative areas. The coalfield stretches across the South of Staffordshire, the North of Worcestershire and an exclave of Shropshire, so local governance – such as it was – up until the nineteenth century was coordinated from the county towns of Stafford and Worcester.

The Municipal Corporations Act of 1835 reformed the existing local government sector and permitted towns to be incorporated as Municipal Boroughs (MB). Walsall had been granted borough status as early as 1627, but it was joined by other towns following this act. In 1888 and 1894, Local Government Acts created administratively and electorally distinct County Boroughs, and a set of Municipal Boroughs, and Rural and Urban District Councils with varying degrees of autonomy from the County Council.

Local government reforms followed in the 1930s, 1950s, 1960s and then in 1974, when the many local authorities were merged into the four Metropolitan Boroughs that exist now: Dudley, Sandwell, Walsall and Wolverhampton (awarded City status in 2008). In that year the new West Midlands county and county council were created, comprising the four Black Country boroughs, plus Birmingham, Solihull and Coventry. West Midlands County Council was abolished in 1986. In 2016 the West Midlands Combined Authority was formed, and in 2017 an elected Mayor of the West Midlands was created.

Appendix 3: Development of municipal authorities in the Black Country

Authority	Historic County	Rural District Council	Urban District Council	Municipal Borough	County Borough	1966 reforms	1974 reforms	Type in 1945	Population in 1945	Population in 1964	Change 1945-1964
Aldridge	Staffordshire		1894	Brownhills		Merged with Brownhills UD	Walsall MB	Aldridge-	20,420	58,900	
Amblecote	Staffordshire	Part of Kingswirford RD	1898			Split between Stourbridge CB and Dudley CB	Dudley MB	Urban District	2,836	3,000	5.80%
Bilston	Staffordshire		1894	1933		Incorporated into Wolverhampton CB	Wolverhampton MB	Municipal Borough	31,600	32,700	3.50%
Brierley Hill	Staffordshire		1894	1934		Incorporated into Dudley CB	Dudley MB	Urban District	47,040	59,500	26.50%
Brownhills	Staffordshire	1877	1894			Merged with Aldridge	Walsall MB	Aldridge-Brownhills UD			
Coseley	Staffordshire		1894			Split between Wolverhampton CB, Dudley CB and West Bromwich CB	Dudley MB	Urban District	29,640	41,300	39.30%
Darlaston	Staffordshire		1894			Incorporated into Walsall CB	Walsall MB	Urban District	20,220	21,500	6.30%
Dudley	Worcestershire			1865	1889	Expanded to incorporate parts of Brierley Hill UD, Sedgley UD, Coseley UD and Tipton UD	Dudley MB	Dudley MB	62,100	63,900	2.90%
Halesowen	Worcestershire and Shropshire	1894	1925	1936			Dudley MB	Municipal Borough	36,800	45,200	22.80%
Heath Town	Staffordshire	1883; incorporated into Wolverhampton 1927				Wolverhampton MB	n/a				

Authority	Historic County Council	Rural District Council	Urban District	Municipal Borough	County Borough	1966 reforms	1974 reforms	Type in 1945	Population in 1945	Population in 1964	Change 1945-1964
Kingswinford	Staffordshire	1894	1934 split between Brierley Hill UD and Seisdon RD			Incorporated into Brierley Hill MB	Dudley MB	n/a-			
Lye & Wollescote	Worcestershire		1894	Incorporated into Stourbridge MB				n/a			
Oldbury	Worcestershire and Shropshire		1894			Amalgamation of Smethwick CB, Oldbury UD and Rowley Regis UD	Sandwell MB	Municipal Borough	35,310	54,200	53,50%
Quarry Bank	Staffordshire		1894	Incorporated into Brierley Hill MB		Incorporated into Dudley MB	Dudley MB	n/a			
Rowley Regis	Worcestershire		1894	1933		Amalgamation of Smethwick CB, Oldbury UD and Rowley Regis UD	Sandwell MB	Municipal Borough	44,780	49,100	9.60%
Sedgley	Staffordshire		1894			Split between Dudley CB, Wolverhampton CB and Seisdon RD	Dudley MB	Urban District	20,700	31,600	52,70%
Seisdon	Staffordshire	1894	1933 expanded to include parts of Kingswinford RD; parts removed to Brierley Hill UD and Wolverhampton CB				South Staffordshire District Council	Rural District			

Appendix 3: Development of municipal authorities in the Black Country

Authority	Historic County Council	Rural District Council	Urban District	Municipal Borough	County Borough	1966 reforms	1974 reforms	Type in 1945	Population in 1945	Population in 1964	Change 1945-1964
Short Heath	Staffordshire		1894 incorporated into Willenhall UD in 1933				Wolverhampton MB	n/a			
Smethwick	Staffordshire		1894	1899	1907	Amalgamation of Smethwick CB, Oldbury UD and Rowley Regis UD	Sandwell MB	County Borough	78,290	67,700	-13.50%
Stourbridge	Worcestershire		1894	1914		Incorporated into Amblecote UD	Dudley MB	Municipal Borough	35,310	45,900	30%
Tettenhall	Staffordshire		1894			Incorporated into Wolverhampton CB	Wolverhampton MB	Urban District	6,727	15,600	132%
Tipton	Staffordshire		1894	1938		Split between West Bromwich CB, Dudley CB and Warley CB	Sandwell MB	Municipal Borough	37,390	38,000	1.60%
Walsall	Staffordshire			1627	1888	Incorporated parts of Willenhall UD and Darlaston UD	Walsall MB	County Borough	107,600	119,900	11.40%
Walsall Foreign	Staffordshire		1894	1934 Incorporated into Walsall CB			Walsall MB	n/a			
Warley						Amalgamation of Smethwick CB, Oldbury UD and Rowley Regis UD	Sandwell MB	n/a			

Authority	**Historic County Council**	**Rural District Council**	**Urban District**	**Municipal Borough**	**County Borough**	**1966 reforms**	**1974 reforms**	**Type in 1945**	**Population in 1945**	**Population in 1964**	**Change 1945-1964**
Wednesbury	Staffordshire			1886			Sandwell MB	Municipal Borough	33,650	34,800	3.50%
Wednesfield	Staffordshire		1894			Incorporated into Wolverhampton CB	Wolverhampton MB	Urban District	14,540	35,100	141%
West Bromwich	Staffordshire			1882	1889	Incorporated parts of Tipton UD	Sandwell MB	County Borough	83,150	97,600	17.40%
Willenhall	Staffordshire		1894; amalgamated with Short Heath UD in 1933			Split between Wolverhampton CB and Walsall CB	Walsall MB	Urban District	28,320	35,200	24.30%
Wolverhampton	Staffordshire			1848	1889	Incorporated Bilston UD, Tettenhall UD and parts of Willenhall UD, Sedgley UD and Coseley UD	Wolverhampton MB	County Borough	147,200	150,200	2%
Total									923,623	1,100,900	19.20%

Selected Further Reading

Secondary sources

Addison, Paul. *No Turning Back: The Peacetime Revolutions of Post-War Britain.* Oxford: Oxford University Press, 2010.

Badger, Samantha J. 'Household Consumption, Food and the Working Class: The Black Country and Coventry 1930-1970.' Unpublished PhD thesis, University of Wolverhampton, 2004.

Bivins, Roberta E. *Contagious Communities: Medicine, Migration, and the NHS in Post-War Britain.* Oxford: Oxford University Press, 2015.

Black Country Roots. West Bromwich: Multistory, 2016.

Black Country Sikhs. West Bromwich: Multistory, 2019.

Boughton, John. *Municipal Dreams: The Rise and Fall of Council Housing.* London: Verso, 2018.

Chinn, Carl. *Black Country Memories (volumes 1-5).* Birmingham: Brewin Books, 2004-2008.

Chitham, Edward. *The Black Country.* Stroud: Amberley Publishing, 2009.

Church, Roy A. *The Rise and Decline of the British Motor Industry.* Cambridge: Cambridge University Press, 1995.

Delaney, Enda. *The Irish in Post-War Britain.* Oxford: Oxford University Press, 2007.

Dick, Malcolm, David J Eveleigh and Janet Sullivan (eds.) *The Black Country: A History in 100 Objects.* Dudley: Black Country Living Museum Publications, 2019.

Duffield, Mark R. *Black Radicalism and the Politics of Deindustrialization: The Hidden History of Indian Foundry Workers in the West Midlands.* Aldershot: Avebury, 1988.

Flinn, Catherine. *Rebuilding Britain's Blitzed Cities: Hopeful Dreams, Stark Realities.* London: Bloomsbury Academic, 2018.

Hennessy, Peter. *Never Again: Britain 1945-1951.* New York: Vintage, 1993.

Hennessy, Peter. *Having It So Good: Britain in the Fifties.* Harmondsworth: Penguin, 2007.

Hirsch, Shirin. *In the Shadow of Enoch Powell: Race, Locality and Resistance.* Manchester: Manchester University Press, 2018.

Jones, Harriet, and Michael D. Kandiah, (eds.) *The Myth of Consensus: New Views on British History, 1945 – 64.* London: Palgrave Macmillan, 1996.

Keith-Lucas, Bryan, and Peter G. Richards. *A History of Local Government in the Twentieth Century.* London: G. Allen & Unwin, 1978.

Kynaston, David. *Austerity Britain, 1945-1951.* London: Bloomsbury Publishing, 2010.

Kynaston, David. *Family Britain, 1951-1957.* London: A&C Black, 2009.

Kynaston, David. *Modernity Britain: 1957-1962.* London: Bloomsbury, 2014.

Langhamer, Claire. *Women's Leisure in England, 1920-1960.* Manchester: Manchester University Press, 2000.

Marwick, Arthur. *British Society Since 1945*. London: Penguin, 1990.

Marwick, Arthur. *The Sixties: Cultural Revolution in Britain, France, Italy, and the United States, c.1958 - c.1974*. Oxford: Oxford University Press, 1998.

McCarthy, Helen. 'Women, Marriage and Paid Work in Post-War Britain'. *Women's History Review* 26, no. 1 (2 January 2017): 46–61.

Millward, Gareth. *Vaccinating Britain: Mass Vaccination and the Public since the Second World War*. Manchester: Manchester University Press, 2019.

Morgan, Kenneth O. *Britain Since 1945: The People's Peace*. Oxford: Oxford University Press, 2001.

Olusoga, David. *Black and British: A Forgotten History*. London: Macmillan, 2016.

Quigley, Paul. 'Black Country Historic Landscape Characterisation'. Archaeology Data Service, 2009. Accessible online at http://archaeologydataservice.ac.uk/archives/view/blackcountry_hlc_2009/.

Ramdin, Ron. *The Making of the Black Working Class in Britain*. London: Verso Books, 2017.

Reeves, Frank. *Race and Borough Politics*. Aldershot: Avebury, 1989.

Schofield, Camilla. *Enoch Powell and the Making of Postcolonial Britain*. Cambridge: Cambridge University Press, 2013.

Singh, Gurharpal, and Darsham Singh Tatla. *Sikhs in Britain: The Making of a Community*. London: Zed Books, 2006.

Smith, Helen. *Masculinity, Class and Same-Sex Desire in Industrial England, 1895-1957*. Basingstoke: Palgrave Macmillan, 2015.

Spencer, Kenneth, Andy Taylor, Barbara Smith, John Mawson, Norman Flynn, and Richard Batley. *Crisis in the Industrial Heartland: A Study of the West Midlands*. Wotton-under-Edge: Clarendon Press, 1986.

Sykes, Richard P. M. 'Popular Religion in Dudley and the Gornals *c.*1914-1965'. Unpublished PhD thesis, University of Wolverhampton, 1999.

Thane, Pat. *Divided Kingdom: A History of Britain 1900 to the Present*. Cambridge: Cambridge University Press, 2018.

Watkiss Singleton, Rosalind. '"Old Habits Persist": Change and Continuity in Black Country Communities: Pensnett, Sedgley and Tipton, 1945-*c.*1970'. Unpublished PhD thesis, University of Wolverhampton, 2010.

Webster, Wendy. *Imagining Home: Gender, Race and National Identity, 1945-1964*. Abingdon: Routledge, 2005.

Williams, Ned. *Black Country Folk At Werk*. Dudley: Uralia Press, 1989.

Williams, Ned. *More Black Country Folk At Werk*. Dudley: Uralia Press, 1990.

Wills, Clair. *Lovers and Strangers: An Immigrant History of Post-War Britain*. London: Allen Lane, 2017.

Zweiniger-Bargielowska, Ina. *Austerity in Britain: Rationing, Controls, and Consumption, 1939-1955*. Oxford: OUP Oxford, 2000.

Primary sources

Abercrombie, Patrick and Herbert Jackson. 'West Midlands Plan' (1948), HLG 71/1262, The National Archives, Kew.

Allen, Walter. *The Black Country.* Paul Elek, 1946.

Birmingham Daily Post (available via British Newspaper Archive, https://www.britishnewspaperarchive.co.uk/)

Black and Ethnic Minority Experience Project (BEME) oral history project 1990-2000, Wolverhampton Archives DX-624

BCLM: Forging Ahead oral history project 2017-2022, Black Country Living Museum

Brennan, Tom. *Midland City: Wolverhampton, Social and Industrial Survey*. London: D. Dobson, 1948.

Department of Economic Affairs. *The West Midlands: A Regional Study*. London: H.M. Stationery Office, 1965.

Drabble, Phil. *The Black Country*. London: Robert Hale Ltd., 1952.

Dudley Herald (available on microfilm at Dudley Archives & Local History)

Foot, Paul. *Immigration and Race in British Politics*. London: Penguin, 1965.

Foot, Paul. *The Rise of Enoch Powell.* Harmondsworth: Penguin, 1969.

MACE (Media Archive of Central England), University of Lincoln.

Petty, John Wilson Angus. *Five Fags a Day: The Last Year of a Scrap-Picker*. London: Secker & Warburg, 1956.

Prem, Dhani R., *The Parliamentary Leper: Colour & British Politics*. Chandigarh: Metric, 1966.

Rich, Doris. 'Spare Time in the Black Country'. In *Living in Towns: Selected Research Papers in Urban Sociology of the Faculty of Commerce and Social Science, University of Birmingham,* edited by Leo Kuper, 299–370. London: The Cresset Press, 1953.

Sissons, Michael, and Philip French, (eds.) *Age of Austerity: 1945-1951*. London: Penguin, 1963.

Smethwick Telephone (available on microfilm at Sandwell Community History & Archives)

Stafford, Jo Mary. *Light in the Dust: An Autobiography.* London: Blake Publishing, 2002.

Staffordshire Advertiser (available via British Newspaper Archive, https://www.britishnewspaperarchive.co.uk/)

Staffordshire County Council. *County Development Plan*. Staffordshire County Council, 1958.

Walsall Observer (available via British Newspaper Archive, https://www.britishnewspaperarchive.co.uk/)

West Midlands Group for Post-War Reconstruction. *Conurbation*. Birmingham, 1948.

West Midland Industrial Development Association Ltd., *Industry in the West Midlands: A Review of Industry in Staffordshire, Shropshire, Worcestershire, Warwickshire and Herefordshire*. London: Ed. J. Burrow & Co, 1954.

Wolverhampton Express & Star (available on microfilm at Wolverhampton City Archives)

Worcestershire County Council. *County Development Plan.* Worcestershire County Council, 1951.

Acknowledgements

I've been making final revisions to *Forging Ahead* during the lockdown of the whole country in the face of the global coronavirus pandemic. It's a strange time to be doing anything, let alone writing. But it has demonstrated once again to me how much I have relied on others' help to get this far. Whilst I have done the writing, and therefore any errors or misjudgements are solely mine, I have done so as part of a huge project: not many historians can say that not only have they written a book, but also contributed towards the building of an entire town. Yet that's what Black Country Living Museum's *Forging Ahead* project is, and it's been a privilege to be part of it.

This strange time has also had some resonance when writing about the end of the Second World War, and the years that followed it. The government has recently introduced economic, social and political measures unthinkable even a year ago: restrictions on movement, financial support for businesses and individuals, state control of railways. Existing inequalities in society have been placed in stark relief by the pandemic, as those labelled 'unskilled' – supermarket workers, NHS cleaners – have found themselves on the front line. Talk has already turned to the dramatic impact this might have on the country in the future, and what Britain might look like as a society in the future feels very much up for grabs. Many of the debates echo those during the Second World War, when Britain – and the world – felt a new political moment approaching. And so it was. The 1930s of hunger marches and general strikes were replaced by the 1940s of welfare state and nationalised industries. It remains to be seen what might happen after 2020, but thinking about the past in a time like this can help us envision what we might want the future to look like – I hope *Forging Ahead* puts the Black Country's history in context while we go through this re-evaluation of ourselves.

I've often read acknowledgements in other history books and marvelled – I didn't think I even knew that many people, let alone had worked with them on a single project. Yet so many people have helped me get this far that I'm not sure I'll even be able to list them all here. Firstly, I would like to thank Mike Gibbs, Dr Malcolm Dick, Dr Jenni Butterworth, Dr Janet Sullivan, John and Averil Maskew and David Beattie at History West Midlands for their invitation to write for them, and their support. Jenni in particular has been a tremendous and constant help throughout, enabling me to develop an idea into a manuscript, and to really improve my writing.

I'd also like to thank Black Country Living Museum, and colleagues past and present. This book is a result entirely of the *Forging Ahead* development. Andrew Lovett, Jonathan Wilson and others encouraged me to turn a report that accompanied our application to the National Lottery Heritage Fund into a manuscript. My colleagues in Collections and Research have been a great support, helping in my research, providing a sounding board, and accompanying me on oral history trips, so thanks (in alphabetical order!) to Nadia Awal, JB, Irene de Boo, Karen Davies, Tom Dipple, Dr Jenny Gilbert, Holly Godward, Tim Hamilton, Steven Hearn, Jess van Hoef, John Hughes, Carol King, Liam Parkes, Chantelle Richards, Tim Shields, Helen Taylor, Debbie Watkins, Mel Weatherly, Clare Weston, and Glenis Williams. There are far too many others in the organisation to name, but I'm grateful to everyone I've worked with.

We also enlisted a fantastic array of local and academic historians to steer our thoughts along the way, so thank you too to everyone who contributed one way or another: Dr Jim Andrew, Prof Maggie Andrews, Dr Paul Belford, Dr Malcolm Dick, Pete Glews, Richard Harper, Keith Hodgkins, Joe Krawec, (soon to be Dr) Anna Muggeridge, Selwyn Owens, Trevor Raybould, Colin Shipley, Dr Janet Sullivan, Connie Wan, Judith Watkin, and Ned Williams. Paul Barnsley was a great help in thinking through nostalgia from a post-industrial perspective. A special thanks goes to academics at Warwick University who helped with the development of the Infant Welfare Centre project and have provided lots of other assistance: Prof Roberta Bivins, Dr Jenny Crane, Prof Angela Davies, Dr George Gosling, Dr Natalie Jones, Dr Gareth Millward, Dr Jack Saunders and Prof Mathew Thomson. My thanks too to the ever-helpful staff at our local archives in the Black Country: Dudley Archives & Local History Service, Sandwell Community History & Archives Service, Wolverhampton City Archives, and Walsall Local History Centre. Particular thanks to those archives and individuals who have given permission to include their pictures in *Forging Ahead*. Thanks to BCLM's Community and Access panel, particularly for reviewing the parts of chapter 4 containing racial slurs. This language and the image of graffiti (p.78) are now, correctly, seen as deeply offensive but have been retained in places to demonstrate how the racism of the era was expressed.

I have had the privilege of presenting about our project to many groups in the Black Country and beyond, and have been very grateful for the feedback: in particular, the CHORD workshop at the University of Wolverhampton, and the Urban History Beyond the Academy conference at Leeds Beckett University, both in 2018. Thanks particularly to Dr Shane Ewen and Dr Tosh Warwick for their invitation to write on *Forging Ahead* for *Urban History* too. My particular thanks go to several people who have read and commented on parts of this book, and whose input has been invaluable: Prof Maggie Andrews, Irene de Boo, Jayne Heathcock, Paul Quigley, Dr Shirin Hirsch, Dr Roz Watkiss Singleton, and especially Dr Malcolm Dick and Prof Carl Chinn who read the entire first draft of the manuscript.

My last batch of thanks goes to the people of the Black Country who have allowed themselves to be studied, scrutinised and interviewed for *Forging Ahead*: I have had the most wonderful time meeting and talking to dozens of people. We have travelled to Oxfordshire, South Wales, and even as far as Great Barr to find you, and we have learnt a tremendous amount from you. Most of all though, my thanks go to another person through whom I acquired my Black Country passport, and without whom I wouldn't be where I am – my wife Tre.

Endnotes

Introduction

1 'Wolverhampton VE Day Celebrations', BBC - WW2 People's War - Wolverhampton VE Day Celebrations, 26 October 2004, http://www.bbc.co.uk/history/ww2peopleswar/stories/08/a3184508.shtml; 'VE Celebrations', *Walsall Observer*, 12 May 1945; 'VE Celebrations', *Staffordshire Advertiser*, 12 May 1945.

2 Although decline is a subjective term, the role of manufacturing in Britain's economy has decreased substantially since the early 1970s, as a share of output, labour and capital. See Stephen Broadberry and Tim Leunig, 'The Impact of Government Policies on UK Manufacturing since 1945', Futures of Manufacturing Project (London: Government Office for Science, 2013). Quoted in David Edgerton, *The Rise and Fall of the British Nation: A Twentieth-Century History* (London: Penguin, 2018). With reference to the Black Country, see particularly Kenneth Spencer et al., *Crisis in the Industrial Heartland: A Study of the West Midlands* (Wotton-under-Edge: Clarendon Press, 1986).

3 Peter Berlyn and Charles Fowler Jnr, *The Crystal Palace: Its Architectural History and Constructive Marvels* (London: James Gilbert, 1851). On the industrial development of the Black Country, see W. H. B. Court, *Rise of Midland Industries, 1600-1838* (Oxford: Oxford University Press, 1938); George Cyril Allen, *The Industrial Development of Birmingham and the Black Country, 1860-1927* (London: G. Allen & Unwin, 1929); T. J. Raybould, *The Economic Emergence of the Black Country: A Study of the Dudley Estate* (Newton Abbot: David & Charles, 1973); Phil Drabble, *The Black Country* (London: Robert Hale Ltd., 1952); Edward Chitham, *The Black Country* (Stroud: Amberley Publishing, 2009).

4 Charles Dickens, *The Old Curiosity Shop* (London: Chapman and Hall, 1841), 44; 'Journals of Queen Victoria', 14 October 1852, RA VIC/MAIN/QVJ (W), Royal Archives; J. B. Priestley, *English Journey* (London: Harper & Brothers, 1934), 89.

5 Elihu Burritt, *Walks in the Black Country and Its Green Border-Land* (London: Sampson Low, Son, and Marston, 1868), 1–2.

6 Allen, *The Industrial Development of Birmingham and the Black Country, 1860-1927*; F. J. Ede, *History of Wednesbury* (Wednesbury: Wednesbury Corporation, 1962), 272; West Midland Group, *Conurbation: A Planning Survey of Birmingham and the Black Country* (Birmingham: Architectural Press, 1948); Tom Brennan, *Midland City: Wolverhampton, Social and Industrial Survey* (London: D. Dobson, 1948); David Palliser. *The Staffordshire Landscape.* (London: Hodder and Stoughton, 1976), 175.

7 Rosalind Watkiss Singleton, '"Old Habits Persist": Change and Continuity in Black Country Communities: Pensnett, Sedgley and Tipton, 1945-*c.*1970' (Wolverhampton, University of Wolverhampton, 2010),
80–81; Walter Allen, *The Black Country* (London: Paul Elek, 1946), 18.

8 Interview with Richard Davenhill, 2016; Chitham, *The Black Country*, 3; 'Tipton surprise at enquiry', *Birmingham Daily Post*, 3 January 1962.

9 For a longer view of the place of these mid-century years, see for example James Vernon, *Modern Britain: 1750 to the Present* (Cambridge: Cambridge University Press, 2017), particularly Part IV; Edgerton, *The Rise and Fall of the British Nation.*

10 Peter J. Larkham, 'Rebuilding the Industrial Town: Wartime Wolverhampton', *Urban History* 29(3), 2002: 388–409; Drabble, *The Black Country*, 209–10.

11 'Small Towns Oppose Absorption', *Birmingham Daily Post,* 8 November 1961.

12 J. Wilson Jones, *The History of the Black Country* (London: Cornish Bros., 1950); Drabble, *The Black Country*; Chitham, *The Black Country* (originally published 1972); Harold Parsons, *The Black Country* (London: Robert Hale Ltd., 1986). Drabble's account can be read alongside memoirs such as John Petty's

Five Fags a Day: The Last Year of a Scrap-Picker (London: Secker & Warburg, 1956) and *The Face* (London: Gentry Books, 1972), and Archie Hill's *A Cage of Shadows* (London: Hutchinson, 1973), both of whom demonstrate a complex relationship with their Black Country home, and a very personal, often graphic, narrative of working-class life in the region.

13 Paul Addison, *The Road To 1945: British Politics and the Second World War*, Revised ed. (London: Random House, 2011); Addison, *No Turning Back*; Peter Hennessy, *Never Again: Britain 1945-1951* (New York: Vintage, 1993); Peter Hennessy, *Having It So Good: Britain in the Fifties* (Harmondsworth: Penguin, 2007); Kenneth O. Morgan, *Britain Since 1945: The People's Peace* (Oxford: Oxford University Oress, 2001); Harriet Jones and Michael D. Kandiah, eds., *The Myth of Consensus: New Views on British History, 1945–64* (London: Palgrave Macmillan, 1996); James Vernon, *Modern Britain*; Arthur Marwick, *British Society Since 1945* (London: Penguin, 1990); Arthur Marwick. *The Sixties: Cultural Revolution in Britain, France, Italy, and the United States, c.1958-c.1974* (Oxford: Oxford University Press, 1998); Dominic Sandbrook, *Never Had It so Good 1956-63* (Boston, MA: Little, Brown, 2005); Dominic Sandbrook, *White Heat: A History of Britain in the Swinging Sixties* (London: Hachette UK, 2015); Rosalind Watkiss Singleton, '"Old Habits Persist"'. It should be noted that Sandbrook's work in particular has been criticised for a shallow use of historical sources and the tendency to recapitulate, rather than interrogate, the views of contemporary commentators.

14 Hennessy, *Never Again*, 105–6.

Chapter 1: A "great recasting of values"

15 Henry DeWolf Smyth, *Atomic Energy for Military Purposes: The Official Report on the Development of the Atomic Bomb under the Auspices of the United States Government, 1940–1945* (Princeton, NJ: Princeton University Press, 1945), 281.

16 Robert Taylor, *The TUC: From the General Strike to New Unionism* (London: Palgrave Macmillan, 2000), 80.

17 Jennie Lee – wife of Minister for Health Aneurin Bevan and seasoned campaigner for women's rights and left-wing causes – was MP for Cannock, which at that time stretched as far as Bentley in the northern part of the Black Country.

18 Rhiannon Vickers and Andrew Gamble, *Manipulating Hegemony: State Power, Labour and the Marshall Plan in Britain* (Basingstoke: Palgrave Macmillan, 2000); Philip Thornton, 'Britain Pays off Final Instalment of US Loan - after 61 Years', *The Independent*, 29 December 2006.

19 Martin Francis, *Ideas and Policies Under Labour, 1945-1951: Building a New Britain* (Manchester: Manchester University Press, 1997).

20 Morgan, *Britain Since 1945*, 42; Kenneth O. Morgan, T*wentieth-Century Britain: A Very Short Introduction* (Oxford: Oxford University Press, 2000), 61.

21 Michael Foot, *Aneurin Bevan: A Biography* (New York: Atheneum, 1973), 78.

22 Amri Beo Dodo, 'A Report on His Recent Journey to England by Chief Amri Beo Dodo of the Gorowa Tribe', 31 May 1955, Institute of Current World Affairs, http://www.icwa.org/wp-content/uploads/2015/10/RFG-9.pdf (accessed 7 April 2020).

23 G. C. Peden, 'Suez and Britain's Decline As A World Power', *The Historical Journal* 55(4), 2012: 1073–96; Caroline Elkins, *Imperial Reckoning: The Untold Story of Britain's Gulag in Kenya* (London: Holt McDougal, 2005).

24 Marwick, *British Society Since 1945*, 100, 110–11. A journalist for *The Economist*, Norman Macrae, invented the character of 'Mr Butskell' to describe the economic consensus. Although there were substantive policy differences, the term 'Butskellism' gained currency in describing the Keynesian economics of the 1950s: Butler himself noted that both Chancellors "spoke the language of Keynesianism… but we spoke it with differing accents and a differing emphasis". See Hennessy, *Having It So Good*, 211.

25 The original member states of the European Economic Community, formed by the Treaty of Rome in 1957,

were Belgium, France, Italy, Luxembourg, the Netherlands and West Germany. In 1960 Britain, along with Austria, Denmark, Norway, Portugal, Sweden and Switzerland established the European Free Trade Association. Hennessy, *Never Again*, 113, 613-18; Hennessy, *Having It so Good*, 491; Morgan, *Twentieth-Century Britain*, 64.

26 Morgan, *Britain Since 1945*, 197; Adam Sharr and Stephen Thornton, *Demolishing Whitehall: Leslie Martin, Harold Wilson and the Architecture of White Heat* (Farnham: Ashgate Publishing, Ltd., 2013), 8; Mark Donnelly, *Sixties Britain: Culture, Society and Politics* (London: Routledge, 2014).

27 The debate amongst historians as to the degree to which the sixties really were 'revolutionary' is of course ongoing. The key supporter of the 1960s as a time of dramatic change is Arthur Marwick, who admittedly describes the decade as lasting from 1958 to 1974. His chief critic is Dominic Sandbrook, who argues for greater continuity of 'traditional' values. See Marwick, *The Sixties*; Sandbrook, *White Heat*.

28 West Midland Group, *Conurbation*, 250; David Kynaston, *Austerity Britain, 1945-1951* (London: Bloomsbury Publishing, 2010), 398.

Chapter two: A "national asset"

29 Roy Peacock, *Ernest and Mary Stevens - The Continuing Legacy* (Birmingham: Thomas Pocklington Trust, 2007).

30 Hopkins, 'England's Men of Iron Forge New Links'; Ned Williams, *More Black Country Folk At Werk* (Dudley: Uralia Press, 1990), 88.

31 R.J. Griffin, 'A Bevin Boy at Baggeridge', *Blackcountryman* 30, no. 1 (1995); R.J. Griffin, 'A Day To Remember', *Blackcountryman* 32, no. 1 (1997); R.J. Griffin, 'Bevin Boys by Ballot', *Blackcountryman* 30, no. 1 (1995); Kynaston, *Austerity Britain*, 103; Spencer et al., *Crisis in the Industrial Heartland*, 12.

32 Addison, *No Turning Back*, 62; 'The Pit That Cried Itself to Death', *Sunday Mercury*, 14 September 1958; R. Newnham, 'The Sinking of Baggeridge Colliery', *Blackcountryman* 1(1), 1967; R. Newnham, 'The Closing Of Baggeridge Colliery', *Blackcountryman* 1(3), 1968.

33 West Midland Group, *Conurbation*, 113.

34 'When Gibbons Fireclay Works of Gornal Led the World in Gas Retorts', *Black Country Bugle*, 26 May 2005; 'Remembering Gibbons Brothers of Pensnett', *Black Country Bugle*, 10 October 2016; John Cooksey, *Brickyards of the Black Country: A Forgotten Industry: Refractories* (Self-published, 2003).

35 'West Midland Industries', in *Industry in the West Midlands: A Review of Industry in Staffordshire, Shropshire, Worcestershire, Warwickshire and Herefordshire*, by West Midland Industrial Development Association Ltd. (Ed. J. Burrow & Co, 1954); Kynaston, *Austerity Britain*, 224–26.

36 W. David Heal, *The Steel Industry in Post-War Britain* (Newton Abbot: David & Charles, 1974), 112; Ede, *History of Wednesbury*, 282–85.

37 Heal, *The Steel Industry in Postwar Britain*, 112.

38 'Visits to Works', *Proceedings of the Institute of Mechanical Engineers* 162 (1950), https://www.gracesguide.co.uk/1950_Institution_of_Mechanical_Engineers:_Visits_to_Works (accessed 7 April 2020); 'World's Smallest Tube Pulls Crowds in London', *The News*, 25 January 1962.

39 G. Sidwell, *Walter Somers Ltd – Times Remembered* (Halesowen: Seth Somers Trust, 1989), 69; 'Queen's Visit to Somers Works (Halesowen) 1957', *Black Country Bugle*, 28 July 2014; W.K.V. Gale, *The Forgemasters - Walter Somers Ltd. a History: 1866 - 1986* (Halesowen: Walter Somers Ltd., 1987); 'Visits to Works'; R.E. Waterhouse, *A Hundred Years of Engineering Craftsmanship: A Short History Tracing the Adventurous Development of Tangye's Limited, Smethwick, 1857-1957* (Smethwick: Tangye Ltd., 1957).

40 David Hall, *Working Lives* (Ealing: Corgi, 2014), 102; S.A. Barnett, 'John Thompson', *History Website*, accessed 28 August 2018, http://www.historywebsite.co.uk/Museum/Engineering/JohnThompson/johnthompson00.htm#menu (accessed 7 April 2020); 'Contract', *Dudley Herald*, 16 February 1962; 'Trade

Fair', *Dudley Herald*, 10 March 1962; 'Trade Fair', *The Guardian*, 5 March 1962.

41 Paul Stamper, 'Only One Way to Scratch up the Dirt', *British Archaeology* 18, 1999; *Made In Oldbury* (Oldbury: Press Services, 1949). The geopolitical economy had always played a major part in the Black Country's industrial history: in the eighteenth century, the blacksmiths of Wednesbury and Darlaston specialised in making gun barrels for England's military. Such intervention was long-lasting: after the Napoleonic Wars ended, and demand for guns dried up, this expertise was poured into one of Wednesbury's staple trades: tube-making. See Priya Satia, *Empire of Guns: The Violent Making of the Industrial Revolution* (New York: Penguin Press, 2018).

42 Hopkins, 'England's Men of Iron Forge New Links'; 'Last Worcestershire Wrought Chain Firm Closing after 108 Years in Business', *County Express*, 17 October 1969. On the history of chainmaking in the region see W.K.V. Gale, 'Handwrought Chains', *Transactions of the Newcomen Society* 29, 1958: 195–204; A. F. Moseley, 'Black Country Chainmakers', *West Midlands Studies* 4, 1970: 56–62; Sheila Christine Blackburn, 'Employers and Social Policy: Black Country Chain-Masters, the Minimum Wage Campaign and the Cradley Heath Strike of 1910', *Midland History* 12(1), 1987: 85–102.

43 'Visits to Works'.

44 'West Bromwich Put a Spring in the Nation's Step', *Black Country Bugle*, 25 June 2015; G.C. Baugh et al., *A History of the County of Stafford*, ed. M.W. Greenslade and R.B Pugh, vol. 17 (London: Victoria County History, 1976); M. Bache, Salter: *The Story of a Family Firm 1760-1960* (West Bromwich: Geo. Salter & Co, 1960).

45 Hopkins, 'England's Men of Iron Forge New Links'; 'West Midland Industries'.

46 Andrew Lorenz, *GKN: The Making of a Business, 1759 - 2009* (Chichester: John Wiley & Sons, 2012); Edgar Jones, *A History of GKN Vol 2: The Growth of a Business, 1918–45* (London: Palgrave Macmillan, 1990).

47 J. Fieldhouse, 'Industries', in *Staffordshire County Handbook* (Stafford: Staffordshire County Council, 1949).

48 C. S. Dingley, *The Story of BIP* (Oldbury: British Industrial Plastics Ltd, 1962); Terry Harrison, Allen Preston, and Roy Spencer, *The Crabtree Story* (Walsall: The Crabtree Society, 2011).

49 'On the Factory Floor at BSR', *Black Country Bugle*, 21 February 2008; Alan R. Cox, *Just for the Record* (Stourbridge: Black Country Society, 1998).

50 Peacock, *Ernest and Mary Stevens*; 'The History of Tala', https://www.talacooking.com/customer/heritage (accessed 28 August 2018).

51 S.H. Walford, 'Architecture In Tension: An Examination of the Position of the Architect in the Private and Public Sectors, Focusing on the Training and Careers of Sir Basil Spence (1907-1976) and Sir Donald Gibson (1908-1991)' (University of Warwick, 2009); 'Prefabricated Houses', *The Times*, 24 December 1943; 'Prefabricated Houses', *The Times*, 23 December 1944.

52 *Rubery Owen Houses* (Darlaston: Rubery Owen Ltd, 1944).

53 Jonathan Wood, ed., Motor Industry of Britain Centenary Book (Acton: Eclat, 1996); Hennessy, *Never Again*, 2006, 105–7; Mark R. Duffield, *Black Radicalism and the Politics of Deindustrialization: The Hidden History of Indian Foundry Workers in the West Midlands* (Aldershot: Avebury, 1988), 9; Worcestershire County Council, 'County Development Plan'.

54 Bev Parker, 'Guy Passenger Motors', *History Website*, http://www.historywebsite.co.uk/Museum/Transport/Buses/Guy/guybuses.htm (accessed 28 August 2018); 'Visits to Works'.

55 Bev Parker, 'Jensen Cars', *History Website*, http://www.historywebsite.co.uk/Museum/Transport/Cars/Jensen.htm (accessed 28 August 2018).

56 Karl Ludvigsen, *BRM V16: How Britain's Auto Makers Built a Grand Prix Car to Beat the World* (Poundbury: Veloce Publishing, 2007)

57 'West Midland Industries'; Duffield, *Black Radicalism*, 8.

58 Duffield, *Black Radicalism*, 58–59.

59 Bill Piggott, *Austin Healey: A Celebration of the Fabulous Big Healey* (Poundbury: Veloce Publishing, 2016), 10.

60 'How to Build a Jaguar', *The Observer*, 29 October 1961; '12,000 Midland Car Workers Made Idle By Disputes', *The Guardian*, 9 September 1961; 'BMC Lays off 2,700 Men Because of Strike', *The Guardian*, 28 March 1962.

61 Bev Parker, 'Bean Cars', *History Website*, http://www.historywebsite.co.uk/Museum/Transport/Cars/Bean/Cars.htm (accessed 28 August 2018)

62 C.S. Dunbar, 'Co-Ordination The Order in Big Group', *Commercial Motor*, 7 October 1955.

63 Other Black Country manufacturers were also involved in Mini components: rear sub-frames were built by Sankey's in Bilston, for instance ('BMC Lays off 2,700 Men Because of Strike'). On Rubery Owen as a case study of industrial decline, see: Roy A. Church, *The Rise and Decline of the British Motor Industry* (Cambridge: CUP, 1995); Timothy Whisler, *The British Motor Industry, 1945-94: A Case Study in Industrial Decline* (Oxford: OUP, 1999); Martin Adeney, *The Motor Makers: The Turbulent History of Britain's Car Industry* (London: HarperCollins Publishers Ltd, 1988); Peter Dunnett, *The Decline of the British Motor Industry: The Effects of Government Policy, 1945-79* (Abingdon: Routledge, 2013).

Chapter 3: "Jobs for all"

64 Colin MacInnes, *Absolute Beginners* (London: Penguin, 1959), 37.

65 Attlee's government included an array of trade unionists, most notably Ernest Bevin, perhaps the most influential trade unionist of the twentieth century, and George Isaacs, chairman of the Trades Union Congress, who became Minister for Labour. Churchill, respectful of the important role played by unions during the war, shifted from his earlier anti-unionism to work closely with unions in his post-war government. See Chris Wrigley, 'Trade Unions, the Government and the Economy', in *Britain Since 1945*, ed. Terry Gourvish and Alan O'Day, Problems in Focus Series (London: Macmillan Education UK, 1991), 59–87; Chris Wrigley, 'Churchill and the Trade Unions', *Transactions of the Royal Historical Society* 11 (2001): 273–93.

66 B.R. Williams, 'The Building Materials Industry', in *The Structure of British Industry*, ed. Duncan Burn (Cambridge: Cambridge University Press Archive, 1958), 309–43; H. Pelling, *The Labour Governments, 1945-51* (London: Palgrave Macmillan, 1984); Daniel Norman Chester, *The Nationalisation of British Industry, 1945-51* (London: H.M. Stationery Office, 1975).

67 Ernie Timmins, *Oral History*, BCLM: Forging Ahead (Birmingham, 2017), Black Country Living Museum.

68 Hennessy, *Never Again*, 2007, 69.

69 Alec Cairncross, *Years of Recovery: British Economic Policy 1945-51* (Routledge, 2013), chapter 14.; Morgan, *Britain Since 1945*, 23; Addison, *No Turning Back*, 62–64; Duffield, *Black Radicalism and the Politics of Deindustrialization*, 30; George J. Barnsby, *A History of the Wolverhampton, Bilston and District Trades Union Council, 1865-1990* (Wolverhampton: Integrated Publishing Services, 1994), 63; H.J. Fyrth and Henry Collins, *The Foundry Workers: A Trade Union History* (Amalgamated Union of Foundry Workers, 1959), 290.

70 'Employment', *Dudley Herald*, 25 June 1955; Watkiss Singleton, '"Old Habits Persist"', 130; Calvert Hutchinson and Bill Orgill, *Oral History*, BCLM: Migration Stories (Black Country Living Museum, 2018), Black Country Living Museum; Worcestershire County Council, 'County Development Plan' (Worcestershire County Council, 1951), Dudley Archives and Local History Service; Department of Economic Affairs, *The West Midlands: A Regional Study* (London: H.M. Stationery Office, 1965), fig. 11; Shirin Hirsch, *In the Shadow of Enoch Powell: Race, Locality and Resistance* (Manchester: Manchester University Press, 2018), 38.

71 Sarah A. Vickerstaff, 'Apprenticeship in the "Golden Age": Were Youth Transitions Really Smooth and Unproblematic Back Then?', *Work, Employment and Society* 17(2), 2003: 269–87.

72 Williams, *More Black Country Folk At Werk*, 9.

73 Watkiss Singleton, '"Old Habits Persist"', 139–40; Colin G. Pooley, '"My Father Found It for Me": Changing Experiences of Entering the Workforce in Twentieth-Century Urban Britain', *Urban History* 42(2), 2015: 290–308; 'Remembering Gibbons Brothers of Pensnett'.

74 Peter Cox, *Oral History*, BCLM: Forging Ahead (Dudley, 2018).

75 On the place of post-war apprenticeships in society, see Vickerstaff, 'Apprenticeship in the "Golden Age"; Sarah Vickerstaff, '"I Was Just the Boy around the Place": What Made Apprenticeships Successful?', *Journal of Vocational Education & Training* 59(3), 2007: 331–47; Selina Todd and Hilary Young, 'Baby-Boomers to "Beanstalkers"', *Cultural and Social History* 9(3), 2012: 451–67.

76 Chance Bros., *Mirror for Chance* (Smethwick: Chance Bros, 1951), 16.

77 'Firm Making More Sophisticated Types of Steel', *The Guardian*, 5 October 1962.

78 'Memories of a Black Country Lad', *Black Country Bugle*, 25 November 2014.

79 Dan Shaw, 'John Thompson Apprenticeship Led to Career Training the next Generation', *Black Country Bugle*, 25 November 2014; '1960s Visit to Snowdonia by Oldbury Workers Recalled', *Black Country Bugle*, 22 March 2016.

80 Carl Chinn, 'Recollections of F.H. Lloyds', *History Website*, http://www.historywebsite.co.uk/articles/Wednesbury1/memories4.htm (accessed 7 April 2020).

81 Chance Bros., *Mirror for Chance*, 16; 'Memories of Darlaston in 1960s', *Black Country Bugle*, 17 April 2016.

82 Waterhouse, *A Hundred Years of Engineering Craftsmanship*; 'Visits to Works'; 'Day Trips for the Apprentices Courtesy of the Mighty Tangyes', *Black Country Bugle*, 14 March 2015; 'My Late Smethwick Cousin Was on Photo', *Black Country Bugle*, 15 April 2015; 'I Had Great Five Years Training at Smethwick Firm', *Black Country Bugle*, 3 February 2016.

83 Watkiss Singleton, '"Old Habits Persist"', 136; Hall, *Working Lives*, 87; Williams, *More Black Country Folk At Werk*, 81.

84 Ned Williams, *Black Country Folk At Werk* (Dudley: Uralia Press, 1989), 20.

85 Hall, *Working Lives*, 96; Watkiss Singleton, '"Old Habits Persist"', 138; Hopkins, 'England's Men of Iron Forge New Links'.

86 William Beveridge, Social Insurance and Allied Services (H.M. Stationery Office, 1942). Quoted in José Harris, *William Beveridge: A Biography* (Oxford: Clarendon Press, 1997), 392.

87 Doris Rich, 'Spare Time in the Black Country', in *Living in Towns: Selected Research Papers in Urban Sociology of the Faculty of Commerce and Social Science*, University of Birmingham, ed. Leo Kuper (London: The Cresset Press, 1953), 313–14; John L. Edwards, *Early Days at BRD* (Self-published, 1995), 102–4; Shelley Pennington and Belinda Westover, *A Hidden Workforce: Women Homeworkers in Britain*, 1850-1985 (Basingstoke: Macmillan International Higher Education, 1989), 152; Watkiss Singleton, '"Old Habits Persist"', 144–51; West Midland Group, *Conurbation*, 127–28.

88 Watkiss Singleton, '"Old Habits Persist"', 147, 156–57, 217–19; Samantha J. Badger, 'Household Consumption, Food and the Working Class: The Black Country and Coventry 1930-1970.' (Unpublished PhD thesis, University of Wolverhampton, 2004), 117; 'Threading Past the Eye of Officialdom', *Birmingham Post*, 15 August 1967.

89 'Interview with Edith Coleman' (Black Country Living Museum, 1999), 1999/055, Black Country Living Museum.

90 Shirin Hirsch, *In the Shadow of Enoch Powell*, 40.

91 Gurharpal Singh and Darsham Singh Tatla, *Sikhs in Britain: The Making of a Community*. (London: Zed Books, 2006), 83; Duffield, *Black Radicalism*, 40, 59; Dhani R. Prem, *The Parliamentary Leper: Colour & British Politics* (Chandigarh: Metric, 1966), 36.

92 Roy A. Church, *Kenricks in Hardware*, 303; A.F. Fellows, *Archibald Kenrick & Sons Ltd: From Casters to Castors* (Self-published, n.d.); Julian Critchley, 'Paternalist Who Runs a £100m Family Business', *The Times*, 7 January 1969.

93 Memories of S.C., in Dudley and Walsall Mental Health Trust, ed., *Reflections* (Dudley and Walsall Mental Health Trust, n.d.).

94 Ansine was being interviewed on his marriage to Joyce Richardson at Wolverhampton's Queen Street Chapel in 1952. He had emigrated from Jamaica after a hurricane had destroyed his father's farm the year before. 'Pair from "Sunshine-Land" Marry in Wolverhampton', *Wolverhampton Chronicle*, 13 August 1952; Hirsch, *In the Shadow of Enoch Powell*, 41.

95 'Visits to Works'.

96 Bache, *Salter*.

97 British Iron & Steel Federation. *Accident Prevention in Hand Rolling Mills in the Iron and Steel Industry.* London: British Iron & Steel Federation, 1959.

98 Bache, *Salter*, 138; Watkiss Singleton, '"Old Habits Persist"', 138; Hall, *Working Lives*, 97; 'He Would Sit on the Step at Home, Completely Shattered', *Black Country Bugle*, 9 March 2014.

99 Williams, *Black Country Folk At Werk*, 23; Waterhouse, *A Hundred Years of Engineering Craftsmanship; Histories of Famous Firms: Midlands Survey Part One*, 1960. Wolverhampton Archives & Local Studies.

100 James Vernon, *Hunger: A Modern History* (Cambridge, MA: Harvard University Press, 2009), 166; 'Vono's Brand New Canteen', *Black Country Bugle*, 6 August 2009.

101 'West Midland Industries'; 'Papers of Rubery Owen Holdings Ltd and Predecessors' (n.d.), Modern Records Centre, University of Warwick, accessed 28 August 2018; Harrison, Preston, and Spencer, *The Crabtree Story*; Percy Eamus, *Made in Oldbury* blog, accessed 28 August 2018, https://madeinoldbury.co.uk/articles/percy-eamus; Martin Prestidge, *Made in Oldbury* blog, https://madeinoldbury.co.uk/articles/martin-prestidge/ (accessed 28 February 2018).

102 'Visits to Works'; Waterhouse, *A Hundred Years of Engineering Craftsmanship; Old Hands*, 16mm (Owen Organisation, 1959), https://player.bfi.org.uk/free/film/watch-old-hands-1959-online

Chapter 4: "Loads of work and loads of jobs"

103 P. Carter, 'An Indian Legacy: FH Lloyd & Co. Ltd India Project (1957-1957)', *Blackcountryman* 46(3), 2013.

104 It should be noted that numbers of imperial workers in wartime West Midlands were small, but not non-existent – Jamaicans were certainly employed and living in hostels, and Indian men were working in foundries in Smethwick. Keith Middlemas, *Politics in Industrial Society: The Experience of the British System since 1911* (London: A. Deutsch, 1979), 277; Ron Ramdin, *The Making of the Black Working Class in Britain* (London: Verso Books, 2017), 86-87; Wendy Webster, *Mixing It: Diversity in World War Two Britain* (Oxford: OUP, 2018); Addison, *No Turning Back*, 64.

105 Kevin Searle, '"Mixing of the Unmixables": The 1949 Causeway Green "Riots" in Birmingham', *Race & Class* 54(3), 2013: 44–64.

106 Hirsch, *In the Shadow of Enoch Powell*, 33; Colin Cross, 'West Midlands Poles Still Hope to Return Home', *Express & Star*, 17 February 1955.

107 *Diana Kay and Robert Miles, Refugees Or Migrant Workers?: European Volunteer Workers in Britain, 1946-1951* (Routledge, 1992); James Walvin, *Passage to Britain: Immigration in British History And Politics*

(Harmondsworth: Penguin, 1984), 105; Johannes-Dieter Steinert, 'British Post-War Migration Policy and Displaced Persons in Europe', in *The Disentanglement of Populations: Migration, Expulsion and Displacement in Postwar Europe, 1944-49*, ed. J. Reinisch and E. White (Basingstoke: Palgrave Macmillan, 2011), 229–50; Aldona Grupas, *Lithuanian Community in the West Midlands after the Second World War* (Amazon, 2013).

108 J. Anthony Hellen, 'Temporary Settlements and Transient Populations. The Legacy of Britain's Prisoner of War Camps: 1940–1948', *Erdkunde* 53(3), 1999: 191–219; Stan Hill, 'PoW Camps for German Prisoners in the Brierley Hill Area', *Blackcountryman* 45(3), 2012: 19; Louis Ambrose, *Oral History*, BCLM: Forging Ahead (Dudley, 2018), 2018/078/001, Black Country Living Museum.

109 Frank Reeves, *Race and Borough Politics* (Aldershot: Avebury, 1989), 12–13; 'Hunt for the Hungarian Wrestler Who Escaped to the Black Country', *Black Country Bugle*, 20 July 2006; 'Coloured Men to Work Again in W'ton Bus Crews', *Express & Star*, 17 January 1955.

110 Enda Delaney, *The Irish in Post-War Britain* (Oxford: Oxford University Press, 2007), 16–19, 203; Catherine Dunne, *An Unconsidered People: The Irish in London* (Dublin: New Island Books, 2003), 4; Matthew Russell, 'The Irish Delinquent in England', *Studies: An Irish Quarterly Review* 53(21), 1964: 136–48; Jennifer Redmond, *Moving Histories: Irish Women's Emigration to Britain from Independence to Republic* (Oxford: Oxford University Press, 2019); Clair Wills, *Lovers and Strangers: An Immigrant History of Post-War Britain* (London: Allen Lane, 2017); Gary P. Freeman, *Immigrant Labor and Racial Conflict in Industrial Societies: The French and British Experience, 1945-1975* (Princeton, NJ: Princeton University Press, 2016); Angela Moran, *Irish Music Abroad: Diasporic Sounds in Birmingham* (Newcastle: Cambridge Scholars Publishing, 2012), 29, 99; Ronan Burtenshaw, 'Ireland's Red Troubadour', *Tribune*, 30 January 2019, https://tribunemag.co.uk/2019/01/irelands-red-troubadour (accessed 7 April 2020); Ultan Cowley, *The Men Who Built Britain: A History of the Irish Navvy* (Dublin: Wolfhound Press, 2001), 130.

111 Enda Delaney, *The Irish in Post-War Britain*, 98–100; Gavin Schaffer and Saima Nasar, 'The White Essential Subject: Race, Ethnicity, and the Irish in Post-War Britain', *Contemporary British History* 32(2), 2018: 209–30; Margaret Feeney, 'Midland Irish: Our Readers Take up the Controversy'. *Birmingham Daily Gazette*. 8 September 1951, sec. Letters to the Editor. Councillor J Beattie, Mayor of Wolverhampton, refuted de Valera's claims outright as "a gross exaggeration of the housing conditions here. Wolverhampton shares with most other large towns in the British Isles the problems created by the acute housing shortage. No doubt some of our Irish visitors are living here in over-crowded conditions, but so, alas, are many of our own population". 'Mr. De Valera Repeats Charges'. *Belfast News-Letter*. 31 August 1951.

112 Colin Cross, 'He Has Travelled Far - 1: From Malta's Sunshine', *Express & Star*, 19 October 1953; Colin Cross, 'He Has Travelled Far - 2: - And Dislikes Our Beer and Weather', *Express & Star*, 20 October 1953; Colin Cross, 'He Has Travelled Far - 3: - And Likes the English Scene', *Express & Star*, 21 October 1953; Colin Cross, 'He Has Travelled Far - 4: An Indian Who Loves Bilston', *Express & Star*, 22 October 1953; Colin Cross, 'He Has Travelled Far - 5: Here with a Purpose', *Express & Star*, 23 October 1953; Colin Cross, 'She Has Travelled Far - 6: From Danzig to W'hampton', *Express & Star*, 24 October 1953. The Gold Coast was modern-day Ghana, which became an autonomous dominion within the Empire in 1957, before winning complete independence in 1960.

113 Manmohan Singh Maheru, *Opportunity and Culture: Four Decades in England* (Wolverhampton: Merridale Publishing, 2012), 84-88; *Black Country Roots*, 2016, 12; Chris Upton, *A History of Wolverhampton* (Chichester: Phillimore, 1998), 131; Philip Donnellan, 'The Colony' (BBC, 1964); 'News', *Express & Star*, 23 January 1955.

114 Peter Fryer, *Staying Power: The History of Black People in Britain* (London: Pluto Press, 1984), 372–73; Hutchinson and Orgill, *Oral History*; Lenny Henry, 'It Feels as If I'm Acting out My Dad's Life', *Daily Telegraph*, 22 June 2013.

115 Hutchinson and Orgill, *Oral History*.

[116] Searle, '"Mixing of the Unmixables"'; 'Evict Poles or We May Act, Say Hostel Britons', B*irmingham Daily Gazette*, 12 August 1949.

[117] Brendan Jackson, 'In the Vernacular', *Where's Our Spake Gone?*, 2013; Carl Chinn, 'From Trinidad to Birmingham', Brumpic, 2012, https://www.brumpic.com/trinidad-to-birmingham/ (accessed 7 April 2020).

[118] Robert Kee, 'Is There a British Colour Bar?' *Picture Post*, 2 July 1949.

[119] Gurharpal Singh and Darsham Singh Tatla, *Sikhs in Britain: The Making of a Community* (London: Zed Books, 2006), 37–44; S. Ram, 'Indians in England: Why Did They Emigrate?' *Population Geography: A Journal of the Association of Population Geographers of India* 9(1–2), 1987: 37–44.

[120] Fryer, *Staying Power*, 373; Duffield, *Black Radicalism*, 77–90; Satnam Virdee, *Racism, Class and the Racialized Outsider* (London: Macmillan International Higher Education, 2014), 120–21.

[121] Reeves, *Race and Borough Politics*, 29; Roberta E. Bivins, *Contagious Communities: Medicine, Migration, and the NHS in Postwar Britain* (Oxford: OUP, 2015), 175; Stephanie Snow and Emma Jones, 'Immigration and the National Health Service: Putting History to the Forefront', *History & Policy*, 8 March 2011, http://www.historyandpolicy.org/index.php/policy-papers/papers/immigration-and-the-national-health-service-putting-history-to-the-forefron (accessed 7 April 2020).

[122] Jordanna Bailkin, *Unsettled: Refugee Camps and the Making of Multicultural Britain* (OUP, 2018); 'News', *Women's Voluntary Service Bulletin*, February 1957.

[123] David Kynaston, *Austerity Britain*, 272; Kee, 'Is There a British Colour Bar?'

[124] Wendy Webster, *Imagining Home: Gender, Race And National Identity, 1945-1964* (Abingdon: Routledge, 2005), 69; David Kynaston, *Modernity Britain*, 1957-1962 (London: Bloomsbury, 2014), 308–9; Paul Foot, *The Rise of Enoch Powell* (Harmondsworth: Penguin, 1969), 107.

[125] Peter Hennessy, *The Prime Minister: The Office And Its Holders Since 1945* (London: Penguin, 2001), 205.

[126] 'Colour Bar at Willenhall Dances? - "No," Says Official', *Express & Star*, 11 March 1952.

[127] Dhani R. Prem, *The Parliamentary Leper: Colour & British Politics* (Chandigarh: Metric, 1966), 58; Foot, *Rise of Enoch Powell*, 50.

[128] Hutchinson and Orgill, *Oral History*.

[129] 'Public's Attitude to Busmen Hardens', *Manchester Guardian*, 26 February 1955; 'Buses Not to Run in Strike Area in Spite of Ruling', *Manchester Guardian*, 19 February 1955; 'Licence Ruling Ignored', *The Times*, 21 February 1955; 'Bus Strikers Get Warning', *Manchester Guardian*, 23 February 1955; 'Town's Decision in Bus Dispute', *The Times*, 23 February 1955; 'Bishops Plead with 450 Busmen', *Daily Mail*, 25 February 1955; 'Three Bad Neighbours', *Daily Mail*, 26 February 1955; 'Driver Refuses to Work with Indian', *Birmingham Daily Gazette*, 4 March 1955; '"Keep Britain White" Label Stuck on Bus', *Express & Star*, 8 September 1955; David Kynaston, *Family Britain*, 1951-1957 (London: A&C Black, 2009), 504; Upton, *A History of Wolverhampton*, 132; Claire Mansour, 'The Cross-National Diffusion of the American Civil Rights Movement: The Example of the Bristol Bus Boycott of 1963', *Miranda* 10, 2014.

[130] Department of Economic Affairs, *The West Midlands*; Kynaston, *Modernity Britain*, 716–21; Hirsch, *In the Shadow of Enoch Powell*, 15; Wills, *Lovers and Strangers*, 67; Stuart Hall, *Familiar Stranger: A Life between Two Islands* (London: Allen Lane, 2017). The term 'West Indian' shifted from aboriginal Caribbean people in the early modern period, to wealthy white settlers during the period of slavery and imperial exploitation, and was only coded primarily as 'black' after the Second World War. Catherine Hall, 'What Is a West Indian?', in *West Indian Intellectuals in Britain*, ed. Bill Schwarz (Manchester: Manchester University Press, 2013).

[131] *Midlands News: Colin Jordan Interview*, 16mm, Newsreel (ATV, 1962), MACE; Foot, *Rise of Enoch Powell*, 51; 'Blackheath Youth Centre', *Birmingham Daily Post*, 7 April 1959.

[132] '"Nights of Violence Are over": Racial Situation Now in Hand Believes Dudley Police Chief', *Express & Star*, 1 August 1962; 'Dudley "Mob Violence" Court Sends Nine to Gaol', *Express & Star*, 1 August 1962; 'Dogs Charge Race Rioters', *Daily Mail*, 1 August 1962; 'Police Alert after Race Riot: Court Told of Cowardly Pack', *The Guardian*, 1 August 1962; 'Rowdies Hunt Coloured People', *The Times*, 1 August 1962; 'Black Hatred Boils over Again at Dudley', *Express & Star*, 2 August 1962; 'Dudley People Told to Keep out of Town Centre at Night', *The Guardian*, 2 August 1962; 'Bottles Thrown at Police from Lorry', *The Times*, 2 August 1962; 'Eleven Arrests on Third Night of Disturbances', *The Times*, 2 August 1962; 'Police Dogs Put Gangs to Flight', *The Guardian*, 3 August 1962; Roy Perrott, 'Behind the Doors of Dudley, Town in Turmoil', *The Observer*, 5 August 1962; 'Dudley's Youth Problems as a Factor in Colour Riots', *The Times*, 2 August 1962; 'Dudley MP Declares... Disturbances Are Nothing to Do with Race Hate', *Express & Star*, 6 August 1962; 'Sikh Provoked, Court Is Told', *The Times*, 24 August 1962.

[133] Michael Hartley-Brewer, 'Smethwick', in *Colour and the British Electorate 1964: Six Case Studies*, ed. N. Deakin (London: Institute of Race Relations, 1965), 77–105.

[134] Smethwick residents were often content to move well away from the town, even if they continued to work there: one interviewee in Pedmore, near Stourbridge, noted a number of neighbours who had moved out of Smethwick to the same new estate in the 1960s. See also Reeves, *Race and Borough Politics*, 12; *Black Country Roots*, 2016, 20. As well as the primary sources noted, this section draws substantially on the contemporary accounts by Paul Foot and Dr Dhani Prem, and more recent historical accounts by Joe Street and Elizabeth Buettner: Paul Foot, *Immigration and Race in British Politics* (London: Penguin, 1965); Prem, *The Parliamentary Leper*; Joe Street, 'Malcolm X, Smethwick, and the Influence of the African American Freedom Struggle on British Race Relations in the 1960s', *Journal of Black Studies* 38(6), 2008: 932–50; Elizabeth Buettner, '"This Is Staffordshire Not Alabama": Racial Geographies of Commonwealth Immigration in Early 1960s Britain', *The Journal of Imperial and Commonwealth History* 42(4), 2014: 710–40.

[135] D. Finney, 'Now Is the Time to Control Immigration', *Smethwick Telephone*, 24 February 1961; D. Finney, 'Committee to Control Immigration', *Smethwick Telephone*, 24 March 1961; Olive B. Pace, 'Anti-Colour Campaign?', *Smethwick Telephone*, 3 March 1961; Foot, *Immigration and Race in British Politics*, 32; Andrew Reekes, 'The West Midlands and Powell's Birmingham Speech', *The Political Quarterly*, 89(3), 2018, 400-408.

[136] 'The *Telephone* and the Colour Problem', *Smethwick Telephone*, 9 June 1961.

[137] 'Colour Bar Speech Causes Angry Scenes at Meeting', *Smethwick Telephone*, 28 April 1961; A local lad, 'The New "Black Hole"', *Smethwick Telephone*, 4 August 1961; John Sanders, 'Diseases Returning', *Smethwick Telephone*, 28 July 1961; Dyno, 'Smethwick Will Soon Be like Mecca', *Smethwick Telephone*, 28 July 1961; '"Colour Bar" Tenants' Threat of a Rents Strike', *The Guardian*, 24 July 1961; 'Rent Strike Was "Only a Token"', *Smethwick Telephone*, 28 July 1961; 'All Quiet on the Price St. Front', *Smethwick Telephone*, 11 August 1961; 'Smethwick Rent Strike Fails', *The Times*, 27 July 1961; 'Church Made into Sikh Temple', *The Times*, 31 July 1961; 'Pakistani Appeal for Help and Good Will', *The Times*, 31 August 1961; 'A Price Street Dividend', *The Guardian*, 6 November 1961; G.W. Baker, 'Life-Time Reader Protests', *Smethwick Telephone*, 25 August 1961.

[138] Prem, *The Parliamentary Leper*, 79.

[139] JEG, 'Can This Be Called the Colour Bar?', *Smethwick Telephone*, 16 June 1961.

[140] 'Migrants - "Stop the Unskilled"', *Express & Star*, 1 August 1962.

[141] 'Immigrants Main Election Issue at Smethwick', *The Times*, 9 March 1964; 'Labour Inquiry over "Immigrant Disturbances"', *The Guardian*, 10 August 1964.

[142] 'Immigrants Main Election Issuc at Smethwick'.

[143] Prem, *The Parliamentary Leper*, 95–134.

144 Dennis D. Wainstock, *Malcolm X, African American Revolutionary* (Jefferson, NC: McFarland, 2008), 149; Stuart Jeffries, 'Britain's Most Racist Election: The Story of Smethwick, 50 Years On', *The Guardian*, 15 October 2014; Chris Arnot, 'Malcolm X in the Black Country', *The Independent*, 3 March 1993; Street, 'Malcolm X, Smethwick, and the Influence of the African American Freedom Struggle on British Race Relations in the 1960s'.

145 'Does Race Count?', *The Economist*, 26 March 1966; Foot, *Rise of Enoch Powell*, 93; Hirsch, *In the Shadow of Enoch Powell*, 43–44.

146 George Kassimeris and Leonie Jackson, 'Negotiating Race and Religion in the West Midlands: Narratives of Inclusion and Exclusion during the 1967–69 Wolverhampton Bus Workers' Turban Dispute', *Contemporary British History* 31(3), 2017: 343–65.

147 Camilla Schofield, *Enoch Powell and the Making of Postcolonial Britain* (Cambridge: Cambridge University Press, 2013), 209.

148 Foot, *Rise of Enoch Powell*, 113–16; J. Enoch Powell, 'Speech to the Annual General Meeting of the West Midlands Area Conservative Political Centre, given in Birmingham', 20 April 1968.

149 Hirsch, *In the Shadow of Enoch Powell*, 53–57.

150 Cited in Hirsch, *In the Shadow of Enoch Powell*, 56.

151 Hirsch, *In the Shadow of Enoch Powell*, 59–61; Schofield, *Enoch Powell and the Making of Postcolonial Britain*, 248; J. Enoch Powell, 'Speech to London Rotary Club, Eastbourne', 16 November 1968.

152 'Mr Powell "Is a Threat to Smooth Race Relations"', *Birmingham Daily Post*, 24 April 1968; Fryer, *Staying Power*, 385; Hirsch, *In the Shadow of Enoch Powell*, 62–65.

153 A. Sivanandan, 'From Resistance to Rebellion: Asian and Afro-Caribbean Struggles in Britain', *Race & Class* 23(2–3), 1981: 111–52.

Chapter 5: An "unlovely heritage"

154 Palliser, *The Staffordshire Landscape*, 171; Drabble, *The Black Country*, 2; L.J. Jay, 'The Black Country of Francis Brett Young', *Transactions of the Institute of British Geographers* 66(1), 1975: 57–72.

155 Priestley, *English Journey*, 110-115.

156 W. G. Hoskins, *The Making of the English Landscape* (London: Hodder & Stoughton, 1955), 171; Allen, *The Black Country*; Stanley H. Beaver, 'Report on Derelict Land in the Black Country' (London: Ministry of Town and Country Planning, 1946); Stanley H. Beaver, 'Rehabilitation of Derelict Land', *Nature*, 166, 1950: 630–32; See also Ben Highmore, 'Playgrounds and Bombsites: Postwar Britain's Ruined Landscapes', *Cultural Politics* 9(3), 2013: 323–36.

157 'West Midland Industries'; Quaestor, 'You Can't Feel Steady Where Every Wall Is Askew', *Express & Star*, 25 March 1957.

158 W.E. Hall, 'Land of Nevermore', *Birmingham Post*, 7 December 1965.

159 Leo Mellor and Mark Rawlinson, 'Cityscape: The Bombed City in the Second World War', in T*he Edinburgh Companion to Twentieth-Century British and American War Literature*, ed. Adam Piette (Edinburgh: Edinburgh University Press, 2012), 462; Janet Thomson, *An Oral History of British Science*, British Library; Michael Lyons, *National Life Story Collection: Artists' Lives*, British Library; J. Wilson Jones, 'From Desolation to Beauty', *Birmingham Daily Gazette*, 28 January 1953; 'West Midland Industries'; Department of Economic Affairs, *The West Midlands*.

160 Drabble, *The Black Country*, 7, 210.

161 Hoskins, *The Making of the English Landscape*, 231.

162 *Blocksidge's Illustrated Dudley Almanack for 1943* (Dudley: E. Blocksidge (Dudley) Ltd., 1943).

[163] West Midlands Group for Post-War Reconstruction. 'West Midlands Plan Interim vol.4 section V, chapter 9, 1948'. TS. LS/WM711/6. Wolverhampton Archives & Local Studies.

[164] Brennan, *Midland City*.

[165] Brennan, Midland City; *Wolverhampton Official Handbook*, Wolverhampton County Borough, 1953 and 1956-7.

[166] West Midland Group, *Conurbation*, 27; Chinn, *Black Country Memories*, vol. 5 (Birmingham: Brewin Books, 2008).

[167] 'Housing at Willenhall', *Walsall Observer*, 9 October 1943; Darlaston UDC and Staffordshire County Council, 'The New Darlaston' (Darlaston UDC, 1962), 2009/0138/001, Black Country Living Museum. 'News', *Walsall Observer*, 9 October 1943.

[168] Rev. F. Brighton, *'The Venice of the Midlands': Ocker Hill (100 Years)* (Dudley: E. Blocksidge (Dudley) Ltd., 1949).

[169] David Smith, *Something Will Turn Up: Britain's Economy, Past, Present and Future* (London: Profile, 2015), 3–4.

[170] In 1957, for instance, two Brierley Hill children contracted paratyphoid after falling into a stretch of the abandoned Pensnett Canal ('Paratyphoid in Canal', *Birmingham Daily Post*, 25 February 1957). Numerous children lost their lives by falling in – the Wyrley & Essington Canal in Wednesfield was a notorious blackspot ('Council Survey of canal danger spots', *Birmingham Daily Post*, 8 December 1966)

[171] Edward Chitham, *West Bromwich: A History* (Bognor Regis: Phillimore, 2009), 192; 'Pirates Raid Coal Boats', *Daily Herald*, 21 December 1950; John Barr, *Derelict Britain* (Harmondsworth: Penguin, 1969), 54; Robert Davies, *Midlands Canals: Memories of the Canal Carriers* (Stroud: Tempus, 2006), 104, 116–18; Harry Hopkins, 'England's Men of Iron Forge New Links', *John Bull*, 12 December 1953.

[172] L.T.C. Rolt, *Narrow Boat* (London: Eyre & Spottiswoode, 1944).

[173] J. Ian Langford, *Stourbridge Canal* (Lapal Publications, 1992), 40; '102 Boats At Canal Rally', *The Times*, 15 August 1962.

[174] Janet C. Sullivan, 'Paying the Price for Industrialisation: The Experience of a Black Country Town, Oldbury, in the 18th and 19th Centuries' (Unpublished PhD thesis, University of Birmingham, 2014); Graham Beckley, *Our Stour* (Halesowen: Black Country Society, 2016); D. Dilworth, *The Tame Mills of Staffordshire* (Bognor Regis: Phillimore, 1976); Terry Langford, 'Pollution History of Black Country Streams', *Blackcountryman* 38, no. 3 (2005); Robert Davies, *Midlands Canals: Memories of the Canal Carriers* (Stroud: History Press), 40.

[175] Walter White, *All Around the Wrekin* (London: Chapman and Hall, 1860), 238; Allan Ahlberg, *The Bucket* (London: Penguin, 2014), 46.

[176] *Black Country Roots* (West Bromwich: Multistory, 2016), 16.

[177] Sullivan, 'Paying the Price for Industrialisation'; 'Memories of Horace Morris', *Black Country Memories Club*, 2001, http://www.blackcountrymemories.org.uk/pages1/morris.htm.

[178] 'Black Country, except as a Name, Must Vanish', *Dudley Herald*, 9 August 1956.

[179] Smith, *Something Will Turn Up: Britain's Economy, Past, Present and Future*; 'News', *Birmingham Daily Post*, 30 January 1962; Clean Air Act 1956 chapter 52, section 1. This Act of Parliament was passed in response to the Great London Fog of 1952 and was extended in 1968. It introduced 'smoke control areas' in towns and cities.

[180] West Midland Group, *Conurbation*, 71.

[181] West Midland Group, *Conurbation*; Staffordshire County Council, 'County Development Plan' (Staffordshire County Council, 1951), LS/S711/13, Wolverhampton Archives & Local Studies.

182 Badger, 'Household Consumption, Food and the Working Class', 75–76; Reconstruction Committee, 'Wolverhampton of the Future' (Wolverhampton County Borough, 1945), DW-23/5/8, Wolverhampton Archives & Local Studies; Peter J. Larkham, *Reconstructing Wolverhampton: The Wartime Reconstruction Plan 'Wolverhampton of the Future'*, Working Paper Series, University of Central England in Birmingham. School of Planning 81 (Birmingham: University of Central England, 2000).

183 Quaestor, 'You Can't Feel Steady Where Every Wall Is Askew'.

Chapter 6: "Different people have different needs"

184 Bev Parker, 'Fallings Park Garden Suburb', *History Website*, http://www.historywebsite.co.uk/articles/FallingsPark/gardensuburb.htm (accessed 14 May 2019). For a general history of housing in the period pre-First World War, see Enid Gauldie, *Cruel Habitations: A History of Working-Class Housing, 1780-1918* (London: George Allen and Unwin, 1974); John Burnett, *A Social History of Housing: 1815-1985*, 2nd ed. (London: Methuen, 1986). In the Black Country, see George J. Barnsby, *A History of Housing in Wolverhampton, 1750 to 1975* (Wolverhampton: Integrated Publishing Services, 1975); Eric Hopkins, 'Working-Class Housing in the Smaller Industrial Town of the 19th Century: Stourbridge – a Case Study', *Midland History* 4(3), 1978: 230–54. Lloyd George's speech can be read in full at Pete Madeley, '"A Fit Country for Heroes": 100 Years since Lloyd George Made Legendary Speech in Wolverhampton', *Express & Star*, 23 November 2018, https://www.expressandstar.com/news/politics/2018/11/23/a-fit-country-for-heroes-100-years-since-lloyd-georges-legendary-wolverhampton-speech/ (accessed 7 April 2020). In Birmingham, such efforts were already being pushed by the future Prime Minister Neville Chamberlain. Andrew Reekes, *More Than Munich: The Forgotten Legacy of Neville Chamberlain* (Birmingham: History West Midlands, 2018), 15-18, 34-41.

185 Paul Quigley, 'Black Country Historic Landscape Characterisation', Archaeology Data Service, 2009, http://archaeologydataservice.ac.uk/archives/view/blackcountry_hlc_2009/; Beaver, 'Report on Derelict Land in the Black Country'; West Midlands Group, 'West Midlands Plan: Interim Vol.1 Sections I and II', 1948, LS/WM711/6, Wolverhampton Archives & Local Studies. For more on council housing in the Black Country and generally, see John Boughton, *Municipal Dreams: The Rise and Fall of Council Housing* (London: Verso, 2018) and the reports on Wolverhampton and Walsall on Boughton's blog, *Municipal Dreams* (https://municipaldreams.wordpress.com/).

186 Beaver, 'Report on Derelict Land in the Black Country'.

187 Watkiss Singleton, '"Old Habits Persist"'; Maria Finch, *BBC Millennium Memory Bank* (Smethwick, 1999), C900/18553, British Library: Sounds.

188 Drabble, *The Black Country*, 209.

189 Barnsby, *A History of Housing in Wolverhampton, 1750 to 1975*, 56; Rich, 'Spare Time in the Black Country'. On the nineteenth-century history of the term 'slum', see particularly A. J. C. Mayne, *The Imagined Slum: Newspaper Representation in Three Cities, 1870-1914* (Leicester: Leicester University Press, 1993).

190 'Slum Clearance', *Express & Star*, 2 September 1954; Willenhall Urban District Council, *Willenhall Town Handbook* (Willenhall: Willenhall Urban District Council, 1956); 'Photograph of Wash-House, Hatton Street, Bradley', June 1955, P/6048, Wolverhampton Archives & Local Studies.

191 Petty, *Five Fags a Day*, 13. "Didicai" is an Anglo-Romani word meaning a person of mixed Romani and non-Romani heritage.

192 Department of Economic Affairs, *The West Midlands*, 39; Boughton, *Municipal Dreams*, 127.

193 Hopkins, 'Working-Class Housing in the Smaller Industrial Town of the Nineteenth Century'; J.W. Willis-Bund, ed., *The Victoria County History of Worcester*, vol. 3 (London: Victoria County History, 1913); 'Doom of a Quaint Dwelling', *Express & Star*, 21 April 1948; 'Survivor of "Mud City"', *Express & Star*, 19 June 1956.

194 Stanley R. Jones, 'West Bromwich (Staffs.) Manor House', *Transactions of the South Staffordshire Archaeological & Historical Society* 17, 1977: 1–63; Baugh et al., *A History of the County of Stafford*; Dave Reeves, ed., *Best of Times - Best of Places: Reminiscences from the Stone Cross Area* (West Bromwich: Sandwell Community Library Service, 1997); Vivian Bird, 'Rare Jewel Is Unearthed in Midlands as Moated Manor House Is Restored', *Birmingham Weekly Post and Midland Pictorial*, 8 November 1957.

195 James Hinton, 'Self-Help and Socialism: The Squatters' Movement of 1946', *History Workshop Journal* 25(1), 1988: 100–126; Reeves, *Best of Times - Best of Places,* 54; 'Co-Operation at Dudley', *The Times*, 17 August 1946; 'Tipton Council's Move', *Birmingham Daily Gazette*, 17 August 1946; 'Told to Leave', *Birmingham Daily Gazette*, 19 September 1946; 'West Midland Squatters Occupy Two More Army Sites', *Express & Star*, 15 August 1946.

196 Barnsby, *A History of Housing in Wolverhampton*, 52; Greg Stevenson, *Palaces for the People: Prefabs in Post-War Britain* (London: Batsford, 2003); Wolverhampton County Borough, *Wolverhampton Centenary Exhibition and Book of the Century* (Wolverhampton: Wolverhampton County Borough, 1948), 82–83.

197 Drabble, *The Black Country*, 4; Wolverhampton County Borough, *Wolverhampton Centenary Exhibition and Book of the Century.*

198 Department of Economic Affairs, *The West Midlands*; H. Atkins, D. Matthews, and S. Robins, *Dudley: The Twentieth Century* (Stroud: Sutton Publishing Ltd, 1999); Dudley County Borough, *Dudley Official Guide* (Dudley: Dudley County Borough, 1956); 'Housebuilding', *Dudley Herald*, 11 August 1954.

199 Department of Economic Affairs, *The West Midlands*; 'Changes in the Capital of the Black Country', *Birmingham Daily Post,* 23 January 1963; Wolverhampton County Borough, *Wolverhampton Town Handbook* (Wolverhampton: Wolverhampton County Borough, 1953). Despite 1,900 acres of land reclaimed from industrial dereliction by 1948, Rowley Regis council had to note that "within this generation, some 50 coal and clay pits were being worked within the Borough, therefore a great deal of thought has to be given to the selection of suitable sites which can be adapted for housing purposes at a reasonable cost". Wednesbury Urban District Council's official handbooks in the 1950s highlighted the seemingly impossible task of "levelling the huge pit-mounds and deep hollows" but also the technological solutions which have enabled them to build Corporation housing. Rowley Regis UDC, *Tenants' Handbook* (Old Hill: Rowley Regis UDC, 1957); Wednesbury Urban District Council, *Wednesbury Town Handbook* (Wednesbury: Wednesbury Urban District Council, 1956).

200 Petty, *The Face*, 49–50; Petty, *Five Fags a Day*; 'Bentley Contrasts: An Outstanding Vision of Golden Loveliness; Ugly Wayside Tips', *Walsall Observer*, 24 April 1943; 'Garden City', *Walsall Observer*, 9 December 1944; 'Industrial Idealism: Rubery, Owen's Ambition: To See Workers Happy', *Walsall Observer*, 9 December 1944; 'Walsall's Housing Hopes', *Walsall Observer*, 9 December 1944; 'Four Towns in One', *Walsall Observer*, 12 May 1945.

201 'Bentley's Future', *Walsall Observer*, 8 May 1943; 'Bentley Common', *Walsall Observer*, 9 October 1943; 'Work to Start on Big Scheme To-Day', *Birmingham Daily Post*, 22 October 1945.

202 'First Brick', *Evening Despatch*, 22 October 1945.

203 Marco Amati, 'Otto Neurath and the Example of 1940s Bilston', in *Engagement and Exhibitionism in the Era of High Modernism*, ed. Robert Freestone and Marco Amati (London: Routledge, 2014); Elain Harwood, 'Neurath, Riley and Bilston, Pasmore and Peterlee', *Twentieth Century Architecture* 9, 2008: 83–96; Iain Boyd Whyte, 'Otto Neurath and the Sociology of Happiness', in *Man-Made Future: Planning, Education and Design in Mid-20th Century Britain* (London: Routledge, 2006), 16–38; Peter J. Larkham, 'People, Planning and Place: The Roles of Client and Consultants in Reconstructing Postwar Bilston and Dudley', *Town Planning Review* 77(5), 2006: 557–82. Phil Drabble's comments on planners are typical of those opposing such intervention.

[204] Rowley Regis UDC, *Tenants' Handbook*.

[205] Drabble, *The Black Country*, 107. Paul Pry was the eponymous main character of a Georgian theatrical farce by John Poole. In the play, Pry was an incurable busybody, idle and meddling – exactly the sort of character Drabble associated with council housing inspectors.

[206] Bev Parker, '37 - 43 Lawley Road, Ettingshall', *History Website*, http://www.historywebsite.co.uk/listed/localist/LawleyRoad.htm (accessed 20 November 2018); 'Changes in the Capital of the Black Country'.

[207] John Boughton, 'Council Housing in Walsall, Part III: Postwar Estates and High-Rise', *Municipal Dreams* blog, https://municipaldreams.wordpress.com/2018/01/09/walsall_council_housing_part_iii/ (accessed 9 January 2018).

[208] Boughton, 'Council Housing in Walsall, Part III'; Miles Glendinning and Stefan Muthesius, *Tower Block: Modern Public Housing in England, Scotland, Wales and Northern Ireland* (New Haven, CT: Yale University Press, 1994); Paul Quigley, *Living in the Sky* (Wolverhampton: Wolverhampton Art Gallery, 2015), http://www.wolverhamptonart.org.uk/wp-content/uploads/2015/04/living-in-the-sky.pdf (accessed 7 April 2020); Barnsby, *A History of Housing in Wolverhampton*, 57.

[209] Glendinning and Muthesius, *Tower Block*; Boughton, *Municipal Dreams*; Quigley, *Living in the Sky*. See Boughton pp.136-138 on Ronan Point.

[210] John Petty, *The Face*, 9. Interview with Mike Warner, 2016.

[211] Detail taken from resources on Ancestry.co.uk, including the 1939 Register, wills and directories.

[212] Kynaston, *Family Britain*, 53.'"Colour Bar" Tenants' Threat of a Rents Strike'.

[213] '"Colour Bar" Tenants' Threat of a Rents Strike'.

[214] 'Amateur Midwives Deliver Pakistani Woman's Baby', *Smethwick Telephone*, 28 April 1961.

[215] Foot, *Immigration and Race in British Politics*, 50; Hutchinson and Orgill, *Oral History*; *Black Country Roots*, 20.

[216] Hirsch, *In the Shadow of Enoch Powell*, 37.

[217] 'Colour Bar by House Builders', *The Guardian*, 12 August 1965; 'House Refused To Coloured Man', *The Times*, 12 August 1965; 'Race Ban on Sale of New House', 16mm, *ATV Today* (ATV, 12 August 1965); 'Rumpus over Colour-Bar Houses', *Daily Mirror*, 12 August 1965; 'News', *Dudley Herald*, 23 January 1962; 'Toured Homes of Coloured', *Birmingham Daily Post*, 27 January 1958; Foot, *Rise of Enoch Powell*, 45; Foot, *Immigration and Race in British Politics*, 50; Hutchinson and Orgill, *Oral History*; *Black Country Roots*, 2016, 20; Reeves, *Race and Borough Politics*, 11; Prem, *The Parliamentary Leper*, 11.

[218] Rachel Yemm, 'Immigration, Race and Local Media: Smethwick and the 1964 General Election', *Contemporary British History* 33(1), 2019; Kassimeris and Jackson, 'Negotiating Race and Religion in the West Midlands'; Hirsch, *In the Shadow of Enoch Powell*, 38; 'Dogs Charge Race Rioters'.

[219] Foot, *Rise of Enoch Powell*, 45.

[220] 'Toured Homes of Coloured'.

[221] 'Smethwick MP Backs Plan to Buy Houses', *Birmingham Daily Post*, 7 December 1964.

[222] Prem, *The Parliamentary Leper*, 138–43.

[223] 'Marshall Street Has Peace and Indifference', *Birmingham Daily Post*, 28 December 1964.

[224] Street, 'Malcolm X, Smethwick, and the Influence of the African American Freedom Struggle on British Race Relations in the 1960s'.

Chapter 7. "Life in the kitchen takes on a new cheerfulness"

225 Cynthia Cashmore, *Oral History*, BCLM: Forging Ahead (Stourbridge, 2018), Black Country Living Museum.

226 R.A. Cook, 'A Black Country Childhood', *Blackcountryman* 33, no. 3 (2000). Quoted in Badger, 'Household Consumption, Food and the Working Class'.

227 Jo Mary Stafford, *Light in the Dust: An Autobiography* (London: Blake Publishing, 2002).

228 John Lester, 'In a Black Country Practice', *Blackcountryman* 36(4), 2003: 15–17.

229 Watkiss Singleton, '"Old Habits Persist"', 111.

230 Angela Davis, *Modern Motherhood: Women and Family in England, 1945-2000* (Manchester: Manchester University Press, 2012), 146.

231 'Life at the Home for Friendless Girls in the 1950s', *Black Country Bugle*, 6 May 2004.

232 Darshan S. Tatla, 'A Passage to England : Oral Tradition and Popular Culture among Early Punjabi Settlers in Britain', *Oral History* 30(2), 2002: 61–72; Shendo Jassal, *Oral History*, BCLM: Forging Ahead (Dudley, 2019), 2019/142/001, Black Country Living Museum; Philomena Lynott and Jackie Hayden, *My Boy*, ed. Niall Stokes (Dublin: Hot Press Books, 2011).

233 Ina Zweiniger-Bargielowska, 'Bread Rationing in Britain, July 1946–July 1948', *Twentieth Century British History* 4(1), 1993: 57–85; Kynaston, *Austerity Britain*, 246; Susan Cooper, 'Snoek Piquante', in *Age of Austerity: 1945-1951*, ed. Michael Sissons and Philip French (London: Penguin, 1963), 35–57.

234 J. S. Allen, *A History of Horseley, Tipton: Two Centuries of Engineering Progress* (Ashbourne: Landmark Publishing, 2000), 156; 'Smethwick Winners in Gas Cookery Contest', *Smethwick Telephone*, June 1951, Sandwell Community History & Archives Service; 'Princess Presents Cookery Awards', *Birmingham Daily Gazette*, 11 July 1951; *Mrs Upton Wins With A Fowl* (British Pathé, 1951), https://www.britishpathe.com/video/mrs-upton-wins-with-a-fowl/; 'Champion Cook By Chance', *Smethwick Telephone*, June 1951.

235 Marianne Monro, *Living Memory* blog, 2018, https://livingmemory.live/story/marianne-monro/ (accessed 7 April 2020); Badger, 'Household Consumption, Food and the Working Class', 134–39; Jack Shaw, 'Everything Is for Harvest Festival', *Birmingham Daily Post*, 1961, LHB34, Newman University; Richard P. M. Sykes, 'Popular Religion in Dudley and the Gornals *c.*1914-1965' (Unpublished PhD thesis, University of Wolverhampton, 1999), 108–11; Watkiss Singleton, '"Old Habits Persist"', 180.

236 Sykes, 'Popular Religion in Dudley and the Gornals *c.*1914-1965', 110.

237 Shaw, 'Everything Is for Harvest Festival'.

238 D.E. Allen, 'Regional Variations in Food Habits', in *The Making of the Modern British Diet*, ed. Derek J. Oddy and Derek S. Miller (London: Croom Helm, 1976), 145

239 *Mr Therm Goes County* (London: The Gas Council, 1951).

240 Cannon (GA) Ltd., *Cannon Cookery Book*, 19th Edition (Bilston: Cannon (GA) Ltd, 1957); Bob Dean, *Oral History*, BCLM: Forging Ahead (Brierley Hill, 2018), 2018/127/001, Black Country Living Museum.

241 Win Downing, *Oral History*, BCLM: Forging Ahead (Dudley, 2017), 2018/076/001, Black Country Living Museum; Janet Thomson, *Oral History*, Oral History of British Science (North Yorkshire, 2010), C1379/20, British Library, https://sounds.bl.uk/Oral-history/Science/021M-C1379X0020XX-0001V0; Cynthia Burgin, *Oral History*, BCLM: Forging Ahead (Dudley, 2017), 2018/010/001, Black Country Living Museum. The phrase 'New Elizabethan' was commonly used in the early 1950s to discuss the flowering of post-war British culture; it did not have the staying power of some other aphorisms, however, and the early 1950s are now, rightly or wrongly, typically more associated with the "tail-end of austerity". Irene Morra and Rob Gossedge, eds., *The New Elizabethan Age: Culture, Society and National Identity after World War II* (London: Bloomsbury Publishing, 2016), 2.

[242] Maggie Andrews, 'Shopping for Identities and Purchasing Fantasies of Domesticity in Post-War Kays Catalogues', in *Gender Construction in Kays Catalogues: 1920 to the New Millennium*, ed. Barbara M. Mitra and Rachel M. Johnson (Cambridge: Cambridge University Press, 2015), 47–60.

[243] Drabble, *The Black Country*, 107.

[244] Paul Reilly, 'Ten Years of Design Centre Awards', *Design* 209, 1966: 58–71; Michael Bennett, *Robert Welch Designs for Old Hall Tableware* (Birkenhead: Appin Press, 2009).

[245] Carl Chinn, 'The Peoples of Birmingham', in *Birmingham: The Workshop of the World*, ed. Carl Chinn and Malcolm Dick (Liverpool: Liverpool University Press, 2016), 9–50.

[246] Hutchinson and Orgill, *Oral History*; *Black Country Roots*, 2016. See also Hirsch, *In the Shadow of Enoch Powell*, 36–37.

[247] Quoted in Singh and Tatla, *Sikhs in Britain*, 147; Parveen Akhtar, *British Muslim Politics: Examining Pakistani Biraderi Networks* (Basingstoke: Palgrave Macmillan, 2013), 39.

[248] Birmingham and the Black Country Sikh Migration Project, *Sikhs: My Story, Our Journey* (Nishkam Centre, 2018).

[249] Lenny Henry, *Who Am I, Again?* (London: Faber & Faber, 2019); Michael McMillan, *The Front Room: Migrant Aesthetics in the Home* (London: Black Dog Publishing, 2009).

[250] Gerard Kemp, 'Have You Frog's Legs?', *Birmingham Daily Post*, 19 March 1956; Interviews with Members of Aman Group, 2019, E2019/033-036, Black Country Living Museum.

[251] Prem, *The Parliamentary Leper*, 44.

[252] Stuart Hall, 'The "West Indian" Front Room', in McMillan, *The Front Room: Migrant Aesthetics in the Home*, 17–23; Daniel Miller, 'Migration, Material Culture and Tragedy: Four Moments in Caribbean Migration', *Mobilities* 3(3), 2008: 397–413.

Chapter 8: Market towns and "local Gothams"

[253] Chitham, *The Black Country*, 118. As early as 1838 William Hawkes-Smith identified "a peculiarity of manner, habit and language" in the Black Country. Chinn, *Black Country Memories*, vol. 5.

[254] Hopkins, 'England's Men of Iron Forge New Links'; Allen, *The Black Country; Crooked Houses Dudley* (British Pathé, 1940), https://www.britishpathe.com/video/crooked-houses-dudley. Although Allen's description of 'Gotham' now conjures up the big city through its association with the Batman comics, it has an older meaning too. Washington Irving gave the nickname to New York City based on a medieval story of the Nottinghamshire village of Gotham, where the residents were supposed to be clever fools.

[255] Allen, *The Black Country*, 27; Brennan, *Midland City*.

[256] Vernon, *Hunger*, 118–58; Kynaston, *Austerity Britain*, 104, 110; Ina Zweiniger-Bargielowska, *Austerity in Britain: Rationing, Controls, and Consumption, 1939-1955* (Oxford: Oxford University Press, 2000), 229.

[257] Halesowen & Hasbury Industrial Co-operative Society, 'General Committee Minutes', 24 November 1948, National Co-operative Archive; Ned Williams, *The Co-Op in Birmingham and the Black Country* (Wolverhampton: Uralia Press, 1993), 95–96.

[258] John Corina, *Spotlight on Self-Service* (Manchester: Co-operative Union, 1949).

[259] Williams, *The Co-Op in Birmingham and the Black Country*, 185–87.

[260] *Questions and Answers on Co-Operative Self-Service* (Manchester: CWS Research Department, 1949).

[261] *Report of the 92nd Annual Co-Operative Congress in the Spa Grand Hall Scarborough May 22nd-25th, 1961* (Manchester: Co-operative Union, 1961).

[262] Kynaston, *Family Britain*, 317; Wolverhampton County Borough, *Wolverhampton Town Handbook.*

[263] Richard Hoggart, *The Uses of Literacy: Aspects of Working-Class Life* (Harmondsworth: Penguin, 1958), 156; 'New Stanton House Marks Beginning of a £500,000 Scheme', *Dudley Herald*, 9 May 1961; Burgin, *Oral History*; Downing, *Oral History*; Philip Body, *Oral History*, BCLM: Forging Ahead (Pensnett, 2017), 2017/455/001, Black Country Living Museum; Fay Wythes, *Oral History*, BCLM: Forging Ahead (Dudley, 2018), 2018/264/001, Black Country Living Museum.

[264] 'Changes in the Capital of the Black Country'; 'A Homely Town – and Not Black', *Birmingham Daily Post*, 5 December 1962; 'Proud Nucleus of a New Borough', *Birmingham Daily Post*, 24 July 1963; 'To Holes and Tips, a Glad Farewell', *Birmingham Daily Post*, 28 November 1962; 'More Aitches - and Fewer Cobbles', *Birmingham Daily Post*, 14 November 1962; 'The Giant of the Black Country', *Birmingham Daily Post*, 20 February 1963.

[265] Rich, 'Spare Time in the Black Country', 319.

[266] Rich, 'Spare Time in the Black Country'; Pat Tyler, 'Modern Wife Gets Best Deal', *Daily Herald*, 11 November 1953.

[267] Abrams, Mark. *The Teenage Consumer: Middle Class and Working Class Boys and Girls. Teenage Consumer Spending in 1959* (London: London Press Exchange, 1961); Rich, 'Spare Time in the Black Country'; Rosalind Watkiss Singleton, '"(Today I Met) The Boy I'm Gonna Marry": Romantic Expectations of Teenage Girls in the 1960s West Midlands', in *Youth Culture and Social Change: Making a Difference By Making A Noise*, ed. Keith Gildart et al. (London: Palgrave Macmillan, 2017), 119–46.

[268] Rich, 'Spare Time in the Black Country', 323.

[269] Foot, *Immigration and Race in British Politics*, 34, 57 Lenny Henry, *Who Am I, Again?* (London: Faber & Faber, 2019); Jassal, *Oral History*.

[270] Tatla, 'A Passage to England'.

[271] Morgan, *Britain Since 1945*, 145; Kynaston, *Family Britain*, 167, 555; Matt Cook, *A Gay History of Britain: Love and Sex Between Men Since The Middle Ages* (Oxford: Greenwood, 2007); Keith Dockray and Alan Sutton, *Politics, Society and Homosexuality in Post-War Britain: The Sexual Offences Act of 1967 and Its Significance* (Stroud: Fonthill Media, 2017); Addison, *No Turning Back*, 98; Helen Smith, *Masculinity, Class and Same-Sex Desire in Industrial England, 1895-1957* (Basingstoke: Palgrave Macmillan, 2015).

[272] Matt Houlbrook, 'For Whose Convenience? Gay Guides, Cognitive Maps and the Construction of Homosexual London 1917-1967', ed. Simon Gunn and R. J. Morris, *Identities in Space: Contested Terrains in the Western City since 1850* (Aldershot: Ashgate, 2001), 165–86; Sebastian Buckle, *The Way Out: A History of Homosexuality in Modern Britain* (London: I.B.Tauris, 2015), 71; Antony Grey, *Quest for Justice: Towards Homosexual Emancipation* (Random House, 2011), 159; 'Murdered Man Identified', *Birmingham Daily Post*, 19 May 1964; '"Double Life" of Murder Victim', *Birmingham Daily Post*, 20 May 1964; Keith Collings, 'Murder-Hunt Detectives Trace Dead Youth's Double Life', *Daily Mail*, 20 May 1964; '5 Questions in Cofton Murder Charge Hearing', *Birmingham Daily Post*, 7 August 1964. See also oral histories from the Birmingham LGBT Community Trust website 'Gay Birmingham Remembered', http://www.gaybirminghamremembered.co.uk

[273] *Blackcountryman* 1(1)

[274] Downing, *Oral History;* Rich, 'Spare Time in the Black Country'; Keith James Farley, *'N Between Times: An Oral History of the Wolverhampton Group Scene of the 1960's* (self-published, 2001), http://www.historywebsite.co.uk/articles/InBetweenTimes/Page0.htm (accessed 7 April 2020); Andy Richards, '50 Years on: Memories of The Beatles' Debut Gigs in Smethwick and West Bromwich', *Birmingham Mail*, 22 November 2012.

[275] Mick Bonham, *John Bonham: The Powerhouse behind Led Zeppelin* (Harpenden: Oldcastle Books Ltd, 2015).

[276] James Nott, *Going to the Palais: A Social and Cultural History of Dancing and Dance Halls in Britain, 1918-1960* (Oxford: OUP, 2015), 275–77; John Williamson and Martin Cloonan, *Players' Work Time: A History of the British Musicians' Union, 1893-2013* (Manchester: Manchester University Press, 2016), 242; George Clay, 'Song and Dance at the Scala', *The Observer*, 22 June 1958; 'Colour Bar Case Raised in Delhi', *The Times*, 27 August 1958; 'Libel and Inter-Racial Friendship', *The Times*, 27 November 1958; 'Bring Your Own Girls, Coloured Men Told', *Daily Mail*, 1 July 1958; 'Axe-Man at Dance Smashes Trumpets', *Daily Mail*, 30 June 1958; 'Band Instruments Damage Charge', *The Times*, 1 July 1958.

[277] Hall, *Working Lives*, 98.

[278] Stafford, *Light in the Dust*.

[279] 'Police Arrival at Dudley Cinema Checked an Ugly Scene', *Dudley Herald*, 8 September 1956.

[280] 'Darlaston Gets Indian Film Shows - but Only Three', *Express & Star*, 31 August 1955; 'Praise for Behaviour of Indians at Special Film Show', *Express & Star*, 12 September 1955.

[281] Upton, *A History of Wolverhampton*, 132; Chitham, *West Bromwich: A History*, 188; Ramdin, *The Making of the Black Working Class in Britain*, 396; 'Proud Nucleus of a New Borough'.

[282] John Burnett, *England Eats Out: A Social History of Eating Out in England from 1830 to the Present* (London: Routledge, 2004), 273–84; Panikos Panayi, *Spicing up Britain: The Multicultural History of British Food* (Reaktion Books, 2008); 'The Night a Fork Slipped', *Birmingham Daily Post*, 2 December 1968; 'Bench Told Men Threw Glasses At Cafe Owner', *Birmingham Daily Post*, 25 January 1963. Restaurant details have been drawn from West Midlands regional telephone directories. Less formal restaurants were of course not always listed – one possible exception appears in the 1958 telephone directory under the name 'H Khan' in Tipton.

[283] Drabble, *The Black Country*, 196.

[284] Callum G. Brown, *Religion and Society in Twentieth-Century Britain* (Harlow: Routledge, 2006), 177–84; Sykes, 'Popular Religion in Dudley and the Gornals c.1914-1965', 112–29; Ann Bastafield, Robert Moseley, and Margaret Vercoe, *Oral History* (Halesowen, 2019), 2019/189/001, Black Country Living Museum; Ned Williams, *Black Country Chapels* (Stroud: The History Press, 2004); Ned Williams, *More Black Country Chapels* (Stroud: The History Press, 2006).

[285] Bernard Ratigan, 'John Hencher's Funeral', Notes from LE2 blog, 14 April 2011, https://bernardratigan1.blogspot.com/2011/04/john-henchers-funeral.html (accessed 7 April 2020); 'Vicar Wants a Wife Just like Ingrid Bergman', *Daily Mirror*, 25 February 1966; 'A "Royal Visit" after 180 Years', *Birmingham Daily Post*, 4 June 1968.

[286] 'New Testament Church of God Harvest Temple Wolverhampton: History', *New Testament Church of God Harvest Temple*, http://www.ntcgharvesttemple.org.uk/history-of-the-church.html (accessed 14 January 2019); 'Dr Oliver A Lyseight', *New Testament Church of God*, https://ntcg.org.uk/about/history/dr-oliver-lyseight/ (accessed 14 January 2019); Oliver A. Lyseight, *Forward March: An Autobiography* (London: G.S. Garwood, 1995); 'Police Chief Opens Place of Worship for West Indians', *Express & Star*, 29 January 1962.

[287] *Sikhs - Tracing the Journey*, 19

[288] Richard Inman, 'Judaism', 15 August 2005, http://www.wolverhamptonhistory.org.uk/people/faith/Judaism (accessed 7 April 2020); *Sikhs - Tracing the Journey*, 19; 'Church Made into Sikh Temple'; '10-Point "Colour Plan" by Mr Griffiths', *The Times*, 1 October 1964.

[289] 'About Us', *Mandir Baba Balak Nath*, http://www.mandirbababalaknath.co.uk/about-us (accessed 14 January 2019).

[290] Drabble, *The Black Country*, 205; Gary Cooper, *Chronicles from the Crown: A History of Crown Green Bowling in the Staffordshire County Region* (Wolverhampton: Staffordshire Country Bowling Association, 2010).

[291] Dodo, 'A Report on His Recent Journey to England by Chief Amri Beo Dodo of the Gorowa Tribe'.

[292] Ronnie Kowalski and Dilwyn Porter, 'Cold War Football: British-European Encounters in the 1940s and 1950s', in *East Plays West: Sport and the Cold War*, ed. Stephen Wagg and David Andrews (Abingdon: Routledge, 2012), 75–76; Nick Miller, 'The Night Wolves Became "Champions of the World" against Honved', *The Observer*, 13 December 2014.

[293] James Leighton, *Duncan Edwards: The Greatest* (London: Simon and Schuster, 2012); Stephen Wagg, 'The Team That Wouldn't Die: On the Mystique of Matt Busby and Manchester United', in *Manchester United: A Thematic Study*, ed. David L. Andrews (London: Psychology Press, 2004), 13–28.

Chapter 9: "Local patriotisms"

[294] Local Government Commission, quoted in 'Beating the Commission in the Black Country (or the Importance of Being Bilston)', *The Guardian*, 8 July 1961.

[295] Thomas Tancred, ed., *First Report of the Midland Mining Commission: South Staffordshire* (London: HMSO, 1843).

[296] Foreword to West Midlands Group for Post-War Reconstruction, 'West Midlands Plan 1:1'.

[297] Peter Shapely, 'Civic Pride and Redevelopment in the Post-War British City', *Urban History* 39(2), 2012: 310–28; Wolverhampton County Borough, *Wolverhampton Centenary Exhibition and Book of the Century*; Wolverhampton County Borough, *Wolverhampton Town Handbook;* Willenhall Urban District Council, *Willenhall Town Handbook;* Sedgley Urban District Council, *Sedgley: The Official Guide* (Ed. J. Burrow & Co, 1963).

[298] 'West Midlands Plan 1:1'.

[299] James Morgan, *Oral History*, BCLM: Forging Ahead (Dudley, 2018).

[300] Mark Freeman, '"Splendid Display; Pompous Spectacle": Historical Pageants in Twentieth-Century Britain', *Social History* 38(4), 2013: 423–55; Tom Hulme, '"A Nation of Town Criers": Civic Publicity and Historical Pageantry in Inter-War Britain', *Urban History* 44(2), 2017: 270–92; Zoë Thomas, 'Historical Pageants, Citizenship, and the Performance of Women's History before Second-Wave Feminism', *Twentieth Century British History* 28(3), 2017: 319–43; Angela Bartie et al., 'Historical Pageants and the Medieval Past in Twentieth-Century England', *The English Historical Review* 133(563), 2018: 866–902; Angela Bartie et al., 'The Pageant of Dudley, 1951', The Redress of the Past, http://www.historicalpageants.ac.uk/pageants/1054/ (accessed 12 April 2019); Gwen Lally, 'Pageant of Dudley: A Historical Pageant Play in Nine Episodes', 13 June 1951, 2001/034/003, Black Country Living Museum; 'Scenes of By-Gone Days Recalled in Dudley Pageant', *Dudley Herald*, 16 June 1951; 'Pageant Attendance Figures Rise after Poor Opening', *Dudley Herald*, 23 June 1951; E.A.D. Naylor, 'Dudley Pageant Scrapbook', 1951, 1996/092/007, Black Country Living Museum; 'Dudley Pageant a Financial Failure', *Birmingham Daily Gazette*, 25 June 1951.

[301] 'History', *South Staffs Water*, https://www.south-staffs-water.co.uk/about-us/our-business/history (accessed 12 December 2018); Trevor Yorke, *Victorian Pumping Stations* (London: Bloomsbury Publishing, 2018), 18.

[302] *Blocksidge's Illustrated Dudley Almanack for 1943*. *Hansard* HC Deb 10 February 1947 vol 433 cc1409-77.

[303] Peter J. Atkins, 'Communal Feeding in War Time: British Restaurants, 1940-1947', in *Food and War in Twentieth Century Europe.*, ed. Ina Zweiniger-Bargielowska, Rachel Duffett, and Alain Drouard (Farnham: Ashgate, 2011), 139–53; Nadja Durbach, 'British Restaurants and the Gender Politics of the Wartime Midday Meal', in *Home Fronts: Britain and the Empire at War, 1939-45*, ed. Mark J. Crowley and Sandra Trudgen Dawson (Woodbridge: Boydell & Brewer, 2017), 19–36; 'Provision of New Civic Restaurant on the Birmingham Street/Fisher Street Site' (County Borough of Dudley, 1948), LD647.95p, Dudley Archives and Local History Service. *Hansard*, HC Deb 28 November 1946 vol 430 cc1796-909.

[304] Historians have been divided about the political intent and extent of the 1944 Act. Butler himself described the Act as an expression of "one nation conservatism", and Brian Simon has emphasised the protection of religion and educational privilege as essentially conservative measures; Kevin Jeffereys has noted the scale and substance of the Act as "a triumph for progressive reform". Paul Addison suggests both are right, which is why it became so widely accepted. Brian Simon, 'The 1944 Education Act: A Conservative Measure?', *History of Education* 15(1), 1986: 31–43; Kevin Jeffereys, 'RA Butler, the Board of Education and the 1944 Education Act', *History* 69(227), 1984: 415–31; Morgan, *Britain Since 1945*, 19, 248; see also Hennessy, *Never Again*, 2006, 156–60

[305] Buettner, '"This Is Staffordshire Not Alabama"'; Prem, *The Parliamentary Leper*, 72.

[306] Desmond Cox, Speaking for Ourselves: An Oral History of People With Cerebral Palsy (Birmingham, 2005), C1134/12/01-03, British Library: Sounds; Jassal, *Oral History*; Marion Brennan, 'I Was Enoch's "Only White Kid in Class": Boy Referred to in Enoch Powell Speech Talks 50 Years On', *Express & Star*, 20 October 2017; 'School Dispersal of Immigrants Costing £17,000', *Birmingham Daily Post*, 21 November 1969. For more on 'bussing' in Britain, see Brett Bebber, '"We Were Just Unwanted": Bussing, Migrant Dispersal, and South Asians in London', *Journal of Social History* 48(3), 2015: 635–61; David L. Kirp, 'The Vagaries of Discrimination: Busing, Policy, and Law in Britain', *The School Review* 87(3), 1979: 269–94.

[307] Lionel Roy McColvin, *The Public Library System of Great Britain: A Report on Its Present Condition with Proposals for Post War Reorganization* (London: The Library association, 1942). A. Black, 'National Planning for Public Library Service: The Work and Ideas of Lionel McColvin'. *Library Trends* 52(4), 2004: 902–23.

[308] 'A Year's Bedtime Stories Cost 1d.', *Birmingham Daily Gazette*, 4 November 1952; 'By Request', *Birmingham Daily Post*, 13 August 1958; 'Proposals for Relieving Pressure on Dudley Central Library', *Birmingham Daily Post*, 2 January 1961; 'Cover Point', *Birmingham Daily Post*, 9 October 1962; W.E. Hall, 'A Chinese God in Dudley', *Birmingham Daily Post*, 28 December 1962; 'Changes in the Capital of the Black Country'; 'Dudley Library Outgrows Building', *Birmingham Daily Post*, 9 July 1963; 'Library Now Has Modern Comforts', *Birmingham Daily Post*, 11 March 1966; 'Punjabi Proves Popular', *Birmingham Daily Post*, 31 August 1967.

[309] '999 Call Led to Quick Arrest', *Birmingham Daily Post*, 13 November 1959; 'Boy Who Dialled 999 Told "Do Not Be Foolish"', *Birmingham Daily Gazette*, 14 October 1953. Advice on Chinese pronunciation for the library badge scheme was provided by the owner of Dudley's new Chinese restaurant Chu Kong.

[310] Petty, *Five Fags a Day*; Petty, *The Face*; Watkiss Singleton, '"Old Habits Persist"', 192–95, 208.

[311] Useful discussions of the representation of crime, and how the Teddy Boys were better understood as a 'moral panic' rather than a genuine crime wave can be found in Stanley Cohen, *Folk Devils and Moral Panics* (Abingdon: Routledge Classics, 2011), and Geoffrey Pearson, *Hooligan: A History of Respectable Fears* (New York: Schocken, 1984).

[312] 'News', *Dudley Herald*, 6 June 1958; 'News', *Dudley Herald*, 19 September 1958; 'News', *Dudley Herald*, 14 April 1962.

[313] Watkiss Singleton, '"Old Habits Persist"', 275; T.R. Fyvel, *The Insecure Offenders* (London: Chatto & Windus, 1961), 17–18; Richard Vinen, *National Service: A Generation in Uniform 1945-1963* (London: Penguin, 2014); Geoffrey Pearson, *Hooligan: A History of Respectable Fears* (New York: Schocken, 1984); Harry Hendrick, 'Histories of Youth Crime and Justice', in *Youth Crime and Justice*, ed. Barry Goldson and John Muncie (Newbury Park, CA: Pine Forge Press, 2006), 3–16; 'Teddy Gang Fought Police To Free Youth', *Birmingham Daily Gazette*, 17 August 1956; 'News', *Express & Star*, 3 September 1956.

[314] 'Dogs Charge Race Rioters'; 'Police Alert after Race Riot: Court Told of Cowardly Pack'; 'Rowdies Hunt

Coloured People'; '11 Held in Race Riot', *Daily Mail*, 2 August 1962; 'Bottles Thrown at Police from Lorry'; 'Dudley's Youth Problems as a Factor in Colour Riots'; 'Police Dogs Put Gangs to Flight'; 'Dudley's Week of Violence: J.Ps Told "Ravening Wolves" Went on Hunt for Black Folk', *Dudley Herald*, 4 August 1962; Perrott, 'Behind the Doors of Dudley, Town in Turmoil'; 'Man Said to Be Riots Ringleader Gets 3 Months', *Dudley Herald*, 11 August 1962.

315 Derek Fraser, *The Evolution of the British Welfare State: A History of Social Policy Since the Industrial Revolution*, Fifth edition (London: Palgrave Macmillan, 2017), 163.

316 Julian M. Simpson, *Migrant Architects of the NHS: South Asian Doctors and the Reinvention of British General Practice (1940s-1980s)* (Oxford: Oxford University Press, 2018); Snow and Jones, 'Immigration and the National Health Service: Putting History to the Forefront'.

317 'Man with His Future behind Him', *Birmingham Daily Post*, 19 February 1963.

318 'New Smallpox Case in Midlands', *Birmingham Daily Post*, 2 January 1962; C. Simpson Smith, 'Smallpox in Staffordshire, 1947; Outbreak at Bilston', *British Medical Journal* 1(4542), 1948: 139–42; 'Annual Report of the Medical Officer of Health' (Borough of Bilston, 1948), Wolverhampton Archives & Local Studies; J.T.A. George, 'Annual Report of the Medical Officer of Health' (Coseley Urban District Council, 1951), Dudley Archives and Local History Service; C.D.L. Lycett and J.T.A. George, 'An Outbreak Of Diphtheria: Influence Of Immunization', *British Medical Journal* 1(4817), 1953: 964–68; 'Road Is Barrier to Spread of Diphtheria', *Birmingham Daily Gazette*, 22 October 1953; J. Aspin, 'Tuberculosis Among Indian Immigrants to a Midland Industrial Area', *British Medical Journal* 1(5289), 1962: 1386–88; Foot, *Rise of Enoch Powell*, 47–53; John Welshman, 'Compulsion, Localism, and Pragmatism: The Micro-Politics of Tuberculosis Screening in the United Kingdom, 1950–1965', *Social History of Medicine* 19(2), 2006: 295–312; Bivins, *Contagious Communities*, 71; Gareth Millward, *Vaccinating Britain: Mass Vaccination and the Public since the Second World War* (Manchester: Manchester University Press, 2019), 53–54.

319 'Polio: Vicar Calls for Sense of Proportion', *Birmingham Daily Post*, 15 July 1958; 'Oldbury Demand for Polio Injections', *Birmingham Daily Post*, 8 April 1959; 'No New Polio Cases in Smethwick', *Birmingham Daily Post*, 19 May 1961; 'Police Escort for Ambulance', *Birmingham Daily Post*, 23 May 1961; 'Child Is Polio Suspect', *Birmingham Daily Post*, 9 June 1961; 'Boy Dies of Polio', *Birmingham Daily Post*, 12 September 1961; 'Polio Suspect at Wolverhampton', *Birmingham Daily Post*, 11 November 1961; 'Tipton Suspects', *Birmingham Daily Post*, 18 November 1961; Richard J Dodds and W.L. Kay, 'Annual Report of the Medical Officer of Health for 1961' (Smethwick County Borough, 1961); Matthew Smallman-Raynor and Andrew Cliff, *Atlas of Epidemic Britain: A Twentieth Century Picture* (Oxford: Oxford University Press, 2012).

320 J.P. Neylon, 'Annual Report of the Medical Officer of Health' (Borough of Bilston, 1958).

321 'Tipton surprise at enquiry'; 'Beating the Commission in the Black Country (or the Importance of Being Bilston)'; '"Bilstonians to Picket Minster's Home"', *Birmingham Daily Post*, 11 July 1961; 'Enquiry to Last "Several Weeks"', *Birmingham Daily Post*, 26 July 1961; 'Bilston Poll', *Birmingham Daily Post*, 29 July 1961; 'Mayor Denies "Propaganda Campaign": Bilston's Referendum', *Birmingham Daily Post*, 9 November 1961; 'Black Country Towns to Fight Merger Plan', *Birmingham Daily Gazette*, 11 January 1954; 'Small Towns Oppose Absorption', *Birmingham Daily Post*, 8 November 1961. 'Inspector Tours Black Country', *Birmingham Daily Post*, 23 November 1961.

322 'Minister Fixes Date for Local Government Reorganisation: Five Boroughs in the Black Country', *The Guardian*, 28 November 1962; West Midland Group, *Conurbation*, 48–57; Urlan A. Wannop, *The Regional Imperative: Regional Planning and Governance in Britain, Europe and the United States* (Abingdon: Routledge, 2014), 45.

Chapter 10: "Never had it so good"

[323] West Midland Group, *Conurbation*, 250. Italics in original.

[324] Drabble, *The Black Country*, 234.

[325] 'Keep Black Country as One, Society Says', *Birmingham Daily Post*, 13 January 1970; J.M. Fletcher, 'What Is the Black Country?', *Blackcountryman* 1(1), 1967: 11–13; John Brimble, 'Society News', *Blackcountryman* 1(1), 1967: 6–10; 'Advertisement for Black Country Folk Songs at the Wolverhampton Folk Song Club', *Blackcountryman* 1(1), 1967: 13. John Fletcher's article defining the boundaries of the Black Country in the very first issue of the *Blackcountryman* set out the society's stall very clearly – even as the region's last colliery made plans for its closure, the BCS considered the exposed South Staffordshire coalfield the defining feature of what constituted the true Black Country. Needless to say, this definition was much challenged, and as this book has demonstrated, a much more expansive definition of the post-war Black Country could be argued.

[326] Joan W. Scott, 'Gender: A Useful Category of Historical Analysis', *The American Historical Review* 91(5), 1986: 1053–75.

[327] Linda Colley, *Britons: Forging the Nation, 1707-1837* (New Haven, CT: Yale University Press, 2005), 6.

[328] Julian Critchley, 'Paternalist Who Runs a £100m Family Business', *The Times*, 7 January 1969; Clifford Webb, 'Moulding a New Identity at Rubery Owen', *The Times*, 6 August 1973.

[329] Brian Harrison, *Seeking a Role: The United Kingdom, 1951-1970* (Oxford: Oxford University Press, 2015), 221.

[330] Morgan, *Britain Since 1945*, 338–43.

[331] Alwyn W. Turner, *Crisis? What Crisis? Britain in the 1970s* (Aurum Press, 2009), 1; Spencer et al., *Crisis in the Industrial Heartland*, 21.

[332] Greig Campbell, 'In the Shadow of Elisabeth', in *Black Country Echoes* (Wolverhampton: Wolverhampton Art Gallery, 2014), 20–22.

[333] Creative Black Country, *Desi Pub* (West Bromwich: Creative Black Country, 2016).

[334] Bev Parker, 'Rubery Owen & Company Ltd.: The Later Years', *History Website*, http://www.historywebsite.co.uk/articles/Darlaston/RO2.htm (accessed 26 March 2019); Spencer et al., *Crisis in the Industrial Heartland*, 46, 52–57, 110, 142.

[335] Dud Dudley, *Mettallum Martis: Or, Iron Made with Pit-Coale, Sea-Coale, &c.* (London: T. M., 1665).

[336] Beveridge, *Social Insurance and Allied Services*.

[337] James Vernon, 'The Local, the Imperial and the Global: Repositioning Twentieth-Century Britain and the Brief Life of Its Social Democracy', *Twentieth Century British History* 21(3), 2010: 375–418.

[338] Campanella, Edoardo, and Marta Dassù. *Anglo Nostalgia: The Politics of Emotion in a Fractured West*. (Oxford: Oxford University Press, 2019), 6.

[339] There is a wide literature on the pros and cons of nostalgia. Particularly relevant here are: Svetlana Boym, *The Future of Nostalgia* (New York: Basic Books, 2001); Tim Strangleman, 'Smokestack Nostalgia, Ruin Porn or Working-Class Obituary: The Role and Meaning of Deindustrial Representation', *International Labor and Working-Class History* 84, no. 1 (7 January 2013): 23–37; Fred Davis, *Yearning for Yesterday: Nostalgia, Art and Society* (New York: The Free Press, 1979); Raphael Samuel, *Theatres of Memory: Past and Present in Contemporary Culture* (London, Verso, 2012).

[340] Jim Evans, 'A Gazetteer of Lock and Key Makers', *History Website*, http://www.historywebsite.co.uk/Museum/locks/gazetteer/gaz01.htm (accessed 7 April 2020).

Index

Note: page references in italics indicate images, information in captions and tables; bold indicates glossary entries.